Law and Lies

Deception and Truth-Telling in the American Legal System

Edited by
AUSTIN SARAT
Amherst College

CAMBRIDGE
UNIVERSITY PRESS

CAMBRIDGE
UNIVERSITY PRESS

32 Avenue of the Americas, New York, NY 10013-2473, USA

Cambridge University Press is part of the University of Cambridge.

It furthers the University's mission by disseminating knowledge in the pursuit of education, learning, and research at the highest international levels of excellence.

www.cambridge.org
Information on this title: www.cambridge.org/9781107108783

First published 2015

A catalog record for this publication is available from the British Library.

Library of Congress Cataloging in Publication Data
Law and lies : deception and truth-telling in the American legal system / edited by Austin Sarat.
pages cm
ISBN 978-1-107-10878-3 (hardback)
1. Deception – United States. 2. Fraud – United States. 3. Torts – United States. 4. Truthfulness and falsehood – United States. I. Sarat, Austin, editor.
KF1271.L39 2015
346.7303–dc23 2015014021

ISBN 978-1-107-10878-3 Hardback

To Ben, with love

Contents

Contributors

Montré D. Carodine is Professor of Law at the University of Alabama.

William N. Eskridge Jr. is John A. Garver Professor of Jurisprudence at Yale Law School.

Mary Anne Franks is Professor of Law at the University of Miami.

Stuart P. Green is Professor of Law at Rutgers Law School–Newark.

Helen Norton is Associate Dean and Associate Professor of Law at the University of Colorado.

Austin Sarat is Associate Dean of the Faculty and William Nelson Cromwell Professor of Jurisprudence and Political Science at Amherst College and Justice Hugo L. Black Visiting Senior Scholar at the School of Law at the University of Alabama.

Norman W. Spaulding is Nelson Bowman Sweitzer and Marie B. Sweitzer Professor of Law at Stanford Law School.

Contributors

Acknowledgments

This volume is the product of a symposium held at the University of Alabama, School of Law on October 10, 2014. I want to thank the colleagues, students, and staff who helped make it such a successful event. I am grateful for the financial support of the University of Alabama Law School Foundation and for the able research assistance of Haley Cambra, Sarah Smith, and Olivia Truax.

Law and Lies

An Introduction

Austin Sarat with Haley Cambra, Sarah Smith, and Olivia Truax

A lie cannot live.

Martin Luther King, speech in Montgomery, AL, 1965

It is necessary to the happiness of man that he be mentally faithful to himself. Infidelity does not consist in believing, or in disbelieving, it consists in professing to believe what he does not believe.

Thomas Paine, *The Age of Reason*

[W]hen we talk about lying, and especially about lying among acting men, let us remember that the lie did not creep into politics by some accident of human sinfulness. Moral outrage, for this reason alone, is not likely to make it disappear . . . . Lies are often much more plausible, more appealing to reason, than reality, since the liar has the great advantage of knowing beforehand what the audience wishes or expects to hear.

Hannah Arendt, "Lying in Politics" in *Crises of the Republic* (1972)

Introduction

Law has a strangely complicated relationship to lies, deception, and truth. Sometimes law takes a hard line on behalf of truth, "the truth, the whole truth, and nothing but the truth," but more often the law looks the other way as lies are told. It tolerates deception, and regards truth as an inconvenient barrier to the attainment of some other value. The American legal system embraces a utilitarian view of lying rather than a strictly Kantian prohibition.[1]

Legal actors sometimes practice deception, if not outright lying, in the service of catching criminals, here we think of the use of undercover agents, and sometimes law forgives lies to those who enforce the law, as in the doctrine of the "exculpatory no."[2] Indeed, law sometimes seems to encourage, if not demand, deception. Here think of "Don't Ask, Don't Tell." Moreover drawing the line between legally tolerated deceptive practices and fraud has proven to be notoriously difficult.[3]

[1] Contrast Immanuel Kant, "On a Supposed Right to Lie From Altruistic Motives," in *Critique of Practical Reason*, ed. Lewis White Beck (Chicago: University of Chicago Press, 1985), 346–350; and Henry Sidgwick, "The Classification of Duties-Veracity," in *The Methods of Ethics*, 7th ed. (London: MacMillan and Co., 1913), 312–319.

[2] See *People v. Brooks*, 51 Ill. App. 3d 800, 1977.

[3] Arthur A. Leff, *Swindling and Selling: The Story of Legal and Illegal Con-games* (New York: Free Press, 1976).

Law and Lies

Law has a strangely complicated relationship to deception. Though it sometimes takes a hard line on behalf of truth – "the truth, the whole truth, and nothing but the truth" – competing values often cause law to look the other way. How and why is lying alternately accepted, condemned, or prosecuted? What are the government's interests in allowing or disallowing lying?

Law and Lies is the first book to thematically address the role of lying in the American legal system. Undercover police agents are permitted to lie in the name of catching criminals, and government officials are permitted to lie in service of national security. In the case of the military's "Don't Ask, Don't Tell" policy, lying was not only permitted, but actively encouraged. A range of illuminating case studies reveal that the government's tolerance of deception is rarely as simple as the "whole truth."

Austin Sarat is William Nelson Cromwell Professor of Jurisprudence and Political Science and Associate Dean of the Faculty at Amherst College and Justice Hugo L. Black Senior Faculty Scholar at the University of Alabama School of Law. He is the author or editor of numerous books, including the recent *A World without Privacy* (2014); *Civility, Legality, and the Limits of Justice* (2014); and *Re-imagining To Kill a Mockingbird: Family, Community, and the* Possibility *of Equal Justice under Law* (2013). His book *When Government Breaks the Law: Prosecuting the Bush Administration* was named one of the best books of 2010 by the *Huffington Post*.

There have been several book-length treatments of lying as a moral, social and/or psychological phenomenon.[4] However, this book is the first to explore lying in and around law. While the subject of law and lies is broad in scope, by way of introduction I offer a few illustrations of the way law deals with and responds to lies and deception.

Lying and the First Amendment

One of the domains in which law's complicated relationship to lies and deception is vividly on display is in the context of the Constitution's First Amendment guarantee of free speech. In a landmark decision in the mid-twentieth century, the Supreme Court took up the question of constitutional protection afforded false statements in and by the media. In *New York Times Co. v. Sullivan*, the city commissioner of Montgomery, Alabama, a man named L. B. Sullivan, filed a libel action against the *New York Times* and four black ministers responsible for a full-page advertisement in the *Times*, which alleged that the arrest of Rev. Martin Luther King Jr. for perjury in Alabama was retaliation for King's efforts to mobilize black voters. The advertisement also included statements about police action against students participating in civil rights demonstrations, some of which were false.

[4] See, for example, Sissela Bok, *Lying: Moral Choice in Public and Private Life* (New York: Random House LLC, 2011); Charles V. Ford, *Lies! Lies!! Lies!!!: The Psychology of Deceit* (New York: American Psychiatric Pub, 1999).

Under Alabama law a publication was libelous *per se* if it was intended to injure a person's reputation or bring that person into public contempt. Once libel *per se* was established, the sole available defense required showing that all statements were entirely factually correct; in this case, however, the advertisements did include minor errors. As a result, the jury found the defendants guilty of libel without any demonstration of malice or material damages to the plaintiff. Alabama's Supreme Court upheld the verdict.

The United States Supreme Court, however, reversed this ruling and expanded constitutional protection for false speech. The Court's unanimous decision stated that "Factual error, content defamatory of official reputation, or both, are insufficient to warrant an award of damages for false statements unless 'actual malice' – knowledge that statements are false or in reckless disregard of the truth – is alleged and proved."[5] This requirement of "actual malice" serves to protect the "erroneous statement (that are) inevitable in free debate."[6] In *New York Times v. Sullivan*, falsehoods were protected in the interest of protecting freedom of the press.

Ten years after *New York Times v. Sullivan*, the Court limited protection of false speech, making a distinction between lies about a public figure and lies about a private individual. In this 1974 case, *Gertz v. Robert Welch*, the majority stated that, because private citizens have access

[5] *New York Times Co. v. Sullivan*, 376 U.S. 254 (1964).
[6] Id.

to fewer ways of counteracting allegations, "the States should retain substantial latitude in their efforts to enforce a legal remedy for defamatory falsehood injurious to the reputation of a private individual."[7]

Recognizing the importance of protecting unpopular opinions from undue prosecutions the Court barred states from imposing a "strict liability" standard for defamation. This ruling allowed states latitude in creating their own libel laws for private individuals, while simultaneously holding that "[u]nder the First Amendment there is no such thing as a false idea." Here again the Court protected "some falsehood in order to protect speech that matters."[8]

Though the decisions in both *New York Times Co.* and *Gertz* centered on falsehoods, neither directly addressed whether or not deceptive, untrue statements (whether malicious or unintentional) comprise a constitutionally protected category of speech. The Court recently took up this question in the context of a Congressional statute, the so called Stolen Valor Act, which imposed criminal penalties on false claims of military honor. The key section of the act reads as follows:

> Whoever falsely represents himself or herself, verbally or in writing, to have been awarded any decoration or medal authorized by Congress for the Armed Forces of the United States, any of the service medals or badges awarded to the members of such forces, the ribbon, button, or rosette

[7] *Gertz v. Robert Welch, Inc.*, 418 U.S. 323 (1974).

[8] Id.

> of any such badge, decoration, or medal, or any colorable imitation of such item shall be fined under this title, imprisoned not more than six months, or both.[9]

In *United States v. Alvarez*, Xavier Alvarez, of Pomona, California, challenged the constitutionality of the Stolen Valor Act after he who was charged for falsely saying, "I'm a retired Marine of 25 years. I retired in the year 2001. Back in 1987, I was awarded the Congressional Medal of Honor. I got wounded many times by the same guy. I'm still around."[10] He was subsequently "sentenced to three years on probation, ordered to do 416 hours of community service, and fined 5,000."[11]

Alvarez appealed to the Ninth Circuit Court of Appeals and won. That Court, in a divided 2–1 ruling, struck down the Stolen Valor Act. The majority held that there was "no authority holding that false factual speech, as a general category unto itself, is among . . . those classes of speech which can be prohibited without any constitutional problem."[12] The Court found that the law did not require prosecutors to show that the defendant had acted with "actual malice," intended to cause injury and his lie had done harm to the reputation of the distinction. Without these provisions, the Stolen Valor Act was, the Ninth Circuit ruled, unconstitutional.[13]

[9] H.R. 3352.

[10] *United States v. Alvarez*, 567 U.S. ___ (2012).

[11] Id.

[12] Id.

[13] *United States v. Alvarez*, 617 F.3d 1198, 1201 (9th Cir. 2010).

The government appealed this decision to the Supreme Court, arguing that false statements of fact are only constitutionally protected when they are "derivative" of the truthful speech that the Amendment is designed to protect.[14] Arguing that false speech does not enjoy the same level of constitutional protection as truthful utterances, the government asserted that "strict scrutiny"[15] is not warranted for those laws that restrict false speech. The government contended that the Stolen Valor Act was constitutional insofar as it outlawed only objective falsehoods, a category of speech that was already unprotected by the First Amendment.

The Supreme Court rejected the government's contention and held that the First Amendment protects lies and deceptive speech, striking down the Stolen Valor Act in a 6–3 decision. Justice Kennedy announced the judgment of the Court "reject[ing] the notion that false speech should be in a general category that is presumptively unprotected."[16] The Court held that "isolated statements in some earlier decisions do not support the

[14] For example, a misstated scientific fact would be protected because falsity is inevitable as science is advanced through debate and discovery.

[15] "Strict Scrutiny" is the most stringent standard of judicial review used by U.S. courts to weigh the government's interests against a constitutional right or principal. To pass the test the law must (1) be justified by a compelling governmental interest, (2) be narrowly tailored, and (3) be the least restrictive means necessary for achieving the interest.

[16] Id., Kennedy's opinion.

Government's submission that false statements, as a general rule, are beyond constitutional protection."[17] False statements, Kennedy argued, are a category of protected speech; therefore, any legislation that seeks to regulate them is subject to "strict scrutiny," a standard under which the Stolen Valor Act failed.

Dissenting, Justice Alito contended that false statements are, as a category, not protected by the First Amendment. Alito wrote, "By holding that the First Amendment nevertheless shields these lies, the Court breaks sharply from a long line of cases recognizing that the right to free speech does not protect false factual statements that inflict real harm and serve no legitimate interest."[18] He argued that "[t]he lies covered by the Stolen Valor Act have no intrinsic value and thus merit no First Amendment protection." Falsehoods, Alito observed, should only be protected insofar as their regulation could have a "chilling effect" on free discourse.[19]

From *New York Times* to *Alvarez* the Supreme Court has given wide latitude for lies and deception. Law tolerates lies and deception as part of its embrace of robust freedom of expression. As Kennedy's *Alvarez* opinion noted, the categorical protection of lies "comports with the common understanding that some false statements are inevitable if there is to be an open and vigorous expression

[17] Id.
[18] *United States v. Alvarez,* 567 U.S. ___ (2012).
[19] Id.

of views in public and private conversation and expression the First Amendment seeks to guarantee."[20]

Perjury and Fraud

Another area in which law's attitude toward lies and deception is on display is in the context of perjury and fraud. In comparison to the contested principles intrinsic to lying and the First Amendment, lying in the context of perjury and fraud seem easier cases. Here the causal relationship between the lie and the damage it creates would appear uncontroversial: a lie told on the witness stand, or to gain material advantage, seems clearly injurious. However, both areas become more complex as statutes with relatively straightforward tenets are applied to the complex world of human interactions.

The most often prosecuted U.S. perjury statute, 18 USC § 1623,[21] states:

> Whoever under oath (or in any declaration, certificate, verification, or statement under penalty of perjury as

[20] Id.

[21] Congress enacted 18 U.S. Code § 1623 to avoid some of the common-law technicalities that developed over the lifetime of the older perjury statute 18 U.S. Code § 1621. When congress passed 1623 it did not repeal 1621, the government can choose the statue that it will prosecute under. Because 1623 outlaws a broader scope of perjury than 1621 and is freed of the many of the common-law requirements, almost all perjury cases are tried under 1623. See Charles Doyle, "Perjury Under Federal Law: A Brief Overview," *Congressional Research Service Report for Congress* (11.5.10).

> permitted under section 1746 of title 28, United States Code) in any proceeding before or ancillary to any court or grand jury of the United States knowingly makes any false material declaration or makes or uses any other information, including any book, paper, document, record, recording, or other material, knowing the same to contain any false material declaration, shall be fined under this title or imprisoned not more than five years, or both.

To prove perjury, "the Government must establish that the defendant (1) knowingly made a (2) false (3) material declaration (4) under oath (5) in a proceeding before or ancillary to any court or grand jury of the United States."[22]

Typically, the third point – "materiality" – is the most ambiguous aspect of a perjury prosecution. Information is usually considered material "if it has a natural tendency to influence, or is capable of influencing, the decision of the decision-making body to which it was addressed."[23] This limits the scope of prosecutable lies to those that could affect the outcome of the case. Lying on the stand about unrelated or digressive matters, for instance, cannot be prosecuted as perjury.

The second criterion for perjury – falsity – has also been a point of legal contention. In *Bronston v. United States*, the Supreme Court ruled that only *patently* false statements could be prosecuted. "It may well be that petitioner's answers were not guileless but were shrewdly calculated to

[22] Id., at 6.
[23] *Kungys v. United States*, 485 U.S. 759 (1988).

evade. Nevertheless ... any special problems arising from the literally true but unresponsive answer are to be remedied through the questioner's acuity and not by a federal perjury prosecution."[24] Misleading or evasive answers to questions are therefore exempt from prosecution due to the ambiguous nature of what constitutes "misleading" testimony.[25] As Justice Kennedy noted in *Alvarez*, lying under oath is criminalized not because it is false but because of its potential to pervert justice: only false statements made with the knowledge of their falsity and with the intent to mislead are criminalized (point one from the perjury statute § 1623, the "knowingly made" criterion). Those made without *mens rea* are exempt.[26]

The criminalization of fraud is similarly focused not on the value of truth for truth's sake, but on the harm done by misleading representations. In *Southern Development Co. v. Silva*,[27] the Supreme Court established the following criteria for proof of fraud: (1) the defendant made a representation in regard to a material fact, (2) the representation was false, (3) the defendant knew the representation was false, (4) the representation was intended to provoke an action by the plaintiff, (5) the plaintiff suffered damage as a result, and (6) in acting, the plaintiff reasonably assumed the representation was true.

[24] *Bronston v. United States*, 409 U.S. 352 (1973).
[25] Id.
[26] See *United States v. Alvarez*.
[27] *Southern Development Co. v. Silva*, 125 U.S. 247 (1888).

As with perjury, materiality is a key issue in fraud cases. To demonstrate materiality, the plaintiff must show that the defendant's statements were not merely false, but that they directly contributed to the damages that the plaintiff incurred.[28]

In contrast to perjury, fraud does not require proof of factual falsity. Courts find fraud in contract cases when a negotiator uses misleading statements to conceal the true nature of the deal. In fraud prosecutions, the issue isn't whether or not a statement was purely factual, but whether it was intended to mislead the other party and conceal a set of facts detrimental to the negotiator's position. In cases of direct lies in negotiations, the courts typically side with the plaintiff, even if the plaintiff's belief in the lies was entirely unjustified. However, when statements of opinion or nondisclosure are involved, the courts tend to be more sympathetic to defendants.[29]

As was the case in the context of the First Amendment, in neither fraud nor perjury cases do courts assert the intrinsic wrong of lies, deception, or false statements. Falsity is criminalized only insofar as it causes demonstrable harm. Thus the complexities attending the constitutional protection of false speech also haunt the ostensibly straightforward perjury and fraud cases.

[28] See Association of Certified Fraud Examiners, "The Fraud Trial" (6), http://is.gd/t7a7ec (July 30, 2013).

[29] See Richard Shell, "When Is It Legal to Lie in Negotiations?" *MIT Sloan Management Review* 32, no. 3 (1991).

Lying by Government Officials

A third arena in which law's relationship to lies is on display involves instances in which government officials themselves use lies and deception, typically in the context of law enforcement or national security. Those officials, it turns out, have fairly broad legal authority to dissemble and deceive. Police may use lies in interrogations, facilitating convictions and presumably promoting public safety by procuring confessions of criminal actions. This is justified by the assumption that an innocent suspect wouldn't be coerced to confess if presented with false information about their supposed "guilt."[30]

Intrinsic misrepresentations about the case are broadly legal; for example, in a murder case interrogators can lie to a suspect by telling him that the murder weapon was found with their fingerprints on it. These lies about the nature of the case itself are not deemed coercive. However, in a 1992 case *Holland v. McGinnis*, the Seventh Circuit Court of Appeals held that lies about *extrinsic* considerations could "overcome" the defendant's "will" by "distorting an otherwise rational choice of whether to confess or remain silent"[31] and are, as a result, not permitted. Extrinsic factors include promises of more favorable treatment in the event of a confession, and misrepresentations of legal principles.

[30] See H. Morley Swingle and Lane P. Thomasson, "Big Lies and Prosecutorial Ethics," *Journal of the Missouri Bar* 66, no. 3 (2012): 84–87 (85), http://is.gd/DDfrOj.

[31] *Holland v. McGinnis*, 963 F.2d 1044, 1050–51 (7th Cir. 1992).

Police, and other law enforcement agents, are also given broad license to lie in contexts other than interrogations: the entire possibility of undercover policing is dependent on legally sanctioned, willful deception.[32] There are, however, limitations on the falsehoods law enforcement agents may tell. For example, though it is okay for law enforcement agents to lie about who they are when delivering a warrant, they cannot lie about the existence of the warrant itself.[33] And, although police may untruthfully misrepresent their status as government agents, they cannot impersonate officials of another branch of the government in order to gain access to information.[34] Prosecutors, however, are given much less latitude when it comes to lying and deception. It is considered professional misconduct for a lawyer to "engage in conduct involving dishonesty, fraud, deceit or misrepresentation" or "commit a criminal act that reflects adversely on the lawyer's honesty, trustworthiness or fitness as a lawyer in other respects."[35]

32 *Lewis v. United States*, 385 U.S. 206, 208 (1966).

33 Frank Connelly, Federal Law Enforcement Training Center, "Consent to Enter or Search by Deception" (3), https://www.fletc.gov/sites/default/files/imported_files/training/programs/legal-division/downloads-articles-and-faqs/research-by-subject/4th-amendment/ConsenttoEnterorSearchbyDeception.pdf.

34 "We think it is clearly improper for a government agent to gain access to records which would otherwise be unavailable to him by invoking the private individual's trust in his government, only to betray that trust." *SEC v. ESM Government Securities, Inc.*, 645 F. 2d 310.

35 American Bar Association Model Rules of Professional Conduct Rule 8.04 (Misconduct).

Courts have long given the government, particularly the executive branch, broad license to lie in the interests of "national security." As former Assistant Secretary of Defense Arthur Sylvester, who served in both the Kennedy and Johnson administrations, put it, "Sometimes, and those times are rare indeed, government officials may be required to fulfill their duty by issuing a false statement."[36] Sylvester claimed that government officials, in their official capacity,[37] have the "duty" to lie to the American people to protect the security of the nation:

> Despite all the lamenting about the credibility gap and the Government's right to lie ... They [the American people] don't want their children surrendered to the savages merely so that the Government could boast it always told the truth, the whole truth, and nothing but the truth.[38]

Sylvester's argument has broadly been accepted in courts within the context of "state secrets."[39]

Lying About Sexual Identity

Finally, in other contexts the government does not just tolerate lying and deception it actively encourages it. Take for

[36] See Sylvester Arthur, "The Government Has a Right to Lie," *Saturday Evening Post*, November 18, 1967.

[37] Id. See "Government officials as individuals do not have the right to lie politically or to protect themselves, but they do always have the duty to protect their countrymen."

[38] Id.

[39] *United States v. Reynolds,* 345 U.S. 1 (1953).

example the military's "Don't Ask Don't Tell" (DADT) policy on homosexuality. Until its repeal in September 2011, closeted homosexuals could serve in the military without harassment or discrimination but openly gay service members were barred from serving.[40] DADT's encroachment on the constitutional values reflected in the due process clauses of the Fourteenth and Fifth Amendments, along with the freedom of speech guaranteed under the First Amendment, was outweighed by the "legitimate governmental interest in maintaining effective armed forces."[41] A desirable *effect* (unit cohesion) justified a rule that encouraged/required misrepresentation and even outright falsity.

"Law and Lies: Deception and Truth-Telling in the American Legal System" suggests that in the American system, what counts as legal or illegal lying is shaped by practical, constitutional, and moral considerations – and these often conflict. Courts seem to agree that falsity may not be morally desirable, but recognize that it can be socially beneficial. Among the questions this book addresses are: How and why are lying and deception accepted, condemned or prosecuted? To what extent is truth outweighed by competing values? What are the government's interests in allowing or disallowing lying: both its own and that of its citizens?

[40] 10 U.S. Code § 654.

[41] See Jody Feder, Congressional Research Service Report for Congress, "'Don't Ask, Don't Tell': A Legal Analysis" September 2, 2009 (p. 4). It can be located at http://fpc.state.gov/documents/organization/130271.pdf.

This book explores the status of the legal treatment of truth in statements made under oath and other statements to government officials, in efforts to impersonate those officials, and in the domain of sexuality and sexual identity. The scholarship presented here examines false and deceptive speech and First Amendment values, fraudulent inducements, and the costs of the legal encouragement of deception. The first three chapters focus on lies in public arenas and contexts and the last two on the legal treatment of lies in the domain of sex and sexuality. The Afterword offers a set of reflections aimed specifically at thinking about the ways legal institutions should respond when the value of truth appears to compete with other values.

In the book's first chapter, "Where the Law Lies: Constitutional Fictions and Their Discontents," Mary Anne Franks discusses the implications of the legal fiction embodied in the Constitution's authorship ... "We the people." Franks defines a lie as the making of an untruthful statement with the intention that the statement be believed to be true, not taking into account suggestions, omissions, or mistakes. Lies, she argues, are embedded in law itself due to the fact that "the people" did not truly ordain and establish the Constitution; rather, a small group of white, property-owning men did, an inconsistency that created lasting inequality in America. The fact that American people know this is a lie does not lessen the harm it causes and can serve to advance the interests of the liars.

The eventual concession of basic rights to women and blacks does not retroactively render these groups part of the "people" who consented to the Constitution. These gestures are, Franks says, at odds with the larger project of equality because reforms have simply added features to the Constitution rather than highlighting its original deception and illegitimacy. Many fundamental legal prohibitions and expectations were shaped before black men or women were able to vote. Constitutional lies produce smaller lies and to reinforce larger, structural lies. The lie of formal equality obscures the reality of lived inequality.

Franks argues that the constitutional lie has generated lasting inequality by examining police abuse, an occurrence directed disproportionately at black men. *Terry v. Ohio* made it legal for police to stop and search individuals if they had "reasonable suspicion" that the person is engaged in criminal activities. The racial disparity in the resulting stops is striking; although black men are stopped more than anyone else, they are less likely to be found with contraband than whites. Furthermore, police officers committing perjury to justify searches and seizures is a widespread and tolerated phenomenon. The effects of police deception for black men include not only the violation of their Fourth Amendment rights, but deprivation of their lives by officers who often go unpunished.

Franks discusses police passivity, an issue that typically affects women and that results in ineffective police responses to violence against women. Women were originally considered "covered" by their husbands under the law, granting their husbands the right of chastisement and marital rape exemption. Even since domestic violence and rape were criminalized, police have avoided making arrests in domestic violence incidents, regarding these occurrences as private matters. When a woman gets a protective order against a man, she entrusts the police with using reasonable means to enforce the order and to arrest the man if he breaks the order. In *Castle Rock v. Gonzales*, the Court held that police officers did not have to arrest a man violating a protection order if they thought it unnecessary, making the protection order a lie. Victims therefore rely on the state for protection, but the state does not have to protect them at all times because the protection orders are lies. Victims of rape who report their abuse to police are frequently met with insensitivity and skepticism. That women cannot rely on the police affects women's liberties and ability to make decisions by forcing them to take into account the need to ensure their own safety.

Lies about consent affect both women and black men, and these lies are also rooted in the constitutional lie. "We the people" assumes consent from groups where there is none and where there never was an option to consent. A consensual search has no inherent limit as to its scope; when police search people, particularly black men, they assume consent to a search with the largest possible scope. Women are assumed to consent to sex unless they engage in obvious refusal or resistance, an assumption that affects the way women who are raped or report rape are treated.

Franks concludes her chapter by suggesting that we approach constitutional lies in such a way as to ensure complete consciousness of their falsity. No rights have been "given" to women and black men but instead have been belatedly acknowledged as rights we should have recognized from the beginning. The Fourteenth Amendment is the closest thing we have to a constitutional truth and promise. Its promise extends to all who are "subjects of [a state's] jurisdiction," and thus it rewrites the inequality present in the Constitution. This Amendment is the foundation for rejecting false claims of equality and exposing how they promote injustice. In the end, Franks embraces Kant's idea of truth as an unconditional duty to all; she argues that tragically the Founding Fathers believed they could be truthful with some people and not others.

Norman Spaulding's chapter offers a critical analysis of the relationship between truth and deception in the American legal system. He begins by claiming that there is an extraordinary amount of inconsistency in the way that law treats deception. On the one hand, certain crimes of deception are regularly prosecuted, while on the other hand, lawyers continuously walk the line of truth and deception in courts without punishment. The purported primary focus of the judicial system is that of seeking the truth, but Spaulding argues that the law allows deception in the very places meant to exclude it.

Spaulding begins his discussion with an observation – that the legal system and the people it serves do not recognize the deception that clearly exists. To do so, he argues, would undermine the purpose and legitimacy of the justice system. He focuses on lawyers, because the realm of litigation is fraught with examples of deception. Lawyers often defend clients who they believe to be guilty, coach witnesses in their testimony, withhold evidence, and sometimes assist clients in committing perjury. And lawyers, Spaulding observes, are some of the most resistant to acknowledging deception in the legal system. When questioned, lawyers respond with outright denial, or admission of the existence of deception, but a denial that it harms anyone in its existing forms. Or, when they acknowledge deception, they blame specific, deceitful lawyers, painting them as the "bad" apples. Spaulding's purpose in identifying these responses is to ask an important question – why is it so difficult for us to talk about the role that deception plays in the law?

As an example of this phenomenon, Spaulding discusses the work of Monroe Freedman, who suggested that it should be permissible for lawyers to assist their clients in committing perjury in the name of preserving lawyer/client confidentiality. At the time it was made, this suggestion created an uproar about the place of deception in a lawyer's practice. Even today, forty years later, the controversy continues as we argue about what it means for a lawyer to "knowingly" make a false statement.

Spaulding claims that it may be impossible to come to a complete and definite answer as to the appropriate role of deception in legal proceedings. This being so, he argues, our job is to productively understand the interdependent relationship between truth and deception in the law, in which the pursuit of the former generates the reality of the latter. He terms this complex, contradictory relationship "the artifice of law."

In the American legal system, the jury has replaced God as the ultimate truth-determining mechanism, and perjury is still only prosecuted in the most crystal-clear of circumstances. These are the first ways in which a system designed to seek the truth produces deception. Spaulding also considers the roots of deception in democracy. In every aspect of the creation and maintenance of democracy, from its inception to every election, there is a disparity between what is said and what is done. Echoing Franks, Spaulding argues that the first deception of the American legal system, he argues, is that the people have power. And this deception is perpetuated as jurors, lawyers, and spectators all participate in the lie that the people are the makers and enforcers of the law.

In the end, Spaulding returns to lawyers. A lawyer, he says, must simultaneously be able to know when a client, witness, or opposing counsel is not telling the truth, and also how to manipulate information without appearing to deceive. The art of lying, as Spaulding calls it, is knowing when this delicate manipulation of information is appropriate and beneficial. In a similar way, the purpose of the law's prohibition of deception – in perjury prosecutions and expectations of lawyers' truthfulness, for example – is not to completely eliminate lies. Rather, these prohibitions create a culturally productive phenomenon that places deception in a productive, interdependent relationship to truth.

In the next chapter, "Lies to, about Being, and to Become the Government," Helen Norton discusses the government's regulation of lies that threaten harm because they involve the government. The First Amendment protects most intentional lies from punishment but excludes harmful speech from protection. Norton discusses the sorts of harmful lies the government punishes: lies to the government, lies that claim to come from a governmental source, and lies that influence specific decisions about who will become part of the government. Norton considers whether and when the First Amendment should permit the government to regulate lies, defining a lie as a speaker's assertion of a fact that is known to be false with the intent that the listener understand the fact to be true.

Laws that prohibit lies to the government aim to protect the public from harm to its collective interests. Perjury laws exemplify laws that prohibit lying to the government in a specific context because of the threat it poses to the integrity of judgments in the legal system. The Federal False Statements Act prohibits lying or submitting false documents to the government so that lies cannot pervert governmental function and inflict harm by diverting government resources. The moral culpability and threat to the public of these sorts of lies stems from the liar's efforts to try to shape the government's behavior, even if such shaping is unsuccessful.

The False Statements Act advances law enforcement's efficiency interests, for often the target of an investigation is not informed that answering a false "no" is a crime until after he has uttered it. Justice Ginsburg calls for the government to focus on punishing aggressive lies toward the government, lies that are known to be unlawful at the time they are uttered, and not on defensive lies, those in response to queries by the government, namely law enforcement.

Lies about being the government, Norton notes, gives the liar an air of trustworthiness and power over the listener. Punishing these lies not only protects innocent people from loss through reliance on false assumptions about authority but also maintains the reputation of, and trust in, the government. Laws that regulate lies about being the government are largely accepted as constitutional because they prevent real harm to the public. These sort of lies are almost always aggressive rather than defensive, revealing their manipulative nature.

Deliberate falsehoods about being the government may sometimes occur in situations in which they have no effect on a listener's decision making, and these sorts of lies are less dangerous. An example of such lies would be children pretending to be police officers. Laws, Norton argues, should therefore take into account the intent of a false statement about being the government before punishing it.

Lies to become the government concern those told by politicians intending to influence voters' choices. These lies are more difficult to regulate because excessive regulation runs the risk of chilling political debate. Regulation of these lies is constitutional when they involve defamation and are motivated by the speaker's malice. However, these sorts of lies seem the least harmful because they occur in campaign contexts, an atmosphere where people expect lies. Nonetheless, Norton claims, if we do not regulate these lies, politicians have more freedom to lie than ordinary citizens, a concerning thought when they are about to become government officials. The next two chapters focus specifically on lying in context of sex. Stuart Green's *Lies and Rape* asks its readers to think about the way deception is treated in the prosecution of rape cases. Green considers both rape and statutory rape cases, noting that when a defendant uses deception into order to induce a partner into having sex, the law does not treat it as rape. However, in cases of statutory rape, when the "victim" deceives the defendant himself into having sex, the case is still generally treated as statutory rape. In other words, when the perpetrator lies to a victim to obtain sex he is not held accountable, but when he is lied *to* by an underage victim, he is prosecuted.

In rape cases, Green argues, the purpose of laws is always to protect the victim's sexual autonomy. He defines the most important facets of sexual autonomy as an individual's rights to decide with whom they want to have sex. In rape cases, Green asks, should rape-by-deception constitute a violation of an individual's sexual autonomy? And in statutory rape cases where the victim herself has used deception to induce the defendant into having sex, can we still say that her sexual autonomy was violated?

Green begins by looking at rape cases in which a violation of sexual autonomy is constituted by a lack of consent, and in which non-consent has, in the past, typically been equated with the presence of force. Green asks readers to consider whether, in cases in which the act of sex would not have occurred absent a form of deception, the deception can be equated with non-consent in the same way as force. In order to answer this question, he distinguishes among different kinds of deception that may cause different levels of harm. Fraud in the factum refers to deception that is central to the nature of the act – deception cases in which the victim does not know that she is having sex. On the other hand, fraud in the inducement refers to types of deception that relate to the act, but are not central to it. The harms of fraud in the inducement are thus referred to as a sort of "collateral" harm.

Although the law does not generally recognize cases involving deception as rape, Green presents two exceptions to the general rule, both of which contain examples of fraud in the factum. The first occurs when the perpetrator induces the victim into having sex by deceiving her into thinking she is undergoing a medical procedure. Here the victim's sexual autonomy is violated because she does not know that she is having sex, and therefore did not have the chance to decide if she wanted it to happen. The second exception to the general rule in laws of rape occurs when the victim is deceived into believing she is having sex with her spouse. This constitutes fraud in the factum and a violation of sexual autonomy because the victim does not know with whom she is actually having sex.

Green also considers one case of fraud in the inducement, which the law typically does not treat as rape. This is the case in which a person with a sexually transmitted disease fails to tell their sexual partner about having the disease before having sex with him/her. In this case, the law treats the act as consensual – that is, the partner knowingly consented to sex – even if the sex would not have occurred had the partner known about the STI. Any harm suffered by the partner as a result of the non-consensual transmission of the disease has no effect on the consensual nature of the act of sex. After discussing these three examples, Green argues that laws prosecuting rape-by-deception should indeed be distinguished according to the nature of the deception involved.

Next, Green considers statutory rape, in which deception plays a very different role. Historically, statutory rape has been treated as a case of strict liability – that is, whether or not the sex was consensual, the defendant will be prosecuted if the intercourse occurred with someone younger than the legal age. This is because of the aforementioned distinction, in which cases of statutory rape presume non-consent on the part of juveniles. Statutory rape laws protect individuals under a certain age from harm, regardless of the specific circumstances of the case. However, Green asks, should the statute still apply if the victim herself deceived the older party into having sex by lying about her age?

His answer is a resounding "no" – when a statutory rape occurs because the victim deceived the defendant into having sex, it seems entirely contradictory to presume that the victim was incapable of consenting to sex. If statutory rape laws exist in order to protect victims, then a victim who induces the older partner into sex by deception essentially inflicts the harm upon herself. For this reason, Green insists that we should abandon the presumption of non-consent in statutory rape cases.

Green concludes by suggesting we need to consider which kinds of deception-induced consent constitute an actual lack of consent that is comparable to that of force, coercion, or incapability. Some types of deception, he argues, *are* serious enough to invalidate consent and violate the law. However, other kinds of deception are not, and for this reason we should refrain from an all-encompassing approach to deception as an invalidator of consent.

In the next chapter William Eskridge argues that American law produces and sometimes even encourages deceit. He includes in his definition of deceit not only intentional lies but also unintentional misrepresentations and lies by omission. This definition of deceit is broader than the other authors' definitions, as most of them only consider intentional lies.

Eskridge focuses on *Kulturkampf*, the anti-homosexual legal regime that produced "Don't Ask, Don't Tell," and the

United States' policy toward inadmissible immigrants as the two major regulatory practices that produce deceit. Law's production of deceit spurs evasion of statutory policies, corruption of institutional and public discourse, and erosion of the rule of law.

Kulturkampf began the civil exclusion of homosexuals who were considered perverts because they practiced sodomy, an illegal act even when consensual. Rather than risk being punished for breaking these laws or being socially excluded, homosexuals denied their sexual practices that, despite the law prohibiting them, they did not think were "wrong." In an attempt to crack down on sodomy, police officers posed as homosexuals and enticed gay men into making explicit offers of sex. Thus the authorities used deceit to expose the evasive concealment and lies of homosexual men.

Eskridge goes on to discuss what he calls criminalized identities that force people to lie to avoid classification as such an identity. With "Don't Ask, Don't Tell," homosexuals had to lie, primarily by omission, about their identities, generating an institutionally sanctioned closet. A similar government sanctioned closet currently affects immigrants who have entered the country without documentation. National immigration laws exclude immigrants from protections and rights enjoyed by citizens. These policies encourage the population of immigrants to misrepresent their status to avoid deportation.

Law generates deceit when there is a gap between what the law demands of people and how people are willing to conduct their lives. Eskridge returns to "Don't Ask, Don't Tell," focusing on how it necessitates lies by omission. People in the military were not allowed to discuss their sexuality, and everyone was assumed to be straight. This assumption created occasions for homosexuals to lie about their sexual orientation. A similar policy of deceit has emerged with the Internal Revenue Service's (IRS) creation of the Individual Taxpayer Identifying Number (ITIN), a number that allows undocumented workers to pay taxes on their earnings without having social security numbers. The government knows that undocumented immigrants work, although they do not have legal authorization to work, and instituted the ITIN so that they can pay income tax. This policy not only tolerates deceit, but raises deceit to the level of conscious national policy.

Eskridge concludes that because the rule of law is not self-sustaining, it must adjust to keep up with social values. Failing to do so is damaging not only to those who must lead lives of deception, but to all who depend on the integrity of the rule of law.

The Afterword by Montré Carodine discusses the implications of thinking about law and lies for the practices of law schools. Carodine argues that law schools themselves have engaged in a variety of deceptive practices. In her view, law schools need to be "more vigilant in self-policing and addressing our own deceptions."

Taken together the works collected in this book explores law's varied relationship to lies, deception, and truth. Rather than a comprehensive overview, this book offers illuminating examples of the ways in which law sometimes prohibits, and sometimes tolerates or encourages, lying and deception. In so doing, it shows that there are few broad conclusions to be drawn from the relationship between law and lying, just as there are no easy conclusions about the nature of lying itself.

1 Where the Law Lies

Constitutional Fictions and Their Discontents

Mary Anne Franks

I. The Constitutional Lie

America is built on a lie. That lie inheres in its foundational text, the Constitution of the United States, which begins in the false claim to speak of and for "we the people" even as the majority of its population – in particular black men and all women – were denied access to the most basic forms of political participation. This act of simultaneous symbolic inclusion and material exclusion has never been fully acknowledged or confronted, which is another way of saying that it has never really ended. As many lies are, America's constitutional lie is generative: it produces other, secondary, mutually reinforcing legal fictions that obscure the deception buried deep in the social and political structure. These fictions serve multiple purposes, including providing reassurance to those holding abstract commitments to equality as well as seducing and subduing excluded groups that might otherwise demand recognition and reparation for injustices done to them. As long as these constitutional fictions persist, the political existence of women and black men remains fundamentally unstable.

To understand these claims, we must first clearly define what is meant by a "lie." Lying can have multiple meanings, and there is considerable philosophical debate over what qualifies as a lie in various contexts. For present purposes, I will use a Kantian definition: "*the making of an untruthful statement with the intention that the statement be believed to be true*."[1] That is, a lie is not a mere suggestive act, omission, or mistake. A lie is an affirmative statement by an entity who knows the statement to be false and who intends to mislead others into believing that it is true. This Kantian conception of lying is usefully supplemented by Freudian insight: the audience we intend to mislead often includes ourselves.

Lies can be harmful or beneficial, portentous or slight, obscure or obvious, or any combination thereof. Here, I take aim at lies embedded in law itself, which as a category tend to be harmful, portentous, and obscure. This is especially true of lies that are "constitutional" in a dual sense, that is, laws that are both foundational to a society

[1] James Edwin Mahon, "The Truth About Kant on Lies," in *The Philosophy of Deception*, ed. Clancy W. Martin (Oxford: Oxford University Press, 2009), 203.

and embedded in a society's actual founding documents. Constitutional lies undermine the intelligibility of the state itself, and the submerged nature of such lies makes challenging them difficult. The self-deception at work in many constitutional lies renders them even more resistant to scrutiny. What follows is a study of the costs of constitutional lies in the United States and strategies to address those costs.

The Constitution is America's binding document; its foundational text; the "supreme law of the land."[2] It is the source of and the ultimate authority on the basic rights afforded to all its citizens, and the basic constraints imposed on all those acting with the power of the state. It is meant to be and believed to be a promise between the governed and the governing. It begins with these famous words:

> We the People of the United States, in Order to form a more perfect Union, establish Justice, insure domestic Tranquility, provide for the common defence, promote the general Welfare, and secure the Blessings of Liberty to ourselves and our Posterity, do ordain and establish this Constitution for the United States of America.[3]

But "the people" did not in fact ordain and establish the Constitution. Nor can it be said that authorized representatives of "the people" did ordain and establish the Constitution. In 1787, a small group of white, property-owning men

[2] U.S. Const. art. VI.

[3] U.S. Const. Preamble.

declared foundational rules that were to govern the entire population. The signatories to the Constitution included not a single representative of women[4] or black people of either gender.[5] As Caroline Forell writes,

[4] "Women had no part in these meetings or in the contested ratification process that began when the document [the Constitution] was submitted to the thirteen states in 1787." Jean H. Baker, *Women and the U.S. Constitution, 1776–1920* (American Historical Association, 2009), 13. As Catharine MacKinnon observed, "No woman had a voice in the design of the legal institutions that rule the social order under which women, as well as men, live. Nor was the condition of women taken into account or the interest of women as a sex represented. To Abigail Adams' plea to John Adams to 'remember the ladies' in founding the United States," he replied, "We know better than to repeal our Masculine systems." Catharine A. MacKinnon, "Reflections on Sex Equality Under Law," *Yale Law Journal* 100 (1991): 1282.

[5] According to Supreme Court Chief Justice Roger B. Taney, "It is difficult at this day to realize the state of public opinion in relation to that unfortunate race which prevailed in the civilized and enlightened portions of the world at the time of the Declaration of Independence and when the Constitution of the United States was framed and adopted. But the public history of every European nation displays it in a manner too plain to be mistaken. They had for more than a century before been regarded as beings of an inferior order, and altogether unfit to associate with the white race either in social or political relations, and so far inferior that they had no rights which the white man was bound to respect." *Dred Scott v. Sandford*, 60 U.S. 393 (1857), 407. Ilya Somin contends, however, quoting Justice Benjamin Curtis' dissent in *Dred Scott*, that a few black men were eligible to participate in the elections for the state conventions that ratified the Constitution and thus are included in the Constitution's "We the People": "I on five of the thirteen original States, colored persons then possessed the elective franchise,

> The "we" has been mythologized to mean that all Americans had a voice in the founding of the new nation when in fact the real "we" was entirely male, white, and propertied. And whether the "we" is described as "people" or "men," the authors had in mind those who resembled themselves. The purportedly universal "we" actually represented a particular gender, a particular race, and a particular class of people.[6]

The authors of the Declaration of Independence expressed the lie even more boldly, claiming that governments are established "deriving their just powers from the consent of the governed."[7] The authors were fully aware that they had obtained no such consent from large segments of the population or from their representatives.[8]

and were among those by whom the Constitution was ordained and established. If so, it is not true, in point of fact, that the Constitution was made exclusively by the white race." Ilya Somin, "Were African-Americans Part of 'We the People' at the Time of the Founding? The Volokh Conspiracy," http://www.volokh.com/2012/09/17/were-african-americans-part-of-we-the-people-at-the-time-of-the-founding/ (September 17, 2012).

[6] Caroline Forell, "Essentialism, Empathy, and the Reasonable Woman," *University of Illinois Law Review* 769 (1994): 770. See also Angela P. Harris, "Race and Essentialism in Feminist Legal Theory," *Stanford Law Review* 42 (1990), 582–583.

[7] Declaration of Independence (1776).

[8] While it is clear that Native Americans were also not included in the ordainment and establishment of the Constitution, the acknowledgment of tribal sovereignty meant that the Constitution did not exert the same control over Native American populations as it did over women and black men.

The observation that the Founding Fathers were not remotely representative of the population they claimed to bind with this document is of course not new. Very few Americans today are unaware of this fact. "We the People" is perhaps the oldest and most well-known "legal fiction" in American history. However, knowledge that a statement is not literally true does not necessarily lessen the harm of the lie. In fact, the very obviousness of a lie can serve to advance the interests of the liars.

One may object that to call these assertions "lies" is inaccurate. The authors of America's foundational texts may have sincerely believed, this argument goes, that they did represent the interests of the entire population, even those that were fully excluded from political participation. That is, that the interests of slaves and women were naturally folded into the declarations made by their masters and husbands, and that it would have simply been beyond comprehension at this point in history to have contemplated either black individuals or women as having separate political interests. This reading is contradicted by many documents written by the Founders themselves, most notably John Adams. Abigail Adams' famous plea to her husband to "remember the ladies" was an eloquent and clear-eyed assessment of the injustice of forming a nation without any form of participation from women: "Remember, all men would be tyrants if they could. If particular care and attention is not paid to the ladies, we are determined to foment a rebellion, and will not hold ourselves bound by any laws in which we have no voice or representation."[9] John Adams' response was both crude and belittling:

> As to your extraordinary code of laws, I cannot but laugh. We have been told that our struggle has loosened the bonds of government everywhere; that children and apprentices were disobedient; that schools and colleges were grown turbulent; that Indians slighted their guardians, and negroes grew insolent to their masters. But your letter was the first intimation that another tribe, more numerous and powerful than all the rest, were grown discontented.[10]

Adams clearly found the possibility of women's political rights even more ludicrous than the idea of political rights for Native Americans or black individuals, all of which he found fit to compare to the idea of political rights for children. That revolutionary proclamations of equality and freedom had encouraged subordinated groups to consider their own liberation apparently moved Adams to mockery. Upon receiving this response, Abigail Adams astutely noted the hypocrisy and inconsistency of her husband's position: "whilst you are proclaiming peace and good will to Men, Emancipating all Nations, you insist upon retaining an absolute power over Wives."[11]

[9] *My Dearest Friend: Letters of Abigail and John Adams*, ed. Margaret A. Hogan and C. James Taylor (Cambridge: Belknap Press of Harvard University Press, 2007), 110.

[10] Id. at 112.

[11] Id. at 116.

John Adams responded far more earnestly to a question about the consent of the governed when it was posed by fellow statesman James Sullivan. In response to Sullivan's suggestion that the voting franchise be extended to white men who did not own property, Adams reflected, "It is certain, in theory, that the only moral foundation of government is, the consent of the people. But to what an extent shall we carry this principle?"[12] Adams warned Sullivan that if the franchise were extended beyond white men who owned property, this would open the floodgates to extending rights to women, children, and perhaps everyone – an outcome Adams clearly found unacceptable.

> Depend upon it, Sir, it is dangerous to open so fruitful a source of controversy and altercation as would be opened by attempting to alter the qualifications of voters; there will be no end of it. New claims will arise; women will demand a vote . . . and every man who has not a farthing, will demand a voice equal with any other, in all acts of state. It tends to confound and destroy all distinctions; and prostrate all ranks to one common level.[13]

Thus it is clear that Adams, like many of the Founders, had certainly contemplated the possibility of political rights for groups such as women and slaves, and resoundingly rejected it. Those who proclaimed the principles of equality and

[12] *The Feminist Papers: From Adams to Beauvoir*, ed. Alice S. Rossi (Lebanon: Northeastern University Press, 1973), 13.

[13] Id. at 15.

freedom in the name of "We the People" were well aware that they were lying. As Catharine MacKinnon observes,

> Equality was not mentioned in the Constitution or the Bill of Rights. The constitutive mind felt no need to guarantee it explicitly. It was apparently neither structurally essential to government nor in danger of loss to the federal power being created. Women who were not slaves were counted as persons, without being mentioned, for purposes of apportionment; slaves of both sexes were explicitly counted as three-fifths of a person. The only purpose of counting either of them was to divide power among white men, who kept the vote, that primitive exercise of citizenship, to themselves. The exclusion of all women as such from the polity was so far a given that the absence of half the population from the founding process was not seen as qualifying its legitimacy – a legitimacy claimed on behalf of "we, the people" no less.[14]

We return, then, to the question of why the Founders lied. Why did they boldly declare that they were exercising their powers with the consent of the governed when they had neither obtained such consent nor felt compelled in any way to obtain it? Why did they not simply write a Constitution

[14] MacKinnon, "Reflections on Sex Equality Under Law," at 1282–1283. See also Mary Anne Case, "'The Ladies? Forget About Them.' A Feminist Perspective on the Limits of Originalism," *Constitutional Comment* 29 (2014): 431–432, "the Framers of both the original Constitution and the post-Civil War Amendments were quite conscious of their interests in preserving their male prerogatives in law."

that told the truth: that an elite portion of the population – white, property-owning men – created rules to be imposed on the entire population? What did they gain, in other words, from lying?

If a lie is, as defined above, a false statement given in order to make others believe it is true, I propose that the Framers intended to mislead both themselves and the non-consenting populations in question. To establish the legitimacy of the great American project, the Framers had to convince themselves that they were acting in the best interests of the excluded. The lie served to protect their self-perception, to reassure them of the justice of their ambition, and to quell attempts by subordinated populations to demand their rights.

One hopes that some of the Framers took note of the irony of their actions, given that the Revolution itself was provoked by the oppression, exclusion, and lack of representation they experienced at the hands of the British. However, as Adams' letters make clear, the Framers believed on some level that the people they were binding without consultation were not fully "people," and that their humanity, such that it was, was adequately represented by Convention delegates. The majestic language of liberty and justice required declarations of fairness and consent; the Framers' claims were delusional, but served important self-legitimating interests.

The lie served the additional purpose of appeasing the vast populations excluded from representation by presenting them with the attractive fiction that they were in fact included. As long as women and black people were kept under strict physical and political control (women by domestic servitude, black men and women by slavery, both groups by complex political and cultural networks of subordination), this abstract rhetoric likely sufficed to keep dissent at bay. Whether either population truly embraced the idea of consent by proxy was likely a moot point, as their options for disagreement were severely limited. As physical and political control began to wane, however, the question of unacknowledged exclusion/fictive inclusion became much harder to ignore. Leaders of the abolitionist movement, which began to gain serious momentum in the 1830s, agitated for various civil and economic rights for women and black men, including the extension of the franchise to black men and women.[15] However, it would be another forty years – after the Civil War had been fought, the Emancipation Proclamation had been issued, and the Thirteenth Amendment had been ratified – before the Fifteenth Amendment, establishing black male suffrage, would be passed in 1870. It would be another fifty years before the Nineteenth Amendment would grant women this most basic right of participation in society.

[15] Although conflicts soon arose over the question of whether black male suffrage and women's suffrage should be urged at the same time, or whether black male suffrage should take first priority. See Ellen Carol DuBois, *Feminism and Suffrage, The Emergence of an Independent Women's Movement in America 1848–1869* (Ithaca: Cornell University Press, 1978), 53–72.

Between 1787 and 1920, then (that is, for the majority of America's existence) the claim that "We the People" had established and ordained the Constitution was an outright lie. Following the concession of basic rights to more than half the population, it remains a lie: the enfranchisement of black men and women, granted 83 and 133 years, respectively, after the establishment of the Constitution cannot retroactively render the foundational claim to consent of the governed any more true.[16] These belated, formal, and

[16] It is instructive to consider how, by contrast, the leaders of the women's suffrage movement essentially "rewrote" the Declaration of Independence in the Declaration of Sentiments at the Seneca Falls Convention in 1848:

When, in the course of human events, it becomes necessary for one portion of the family of man to assume among the people of the earth a position different from that which they have hitherto occupied, but one to which the laws of nature and of nature's God entitle them, a decent respect to the opinions of mankind requires that they should declare the causes that impel them to such a course.

We hold these truths to be self-evident: that all men and women are created equal; that they are endowed by their Creator with certain inalienable rights; that among these are life, liberty, and the pursuit of happiness; that to secure these rights governments are instituted, deriving their powers from the consent of the governed. Whenever any form of government becomes destructive of these rights, it is the right of those who suffer from it to refuse allegiance to it, and to insist upon the institution of a new government, laying its foundation on such principles, and organizing its powers in such form, as to them shall seem most likely to effect their safety and happiness. Sally G. McMillen, *Seneca Falls and the Origins of the Women's Rights Movement* (Oxford: Oxford University Press, 2008), 237.

incomplete gestures toward equal citizenship for black men and women are no more than the least the state could have done.

In fact, these corrective gestures are in some respects at odds with the larger project of equality and justice. This is partly because they simply add features to the Constitution rather than highlighting its original deception and illegitimacy. The Fifteenth and Nineteenth Amendments do not acknowledge the injustice and unintelligibility of the union as it was before them. They are merely prosaic declarations that, from this point on, there will be no denials of the right to vote based on the categories of race or sex.

But what of all the laws created, enforced, or revised in the 83 years before a significant minority was allowed to vote, and 133 years before half the population received even the most basic political right? What of the legal, social, and political institutions that were built up over years without contribution from women or African-American men? Their power to bind the populations that had no say in their creation is not questioned. There is no acknowledgment, in the amendments or elsewhere in the Constitution, of the radically unjust imposition of power over non-consenting individuals or reflection on what this imposition means for the continuing legitimacy of the government. In other words, there is no real acknowledgment of the constitutional lie and its effects.

And who would call for such an acknowledgment now? For the majority of this country's history, the lie has been allowed to flourish. That lie has formed the legal basis of our society itself and has provided the outer limits of all of our laws for more than a century. Our fundamental legal prohibitions and expectations were shaped long before either black men or women got the vote; the concept of *stare decisis* compels us to honor and defer to what has come before except in extreme circumstances. Openly recognizing the long-held lie would not only create administrative and organizational problems, but also psychological ones. Humans are not well-suited to radical change; inertia is one of the most difficult forces to overcome. It requires far less legal, cognitive, and psychological energy to participate in the legal fiction of constitutional truth than to try to expose and battle its comprehensive reach.[17]

Is it so bad to embrace the legal fiction, to continue to regard our Constitution and the laws that flow from or are restrained by it as though they really were built on the consent of the governed? One can reasonably argue that it is better for social order that we refrain from scrutinizing long-established lies, lest we become overwhelmed by chaos and resentment. However, constitutional lies inflict

[17] Nietzsche claimed that mankind only seeks truth to the extent that it is reassuring and positive: "In a . . . limited way man wants the truth: he desires the agreeable life-preserving consequences of truth, but he is indifferent to pure knowledge, which has no consequences; he is even hostile to possibly damaging and destructive truths." Friedrich Nietzsche, "On Truth and Lie in an Extra-Moral Sense," http://oregonstate.edu/instruct/phl201/modules/Philosophers/Nietzsche/Truth_and_Lie_in_an_Extra-Moral_Sense.htm.

constitutional harms, and pretending not to see them does not make them any less real. The failure to recognize and denounce the constitutional lie means that constitutional existence of the excluded will always be precarious. Put another way, the lie of abstract equality serves to obscure the reality of lived inequality. This obscurity is compounded by the tendency of constitutional lies to proliferate: they produce smaller lies that reinforce and disguise the larger, structural lies.

The repressed truth – that women and black men were treated fundamentally as objects and not subjects of the law – resurfaces in multiple ways and in particular practices of legal deception. The examples I will focus on here are the lies that structure law enforcement abuses, which disproportionately burden black men, and the lies that structure law enforcement passivity, which disproportionately burden women. These deceptive and repressive practices have common origins in the lies that structure the concept of consent.

II. Lies and Law Enforcement Abuse

In the years following Emancipation, as African-Americans began to gain political and civil rights, groups of white racists engaged in lynching campaigns intended to terrorize blacks back into submission. Although lynching is accurately described as a form of extra-legal "mob justice," law enforcement often played a role in these attacks, with officials sometimes participating directly in the torture or deliberately turning a blind eye to mobs so that the attacks could be carried out.[18]

Lies played a key role in these violent killings, which included hangings, shootings, setting on fire, beatings, and genital mutilation. The proffered justification for these acts of violence was that they were punishment for heinous crimes, including rape and murder, committed by black individuals. The journalist Ida B. Wells chronicled not only the brutality but also the deception at work in lynching, demonstrating the falsity of many of the claims of black violence.[19] A considerable number of the alleged rapes of white women by black men were wholly unsupported by evidence; in several cases, allegations of sexual assault were clearly used to disguise consensual sexual relations between black men and white women that were inadvertently brought to light.[20] The summary violence delivered in the cases that may have had some basis in reality stood in sharp contrast to the process and punishment afforded white men accused of similar crimes.[21] As African-Americans made political and social gains, the myth of the "black beast" was used to stir up white fear and sexual

18 See generally *Southern Horrors and Other Writings: The Anti-Lynching Campaign of Ida B. Wells, 1892–1900*, ed. Jacqueline Jones Royster (Boston: Bedford/St. Martin's, 1997).

19 Id.

20 Royster, *Southern Horrors* at 54.

21 Robert A. Gibson, *The Negro Holocaust: Lynching and Race Riots in the United States, 1880–1950* (Yale-New Haven Teachers Institute).

anxiety.[22] That myth was promoted even as white men's rape of black women – a common occurrence during the slavery era and after – was well-known and accomplished in most cases with impunity.[23]

By the middle of the twentieth century, lynchings had all but stopped, and the civil rights movement demanding racial equality was gaining momentum. The Civil Rights Act of 1964 spelled a formal end to the most overt forms of racial discrimination in schools and public accommodations, and the Voting Rights Act of 1965 did the same with regard to voting. However, these reforms were met with considerable resistance and resentment on the part of the white population, and tensions between whites and blacks ran high throughout the 1950s and 1960s. Law enforcement continued to turn a blind eye to crimes committed by whites against blacks, whereas allegations of crimes committed by blacks against whites were often met with swift brutality.

In 1968, the Supreme Court held that law enforcement had the power to stop and frisk individuals based on what would come to be called "reasonable suspicion": "specific reasonable inferences which [a police officer] is entitled to draw from the facts in light of his experience"[24] that a person

[22] Danielle L. McGuire, *At the Dark End of the Street: Black Women, Rape, and Resistance – A New History of the Civil Rights Movement from Rosa Parks to the Rise of Black Power* (New York: Random House, 2010), 25–28.

[23] McGuire, *At the Dark End of the Street.*

[24] *Terry v. Ohio*, 392 U.S. 1 (1968).

is engaged in criminal activity. The suspicious behavior in the case at issue, *Terry v. Ohio*, involved two African-American men strolling past a store window several times and looking in. The Court made much of the fact that Officer McFadden, who stopped and frisked the men (finding a weapon in the coat pocket of one), had thirty-nine years of experience on the force.[25] In this and many cases that followed, the Court adopted a highly deferential approach to law enforcement.

In his opinion for the majority, Justice Earl Warren alluded to the tense relations between police officers and the black community in the midst of the civil rights movement, noting "the wholesale harassment by certain elements of the police community, of which minority groups, particularly Negroes, complain,"[26] and acknowledged the indignity imposed by the stop and frisk procedure. However, he was ultimately unconcerned that police would abuse their discretion with this newly established right to stop and search citizens without probable cause. By contrast, Justice Douglas, the sole dissenter, called the ruling a "step down the totalitarian path."[27] To get a fuller sense of Justice Douglas' concerns, it is useful to consider his majority opinion in a case that came just four years later, this one involving the convictions of several people for "vagrancy."

[25] Id. at 27.
[26] Id. at 14.
[27] Id. at 38.

In *Papachristou v. City of Jacksonville*,[28] the Court was tasked with determining the constitutionality of a Florida anti-vagrancy statute that prescribed criminal punishment for individuals who engaged in the following activities:

> Rogues and vagabonds, or dissolute persons who go about begging, common gamblers, persons who use juggling or unlawful games or plays, common drunkards, common night walkers .... lewd, wanton, and lascivious persons ... persons wandering or strolling around from place to place without any lawful purpose or object, habitual loafers, disorderly persons, persons neglecting all lawful business and habitually spending their time by frequenting houses of ill fame, gaming houses, or houses where alcoholic beverages are sold or served, persons able to work but habitually living upon the earnings of their wives or minor children.[29]

Justice Douglas declared that the kinds of activity prohibited by the statute were "historically part of the amenities of life as we have known them" that "have dignified the right of dissent and have honored the right to be nonconformists and the right to defy submissiveness. They have encouraged lives of high spirits rather than hushed, suffocating silence."[30] Justice Douglas observed, in addition, that this kind of vague ordinance would no doubt be enforced more often against disfavored populations.

[28] *Papachristou v. City of Jacksonville*, 405 U.S. 156 (1972).
[29] Id. at note 1.
[30] Id. at 165.

> Those generally implicated by the imprecise terms of the ordinance – poor people, nonconformists, dissenters, idlers – may be required to comport themselves according to the lifestyle deemed appropriate by the Jacksonville police and the courts. . . . It results in a regime in which the poor and the unpopular are permitted to "stand on a public sidewalk" . . . only at the whim of any police officer.[31]

For these reasons, the Court unanimously struck down the ordinance as unconstitutionally vague and overbroad.

In *Terry*, the majority noted the possibility of law enforcement harassment in determinations of suspicious behavior, but ultimately expressed confidence that law enforcement could be trusted to exercise its discretion. In *Papachristou*, the majority was concerned that broad vagrancy laws might allow law enforcement to single out disfavored populations for harassment.

It is *Terry*'s legacy, rather than *Papachristou*'s, that has carried the day, at least in cases that often involve black defendants or law enforcement practices that disproportionately target black individuals. Since *Terry*, the Court has ruled in favor of police action in a succession of increasingly invasive stops and frisks provoked by decreasingly suspicious behavior, including sitting in one's car in a "high-crime area,"[32] running from police officers in a "high-crime

[31] Id. at 170.

[32] *Adams v. Williams*, 407 U.S. 143 (1972) (police officer acting on an informant's tip reached his hand into waistband of defendant's pants to search for gun).

area,"[33] and walking in the opposite direction from police officers.[34] Stop and frisk practices are now widespread in many cities and are triggered by behavior such as wearing baggy clothing or, according to many African-Americans who are stopped, simply engaging in public activities while black. The racial disparity in the stops is impossible to ignore, especially when considered alongside "hit" rates (the number of searches that actually reveal contraband). In nearly every city where empirical data has been gathered, police overwhelmingly stop racial minorities more than any other group, even though whites are more likely to be found with contraband. To take New York City as an example, black and Latino males between the ages of 14 and 24 accounted for 41.7 percent of stops in 2012, despite making up only 4.7 percent of the population.[35] Nine out of ten people searched in New York in 2011 were completely innocent. According to data gathered from studies in Los Angeles (with New York, Illinois, Minnesota, Rhode Island, Missouri, and West Virginia reporting similar results), blacks are forty-two percent less likely than whites to be found with weapons; twenty-five percent

[33] *Illinois v. Wardlow*, 528 U.S. 119 (2000) (police officers chased defendant and immediately searched the bag he was holding, despite having no informant's tip or other reason to believe defendant was engaged in illegal activity).

[34] *Minnesota v. Dickerson*, 508 U.S. 366 (1993) (Court takes no issue with police stopping a man after he walks in the opposite direction from them; finds that manipulation of object found in man's pocket violated the "plain touch doctrine").

[35] New York Civil Liberties Union, http://www.nyclu.org/files/stopandfrisk-factsheet.pdf (2011).

less likely than whites to be found with drugs; and thirty-three percent are less likely than whites to be found with other contraband.[36]

It may have been mere coincidence that the defendant in *Terry* was African-American and that some of the defendants in *Papachristou* were white, but these subsequent rulings and police practices have made it abundantly clear that police treat racial minorities very differently from whites. But are these practices lies according to the definition outlined above? Although these police practices are not lies in themselves, the claim that police are "colorblind" and make judgments based only on objective evaluations of a person's conduct is a lie.[37] Eduardo Bonilla-Silva refers to whites' proclamations of color-blindness as "sincere fictions," a term he borrows from Vera Hernán and Joe R. Feagin, who used the term to illustrate how the lies white people tell themselves make it possible to avoid confronting "the brutal realities of U.S. racial relations."[38] The deception at work in law enforcement practices has a whole-sale discriminatory effect on African-American and other racial minority populations. Although it may have been plausible that some police departments were unaware of racial

[36] See L. Song Richardson, "Police Efficiency and the Fourth Amendment," *Indiana Law Journal* 87 (2012): 1145.

[37] See Eduardo Bonilla-Silva, *Racism Without Racists: Color-Blind Racism and the Persistence of Racial Inequality in the United States* (Oxford: Rowman and Littlefield Publishers, 2003).

[38] Vera Hernán et al., "Superior Intellect? Sincere Fictions of the White Self," *The Journal of Negro Education* 64 (1995): 257. The authors borrowed the term in turn from Pierre Bourdieu.

bias in their stop and frisk policies two decades ago, recent research has conclusively shown that racial bias infects nearly all interactions that police have with the communities they are tasked with protecting.[39] Now individual police officers and departments are very much aware that racial bias affects the way they perform their duties, but they nonetheless continue to insist that this is not the case.

Compounding and helping to obscure the lie of colorblindness in law enforcement are the lies embedded in routine police practices. Police mendacity is such an open secret that it has its own neologisms: "testilying" and "blue lies." Police perjury, whether before magistrates in order to obtain warrants or in court to retroactively justify an illegal search or seizure, is widespread and routinely tolerated. As Bennett Capers describes it,

> Blue lies are so pervasive that even former prosecutors have described them as "commonplace" and "prevalent." Surveyed prosecutors, defense attorneys, and judges believed perjury was present in approximately twenty percent of all cases. A separate survey of police officers was even more sobering. Seventy-six percent of responding

[39] As Michelle Alexander describes it, "it is no longer permissible to use race, explicitly, as a justification for discrimination, exclusion, and social contempt. So we don't. Rather than rely on race, we use our criminal justice system to label people of color 'criminals' and then engage in all the practices we supposedly left behind . . . . We have not ended racial caste in America; we have merely redesigned it." Michelle Alexander, *The New Jim Crow: Mass Incarceration in the Age of Colorblindness* (New York: The New Press, 2012).

officers agreed that officers shade the facts to establish probable cause; forty-eight percent believed judges were often correct in disbelieving police testimony.[40]

However, even these shockingly high estimates don't come close to painting the real picture of police deception. Only a tiny minority of cases involving police abuse or lies ever makes it to court. One of the profound ironies of the exclusionary rule, which is the only real remedy for criminal procedure violations in most cases, is that it only benefits individuals with something to hide. The illegal searches and seizures that turn up nothing – that is, the searches and seizures of completely innocent people – will almost never make it to court or into casebooks. That is as stacked a deck as any officer could want: the public/jury/judge/law students only learn about searches that turn up something, which has the dual effect of making police officers seem like geniuses (their suspicions are always correct!) and virtually ensuring that the defendant will be convicted because anyone found with contraband is unlikely to overcome the impression that he is guilty.

As if the law wasn't tolerant enough of police deception, the Supreme Court has handed down several decisions that encourage and reward the police for lying. In *Murray v. U.S.* (1988), police officers illegally broke into a warehouse that they had probable cause to believe contained drugs.[41] Upon

40 I. Bennett Capers, "Crime, Legitimacy, and Testilying," *Indiana Law Journal* 83 (2008): 871.

41 *Murray v. U.S.*, 487 U.S. 533 (1988).

confirming that there were in fact drugs in the warehouse, the police officers left everything as it was and went to a magistrate to get a search warrant. They made no reference to the fact that they had entered the warehouse illegally, relying solely on evidence of probable cause they had obtained prior to the illegal entry.[42] The search warrant was granted and the officers returned to the warehouse, legally entered the premises, and seized the drugs. The Supreme Court ruled that, although there was no question that the police had violated the defendant's Fourth Amendment rights when they engaged in the illegal initial search, the second search was "untainted by the initial illegality."[43] The Court did not seem to mind the fact that the police had effectively lied to the magistrate in obtaining the warrant to conduct the "legal" search. By omitting the fact that their strongest reason for suspecting there was marijuana in the warehouse was because they had been inside and seen it, the police intentionally misled the magistrate to believe that they were basing their probable cause on other factors so that he would grant the warrant. As Justice Marshall pointed out in dissent, this decision encourages police to engage in confirmatory searches, in fact removing any incentive they might have not to do so:

> any confirmatory searches will result in the discovery that no evidence is present, thus saving the police the time and trouble of getting a warrant. If contraband is discovered,

[42] Id. at 536.
[43] Id. at 538.

> however, the officers may seek a warrant to shield the evidence from the taint of the illegal search. The police thus know in advance that they have little to lose and much to gain by forgoing the bother of obtaining a warrant and undertaking an illegal search.[44]

Before *Murray*, police could and did simply fabricate tips from unidentified informants. However, this practice carried a risk: if "Old Reliable" was wrong enough times, that is, if enough searches turned up nothing, the magistrate might stop issuing warrants to that police officer. After *Murray*, however, "there is no such fear, because the fictitious 'Old Reliable' will always be right! His 'tip' will always lead to evidence because the police will have found it in advance."[45]

In 1996, the Supreme Court issued a unanimous decision that further rewarded and incentivized racialized police deception. In *Whren v. U.S.*, the Court declared that pretextual stops – that is, stopping a defendant for some reason other than the one officially articulated – did not violate the Fourth Amendment.[46] Justice Scalia wrote, "subjective intentions play no role in ordinary, probable-cause Fourth Amendment analysis."[47] A police officer can stop a defendant on the basis of his race so long as there is

[44] Id. at 547.

[45] Craig M. Bradley, "*Murray v. United States*: the Bell Tolls for the Search Warrant Requirement," *Indiana Law Journal* 64 (1989): 917–918.

[46] *Whren v. U.S.*, 517 U.S. 806 (1996).

[47] Id. at 813.

an independent justification for the stop. Given that there are hundreds of traffic regulations that a person might violate if she is followed long enough, this ruling made it possible to stop anyone for any minor reason – or for no reason at all, given how easily an officer can lie about what he has seen. Proof that police officers do exactly this has been obtained on numerous occasions.[48] The ubiquity of recording devices has made it possible to learn how police officers tell citizens that they failed to signal or come to a complete stop at a stop sign even though citizens protest that this is false, calmly announce that they are "in fear of their lives" despite no sudden or suspicious movement by the detained person,[49] or repeatedly order a citizen to "stop resisting arrest" when it is abundantly clear that the citizen is doing no such thing.[50]

As recent events have grimly highlighted, the consequences of police deception can be far more serious even than this. The August 2014 shooting of an unarmed black

48 Joanna Rothkopf, "'I'm Not Your Brother!' Video Reveals Police's Stunning Double-Standard for Black Americans," *Salon*, http://www.salon.com/2014/08/29/st_paul_cops_tase_and_arrest_black_man_for_waiting_to_pick_his_kids_up_from_preschool/ (August 29, 2014).

49 Gary Webb, "Driving While Black," *Esquire*, http://www.esquire.com/features/driving-while-black-0499.

50 Alyson Shontell, "Man Facing Years in Jail After Dash Cam Video Shows Scary Police Behavior," *Business Insider*, http://www.businessinsider.com/marcus-jeter-dash-cam-video-2014-8?IR=T (August 27, 2014).

teenager named Michael Brown[51] was only one in a series of deaths of unarmed black men at the hands of police that month. The repeated lie by police and those invested in believing them is that these shootings were all justified by the actions of the victims. In some cases we know these are lies because film footage reveals the truth, and in some cases the available evidence strongly demonstrates that white suspects exhibiting similar or in many cases much more aggressive behavior are rarely killed or even badly injured by police. Whatever aggression unarmed Michael Brown may have shown toward Darren Wilson before Wilson shot him at least six times surely could not compare to the white men defending their criminal defiance of federal law by pointing guns at federal agents at the Bundy Ranch, and yet the agents there retreated without firing a shot.[52] A black man who had picked up a toy gun in Wal-Mart was shot on sight,[53] whereas none of the many men carrying assault rifles and other weapons in stores and on

[51] "Michael Brown's Shooting and Its Immediate Aftermath in Ferguson," *New York Times*, http://www.nytimes.com/interactive/2014/08/12/us/13police-shooting-of-black-teenager-michael-brown.html?_r=0 (August 9, 2014).

[52] Brad Friedman, "*Cliven Bundy v. Ferguson*'s Peaceful Demonstrators: A Tale of Two Protests," *Salon*, http://www.salon.com/2014/08/18/cliven_bundy_vs_fergusons_peaceful_demonstrators_a_tale_of_two_protests/ (August 18, 2014).

[53] Andres Jauregui, "Cop Who Killed John Crawford III at Ohio Walmart Shot Him 'On Sight,'" *Huffington Post*, http://www.huffingtonpost.com/2014/08/27/john-crawford-killed-walm_n_5721676.html (August 27, 2014).

public streets as part of alleged "open-carry" demonstrations have been shot or assaulted.[54] An unarmed, mentally ill black man in LA was shot in the back while lying down following an "investigative stop;"[55] meanwhile in St. Louis, not a single shot was fired when a white robbery suspect assaulted two cops, breaking the hand of one of them.[56] An analysis of federally collected data on police shootings showed that young black males are twenty-one times more likely than their white counterparts to be shot by police.[57]

The constitutional consequences of police deception for black men in particular include the evisceration not only of their Fourth Amendment rights, but also, in far too many cases, the permanent deprivation of their lives. The constant police surveillance and scrutiny of black men is

[54] Ryan Broderick, "A Bunch of Gun Activists Wore Assault Weapons While Walking Around the Baby Clothes Aisle at Target," *BuzzFeed*, http://www.buzzfeed.com/ryanhatesthis/moms-versus-assault-weapons-in-target (June 4, 2014).

[55] Thomas Johnson, "Ezell Ford: The mentally Ill Black Man Killed by the LAPD Two Days After Michael Brown's Death," *The Washington Post*, http://www.washingtonpost.com/news/morning-mix/wp/2014/08/15/ezell-ford-the-mentally-ill-black-man-killed-by-the-lapd-two-days-after-michael-browns-death/ (August 15, 2014).

[56] "Police: Suspect Hides in Woman's Basement, Assaults Officers," KMOV, http://www.kmov.com/news/crime/Police-Suspect-hides-in-womans-basement-assaults-officers-271009211.html.

[57] Ryan Gabrielson et al., "Deadly Force, in Black and White," *ProPublica*, http://www.propublica.org/article/deadly-force-in-black-and-white (October 10, 2014).

underwritten by the threat of execution.[58] This reality constrains their constitutional rights to liberty and privacy, as well as making a mockery of racial equality.

III. Lies and Law Enforcement Passivity

Violence against women, including physical assault, rape, and stalking, is an epidemic in the United States. More than a third of women have experienced some form of violence by an intimate partner in their lifetimes[59]; victimizations by strangers or casual acquaintances make this number even higher. However, law enforcement response – and legal response more generally – to violence against women has been so lackluster and ineffective as to tacitly encourage and legitimize this violence.[60]

[58] See Isabel Wilkerson, "Mike Brown's Shooting and Jim Crow Lynchings Have Too Much in Common. It's Time for America to Own Up," *The Guardian*, http://www.theguardian.com/commentisfree/2014/aug/25/mike-brown-shooting-jim-crow-lynchings-in-common (August 25, 2014).

[59] National Center for Injury Prevention and Control (CDC), *National Intimate Partner and Sexual Violence Survey 2010*, 2, http://www.cdc.gov/violenceprevention/pdf/nisvs_report2010-a.pdf (hereafter *NISVS 2010*).

[60] "Condescending, demeaning, hostile, humiliating, and indifferent judicial treatment of female victims of sexual assault is not uncommon. Government commits this inequality and should rectify it. Law has a choice. It can inscribe this misogyny on society yet more authoritatively, promoting sex inequality, or it can move against it by promoting sex equality. Sexual assault cannot be treated as gender neutral because sexual assault is not gender neutral. The law of sexual assault cannot be treated as private

Until the mid-1800s in much of the western world, including the United States, men's violence toward their wives was considered a right, not a crime. The doctrine of coverture, which maintained that a married woman was "covered" by her husband under the law and thus did not have her own rights and responsibilities, included both a "right of chastisement" and what would later be called the "marital rape exemption."[61] Domestic violence and rape are now recognized as crimes, but law enforcement still often regards them as private matters that do not warrant police interference, and demonstrates skepticism and hostility toward victims.

For decades, "arrest avoidance" was official police policy toward domestic violence incidents,[62] as police did not view men beating their wives as a conduct that should be punished by jail. Some argue that the pendulum has now swung too far in the opposite direction with the adoption of mandatory arrest and "no-drop" policies in some states (measures that also sometimes do a poor job of protecting victims), but these reforms were intended to address the longstanding lack of law enforcement response to domestic violence.

action because it is government action. Women are not receiving equal protection of the laws. The equal protection clause is inconsistent with state law that promotes sex inequality. The law of sexual assault commands Fourteenth Amendment scrutiny." MacKinnon, "Reflections on Sex Equality Under Law" at 1306–1307.

61 See Reva B. Siegel, "'The Rule of Love': Wife Beating as Prerogative and Privacy," *Yale Law Journal* 105 (1996): 2122–2129.

62 See Roslyn Muraskin, *Women and Justice* (Amsterdam: Routledge, 2005), 104–114.

One of the few measures victims of violence can take to grant them some security and peace of mind is the protection order. Protection orders, also called "stay away" or restraining orders, set out specific conditions of no-contact between an abuser and his victim. As many abusers and victims share custody of children, these orders often detail the days and times that each parent is to see the children. Protection orders often include mandatory arrest language, e.g.,

> "(a) Whenever a restraining order is issued, the protected person shall be provided with a copy of such order. *A peace officer shall use every reasonable means to enforce a restraining order.*
>
> "(b) A peace officer shall arrest, or, if an arrest would be impractical under the circumstances, seek a warrant for the arrest of a restrained person when the peace officer has information amounting to probable cause that:
>
> > "(I) The restrained person has violated or attempted to violate any provision of a restraining order; and
> >
> > "(II) The restrained person has been properly served with a copy of the restraining order or the restrained person has received actual notice of the existence and substance of such order.[63]

[63] *Castle Rock v. Gonzales*, 125 S.Ct. 2796, 2805 (2005).

This was in fact the exact language printed on the protection order issued to Jessica Gonzales (now Lenahan) against her ex-husband, Simon Gonzales, in light of his years-long history of beating, raping, and terrorizing Jessica. The couple had three children together, and Simon was allowed to see the girls on designated days. One day, Jessica realized that the girls had gone missing from the yard. Simon was not scheduled to see them that day, and she feared that he had abducted them. She immediately called the police and showed them the protection order when they arrived. The police informed her that there was nothing they could do until the girls had been gone for a longer amount of time. Jessica emphasized that Simon was unstable and dangerous, but the police were unmoved, even chiding her at one point that she shouldn't be worried because the "girls were with their father." Jessica continued to call the police as the hours went by, but received the same reaction, even when Simon called to taunt Jessica with the information that he had the girls. All in all, she reached out for help from the police nine times that night. Around 3 am, Simon pulled up to the Castle Rock police station and opened fire. The police returned fire, and when the shootout ended with Simon's death, the bodies of Jessica's three daughters were found in his truck.[64]

Jessica filed a §1983 claim against the Castle Rock police department, arguing that the police had deprived her of her

[64] Id. at 2802–2803.

due process rights by failing to enforce the restraining order. The Tenth Circuit agreed, holding that

> this statutory provision – especially taken in conjunction with a statement from its legislative history, and with another statute restricting criminal and civil liability for officers making arrests – established the Colorado Legislature's clear intent "to alter the fact that the police were not enforcing domestic abuse retraining orders," and thus its intent "that the recipient of a domestic abuse restraining order have an entitlement to its enforcement." Any other result, it said, "would render domestic abuse restraining orders utterly valueless."[65]

The case went up to the Supreme Court, where Justice Scalia, writing for the majority, disagreed with the Tenth Circuit's conclusion. He argued that police officers necessarily always retain "discretion" over when and how to make arrests, and as such a mandatory arrest measure could not be taken literally.[66] In other words, the Court held that the protection order was a lie, and that this lie did not violate any of Jessica Gonzales' constitutional rights. Even if the order meant what it said, Scalia found, it would not implicate any property interest guaranteed by the Fourteenth Amendment.[67]

Justice Stevens wrote a blistering dissent, pointing out that the entire purpose of mandatory arrest language was to

[65] Id. at 2805.
[66] Id. at 2806.
[67] Id. at 2809.

address and correct the historic under-enforcement of protections against domestic violence.[68] Justice Stevens observed that the protection order assured Jessica of certain action that would be taken on her behalf, and the police failed to provide that action:

> if respondent had contracted with a private security firm to provide her and her daughters with protection from her husband, it would be apparent that she possessed a property interest in such a contract. Here, Colorado undertook a comparable obligation, and respondent – with restraining order in hand – justifiably relied on that undertaking. Respondent's claim of entitlement to this promised service is no less legitimate than the other claims our cases have upheld, and no less concrete than a hypothetical agreement with a private firm. The fact that it is based on a statutory enactment and a judicial order entered for her special protection, rather than on a formal contract, does not provide a principled basis for refusing to consider it "property" worthy of constitutional protection.[69]

Domestic violence experts characterized the ruling as a devastating blow to victims that made protection orders quite literally not worth the paper they are printed on.[70] Victims are told to rely on the state to protect them, but

[68] Id. at 2817–2818.

[69] Id. at 2815.

[70] See Zanita Fenton, "State-Enabled Violence: The Story of Town of *Castle Rock v. Gonzales*," in *Women and the Law Stories*, eds. Elizabeth Schneider and Stephanie Wildman (New York: Thomson Reuters, Foundation Press, 2011).

that the state can always decline to do so. The state presents protection orders as the only legitimate response to the threat of domestic violence. They are written as promises to protect victims. If the state is not obligated to honor those orders, then that promise is broken from the beginning – it is a lie. This lie not only leaves women vulnerable to the whims of police, but also deprives them of addressing the situation themselves through self-help. This lie, such as the lie of police abuse, costs citizens not only their constitutional rights to due process but also, in many cases, their very lives.

Police deception and passivity have similarly destructive effects in the context of sexual assault. In 2010, there were nearly 1.3 million rapes of women in the United States.[71] One in five women will be raped in her lifetime. This risk increases for female college students, 1 in 4 of whom will be raped.[72] Most of these sexual assaults will never be officially

[71] National Center for Injury Prevention and Control (CDC), *NISVS 2010* puts the number at 1,270,000 (18). This figure is considerably higher than the number reported by the *National Crime Victimization Survey*, which counted 188,380 rapes in 2010. Jennifer L. Truman, U.S. Dept. of Just., Pub. No. 235508, *National Crime Victimization Survey 2010*, http://bjs.gov/content/pub/pdf/cv10.pdf. There is compelling evidence demonstrating that the National Crime Victimization Survey's study is badly flawed (including lack of privacy controls and a definition of rape that excludes incapacitation) that the CDC study is far more accurate. See Nat. Research Council, *Estimating the Incidence of Rape and Sexual Assault*, eds. Candace Kruttschnitt et al. (2014).

[72] Bonnie S. Fisher, Francis T. Cullen and Michael G. Turner, Nat. Inst. of Just., Pub. No. 182369, "The Sexual Victimization of College

counted. More than eighty percent of rapes are never even reported to the police. The reasons for this are complex, but they include a fear of not being believed, being forced to undergo an invasive and humiliating investigation, and a lack of confidence in the police's willingness or ability to find and prosecute the perpetrators – all, sadly, reasonable concerns.[73]

Victims who do report their rapes to the police are frequently met with insensitivity, incompetence, and skepticism. Recent research by law professor Corey R. Yung reveals that in addition to discouraging rape victims from filing reports, police departments around the country have been deliberately and systematically suppressing the number of reported rapes for more than a decade.[74] Yung estimates that as many as a million rapes have gone uncounted during this period: "America is in a crisis of sexual violence that has gone undetected because police departments across the country systemically underreport rape."[75] That is, police

Women," https://www.ncjrs.gov/pdffiles1/nij/182369.pdf (2000). The study estimated that between 1 in 4 and 1 in 5 college women experience completed or attempted rape in their college years.

[73] See Nat. Research Council, *Estimating the Incidence* (36): "Conducted in 1989–1991, the National Women's Study . . . collected information on rape and sexual assault. It estimated that 84 percent of rape victims did not report their victimization to police (Kilpatrick, Edmunds, and Seymour, 1992). Tjaden and Thoennes (2006) reported a similar percentage (81 percent) of nonreporting from the *National Violence Against Women Survey*."

[74] Corey Rayburn Yung, "How to Lie with Rape Statistics: America's Hidden Rape Crisis," *Iowa Law Review* 99 (2014): 1204.

[75] Id.

departments, in addition to treating victims with disrespect and hostility, have been engaged in outright deception regarding the incidence of reported rapes. Many colleges and universities have come under fire in the wake of similar reports that they have been deliberately underreporting sexual assaults.[76]

The examinations rape victims must undergo as part of the investigative process are extremely invasive, painful, and can take several hours to complete.[77] Victims who endure this process may have done so for nothing: there is an estimated backlog of 400,000 untested rape kits collecting dust in the United States.[78] This backlog is created in part by the choices that police make to focus on drug crimes instead of sexual assaults.[79] Bearing in mind that as little

[76] Danielle Dirks, "Surveys Will Reveal the True Numbers of Sexual Assault Survivors on Campus," *New York Times*, http://www.nytimes.com/roomfordebate/2014/08/12/doing-enough-to-prevent-rape-on-campus/surveys-will-reveal-the-true-numbers-of-sexual-assault-survivors-on-campus (August 12, 2014).

[77] "Sexual Assault Information & Resources: Immediate Physical Safety and Medical Options," Wheaton College, http://wheatoncollege.edu/sexual-assault/home/frequently-asked-questions/relationship-violence/.

[78] Nat. Inst. of Just., Pub. No. 209274, *2004 Annual Report*, https://www.ncjrs.gov/pdffiles1/nij/209274.pdf; Hillary Hylton, "The Dark Side of Clearing America's Rape Kit Backlog," *Time Magazine*, http://nation.time.com/2013/09/07/the-dark-side-of-clearing-americas-rape-kit-backlog/ (September 7, 2013).

[79] See Bill Piper, "Thousands of Rapists Are Not Behind Bars Because Cops Focus on Marijuana Users," *Huffington Post*, http://www.huffingtonpost.com/bill-piper/rape-kit-backlog_b_5504287.html (August 17, 2014).

as twenty percent of all rapes are reported to the police, only thirty-seven percent of those cases are prosecuted,[80] and of those, only eighteen percent result in convictions.[81]

There is a vast spectrum of abuse aimed disproportionately at women that laws and law enforcement fail to acknowledge, investigate, or deter. In addition to the odds of physical violence and sexual assault, one in six women will be stalked in her lifetime[82] and up to eighty percent of women have experienced street harassment (including sexual threats and groping).[83] The frequency and intensity of these forms of abuse detract from women's liberty in numerous ways, including inhibiting how women perform in school and work, what profession they choose, where they will live, what transportation they can take, what clothes they can wear, and when and how to exit an intimate relationship they no longer wish to continue. In short, women are denied the basic freedoms that most men enjoy: Put another way, women are denied basic equality.

80 Tyler Kingkade, "Prosecutors Rarely Bring Charges in College Rape Cases," *Huffington Post*, http://www.huffingtonpost.com/2014/06/17/college-rape-prosecutors-press-charges_n_5500432.html (June 17, 2014).

81 Id.

82 *NISVS 2010*, at 3.

83 Deborah M. Thompson, "'The Woman in the Street': Reclaiming the Public Space from Sexual Harassment," *Yale Journal of Law & Feminism* 6 (1994). See also Stop Street Harassment, *Unsafe and Harassed in Public Spaces, A National Street Harassment Report* (2014), http://www.stopstreetharassment.org/wp-content/uploads/2012/08/2014-National-SSH-Street-Harassment-Report.pdf (reporting that 57% of women had experienced street harassment).

That denial of equality is written into the law itself and is exercised through the lies of the law and of law enforcement practice. As Catharine MacKinnon has argued in great detail, the inequality of women is constituted and sustained through legal institutions.

> Women's situation combines unequal pay with allocation to disrespected work; sexual targeting for rape, domestic battering, sexual abuse as children, and systematic sexual harassment; depersonalization, demeaned physical characteristics, and use in denigrating entertainment; deprivation of reproductive control and forced prostitution. These abuses have occurred, in one form or another, for a very long time in a context characterized by disenfranchisement, preclusion from property ownership, ownership and use as object, exclusion from public life, sex-based poverty, degraded sexuality, and a devaluation of women's human worth and contributions throughout society. Like other inequalities, but in its own way, the subordination of women is socially institutionalized, cumulatively and systematically shaping access to human dignity, respect, resources, physical security, credibility, membership in community, speech, and power.[84]

The passivity and deception of the law regarding the wide range of destructive conduct directed at women plays a central role in maintaining women's subordinated status.

[84] MacKinnon, "Reflections on Sex Equality Under Law" at 1298–1299.

IV. Lies About Consent: The Constitutional Ghost

The second-class status afforded to women and black men converges at many points, most poignantly in the legal violence done to the concept of consent. Recall that the Declaration of Independence boldly claimed that Governments "derive their just powers from the consent of the governed" even as the consent of women and black men was never so much sought, to say nothing of obtained. Their consent was presumed, imposed, and asserted in "We the People," the first constitutional lie. This was only the first of the legal distortions of consent that have disproportionate effects on the lives of women and black men.

In the 1972 case *Schneckcloth v. Bustamonte*, the Supreme Court wrestled with how to define "voluntary consent" in the context of the Fourth Amendment.[85] Although the Fourth Amendment forbids unreasonable searches and seizures, the Court reasoned that citizens must have the freedom to consent to searches and seizures if they so wished. Such consent would render the need for a reasonableness analysis unnecessary, because the law would merely need to respect the citizen's right to exercise his autonomy. Specifically, the Court was faced with the question of whether consent to a search or seizure could be considered voluntary if the citizen was unaware that he had the right to say no. The majority held that consent given

[85] *Schneckcloth v. Bustamonte*, 412 U.S. 218 (1973).

without the knowledge that one is allowed to refuse could constitute valid consent. "Voluntariness is a question of fact to be determined from all the circumstances, and while the subject's knowledge of right to refuse is a factor to be taken into account, the prosecution is not required to demonstrate such knowledge as a prerequisite to establishing voluntary consent."[86]

This holding should be considered yet another constitutional lie. Justice Marshall's vehement dissent questioned "how a decision made without knowledge of available alternatives can be treated as a choice at all."[87] Indeed, how can one claim that submitting to an authority when one believes there is no other alternative is a choice, to say nothing of a voluntary and consensual choice?

The decision in *Schneckcloth* opened the door to a vast number of search possibilities. A consensual search has no inherent limitations of scope; if a citizen does not specify the scope of his consent, a search can far exceed what would be allowed through ordinary probable cause determinations and certainly what would be permissible under search warrants, which have built-in requirements of specificity and scope. Unsurprisingly, police officers openly admit they try to get consent to searches for which they don't think they can or want to get a warrant. They prefer to get consent even for searches where they do have probable cause or a warrant because a search authorized by the former will almost

86 Id. at 227.
87 Id. at 284.

always be more expansive in scope than a search authorized by the latter.[88] According to some estimates, ninety-eight percent of all warrantless searches are "consensual."[89] That is a suspiciously high number even for the loose conception of consent allowed in *Schneckcloth*; one suspects that in some appreciable number of these cases, police officers have used manipulation or outright lies to either obtain consent before the search, or to invoke consent after.

In the Fourth Amendment search and seizure context, which disproportionately affects black men, consent is effectively treated as the default, and only compelling evidence can move this setting. Compelling evidence in this context must go beyond showing merely that the citizen did not know he could say no, was too afraid to do so, or did not believe that saying no would have any effect. This is an equally accurate description of how the concept of consent tends to operate in the context of sexual assault, which disproportionately affects women. Women are presumed to consent to sex unless they engage in obvious signs of refusal or resistance,[90] and even in cases where it is clear that a woman "consented"

[88] See Tracy Maclin, "The Good and Bad News About Consent Search in the Supreme Court," *McGeorge Law Review* 39 (2008): 31.

[89] Ric Simmons, "Not 'Voluntary' but Still Reasonable: A New Paradigm for Understanding the Consent Search Doctrine," *Indiana Law Journal* 80 (2005): 773.

[90] See Susan Estrich, *Real Rape* (Cambridge: Harvard University Press, 1987).

only in the sense that she feared she would be physically harmed if she did not, the law treats that consent as voluntary.[91]

And why should it not be so, given that the consent of women and black men was presumed by the founding document of America itself? States, no less than individuals, are creatures of habit, and the habit of lying about consent began early in this country's history. If the Founding Fathers themselves never saw women or black men as fully realized human beings with the power to make decisions in their own interests, and chose to claim a bold fiction of ruling with consent instead of acknowledging the reality of ruling with brute force, we should not be surprised by the continuation throughout history of this subtle, subjugating deception.

V. Attacking the Lie: The Fourteenth Amendment

According to Lon Fuller, "a fiction becomes wholly safe only when it is used with a complete consciousness of its falsity."[92] This, I submit, is how we should address constitutional lies: by ensuring the complete consciousness of their falsity. Formal equality is fictive equality, and the failure to recognize it as such is to allow equality to remain merely fictive. We must reject the legal fiction that our

[91] See *State v. Rusk*, 289 Md. 230 (1981).

[92] Lon L. Fuller, *Legal Fictions* (Stanford: Stanford University Press, 1967), 10.

Framers believed that all men are created equal and that "men" signified the family of humankind, including women. They did not believe either of these things. Women and black men were excluded from the start, and their full subjecthood remains an ongoing project. Decades of injustice and inequality cannot be undone by formal declarations of universality, and the implied promise that the Constitution makes to the American people – now all American people – can only be delivered by recognizing that the past leaves its marks. Neither the Founding Fathers nor any of the successive leaders of this country have "given" rights to women and men; they have only belatedly acknowledged what should have been recognized from the beginning.

The Fourteenth Amendment, although also deeply flawed, is our current best approximation of a genuine constitutional truth and promise.

> All persons born or naturalized in the United States, and subject to the jurisdiction thereof, are citizens of the United States and of the Sate wherein they reside. No State shall make or enforce any law which shall abridge the privileges or immunities of citizens of the United States; nor shall any State deprive any person of life, liberty, or property, without due process of law; nor deny to any person within its jurisdiction the equal protection of the laws.[93]

[93] U.S. Const. amend. XIV.

Even though Section 1 of the Fourteenth Amendment is undermined by Section 2's invocation of "male inhabitants,"[94] the literal meaning of this passage comes the closest to providing a right to equality of any of our founding texts. The Amendment contains no assertion of false consent or fictive solidarity. It is a promise issued from the state to all those who are "subject to its jurisdiction," a declaration of the state's responsibilities to the citizen. It is the state that must meet the obligations to the citizen, not the other way around. This Amendment provides the basis, in theory, for rejecting every false claim of equality, of inclusion, of fairness and to expose how they urge submission to injustice.[95]

[94] Section 1 of the Fourteenth Amendment "suggested to some that women might enjoy all the rights and privileges of citizenship, including the right to vote. This, however, was hardly the intent of radical Republicans, who sensed that privileging former male slaves was all the nation could bear. Thus, the amendment's second paragraph introduced wording that clearly discriminated against women." McMillen, *Seneca Falls* at 164. Justice Antonin Scalia, among others, has publicly asserted that the Fourteenth Amendment does not prohibit gender discrimination. See Jillian Rayfield, "Scalia: 14th Amendment Doesn't Protect Women Against Discrimination," Talking Points Memo, http://talkingpointsmemo.com/dc/scalia-14th-amendment-doesn-t-protect-women-against-discrimination (January 4, 2011).

[95] "Women are not receiving equal protection of the laws. The equal protection clause is inconsistent with state law that promotes sex inequality. The law of sexual assault commands Fourteenth Amendment scrutiny." MacKinnon, "Reflections on Sex Equality Under Law" at 1307. The endorsement of the Fourteenth Amendment as a vehicle for gender equality does

The Fourteenth Amendment is the Constitution's Kantian moment. The exacting truthfulness that Kant insisted we must never abandon can be found in this

not signify a rejection of the compelling arguments in favor of an Equal Rights Amendment. In particular, I find Reva Siegel's observations on the limitations of the Fourteenth Amendment's potential for addressing gender inequality quite persuasive. Siegel argues that the demands of sex equality are qualitatively and historically distinct from the demands of racial equality, and that the Fourteenth Amendment is ill-equipped to serve the former. "First, the framers of the Fourteenth Amendment were thinking about questions of race discrimination, not sex discrimination. Thus, it is appropriate for courts to apply a less rigorous standard of review to questions concerning equal citizenship for women; bluntly put, the nation never made a collective constitutional commitment to respect women as equals of men. Second, and very much related to this lack of constitutional history, the difference in standards reflects a pervasive intuition that the problem of sex discrimination is not as grave, harmful, or significant in American history as the problem of race discrimination. The case law presents sex discrimination as a problem involving old-fashioned ways of thinking – '"archaic and overbroad" generalizations' about differences between the sexes. Sex discrimination, so understood, grows out of evolving customary norms, rather than a long trail of state-sponsored coercion. Third, underneath it all, there is a sense that sex discrimination is at root different from race discrimination. Sex distinctions are not always harmful (or based on animus) the way race distinctions are; it is not clear that we are prepared to embrace a model of sex blindness, in matters of love or war." Reva B. Siegel, "She the People: The Nineteenth Amendment, Sex Equality, Federalism, and the Family," *Harvard Law Review* 115 (2002): 954–956.

unconditional declaration of equal treatment. In his famous response to Benjamin Constant on the subject of lying, Kant exposed the unintelligible exceptionalism at the heart of Constant's criticism. Constant argued, "To tell the truth is a duty, but is a duty only with regard to the man who has a right to the truth."[96] First, Kant points out, "truth is not a possession the right to which can be granted to one person but refused to another."[97] The idea that one could subject truth to the subjective determinations of who should be considered deserving is fundamentally unintelligible.[98] Moreover, Kant writes, "the duty of truthfulness ... makes no distinction between person to whom one has this duty and to whom one can be excused from this duty; it is, rather, an unconditional duty which holds in all circumstances."[99]

The Framers no doubt believed that they had the right and the capacity to grant truth to some people and not others. They also doubtless believed that they could take exception from the duty to tell the truth to those who were

[96] Immanuel Kant, "On a Supposed Right to Lie Because of Philanthropic Concerns," in *Grounding for the Metaphysics of Morals*, trans. James W. Ellington (Hackett Publishing Company, 1981), 66.

[97] Id.

[98] This is why I take the position that Section 1 and Section 2 of the Fourteenth Amendment are fundamentally incompatible, and that the latter should be considered an incoherent attempt to limit the clear import of the former.

[99] Id.

not deserving of truth. However, truth is not subjective or consequentialist, and the moment we convince ourselves that we can decide which humans do and do not deserve to be told the truth, we have abandoned the coherence of our constitutional project.

2

The Artifice of Advocacy

Perjury and Participation in the American Adversary System

Norman W. Spaulding*

> The basic purpose of a trial is the determination of truth, and it is self-evident that to deny a lawyer's help through the technical intricacies of a criminal trial . . . is to impede that purpose and to infect a criminal proceeding with the clear danger of convicting the innocent.
>
> – *Tehan v. U.S. ex rel. Shott*, 382 U.S. 406, 416 (1966)

> False testimony in a formal proceeding is intolerable. We must neither reward nor condone such a flagrant affront to the truth-seeking function of adversary proceedings.
>
> – *United States v. Mandujano*, 425 U.S. 564, 576–77 (1976)

> When my love swears that she is made of truth, I do believe her, though I know she lies.
>
> – William Shakespeare, Sonnet 138

* I am grateful to Austin Sarat and the other contributors to this volume for insightful comments and criticism. I am also grateful to Ticien Sassoubre, as always, for improving the project at every phase.

As moral philosophers seem to take delight in pointing out, there is no small duplicity in the way the law addresses deception. On the one hand, certain forms of serious deception are criminally proscribed or may result in civil liability,[1] lawyers are subject to discipline for "engag[ing] in conduct involving dishonesty, fraud, deceit or misrepresentation,"[2] and "truth" is said to be the paramount objective of adjudication. On the other hand, lawyers regularly defend clients they believe to be guilty, they file technically non-frivolous suits of doubtful moral or social value, they coach friendly witnesses to "perfect" their testimony while using cross-examination to destroy the credibility of adverse witnesses whom they believe to be truthful, they withhold material evidence when it has not been properly requested by an adversary, and although courts and prosecutors can punish some forms of misconduct in litigation, people injured by misrepresentations made in court are generally prohibited from suing.[3] Out of court lawyers

[1] The principal offenses related to giving testimony are perjury, see 18 U.S.C. §§ 1621, 1623, and subornation of perjury, see 18 U.S.C. § 1622. The principal offense relating to official investigations is making false statements, see 18 U.S.C. § 1001. Perjury is also grounds for an enhancement of sentence. See U.S. Sentencing Guidelines §3C1.1. The principal source of civil liability is the common law doctrine of fraud.

[2] ABA Model Rule of Professional Conduct 8.4.

[3] Absolute immunity extends to prosecutors and other government officials who make misrepresentations in court. See *Imbler v. Pachtman*, 424 U.S. 409 (1976) (upholding immunity of prosecutor from civil damages liability where prosecutor was alleged to have knowingly introduced perjured testimony). On the litigation

bluff, puff, spin, and trade on the goodwill, ignorance, and cupidity of others.

When the law "swears that she is made of truth" should we believe her? We know it's a lie.

I. Taking Deception Seriously

All manner of harms are said to flow from this duplicity. Deception itself is wrong, the philosophers tell us. Victims of deception suffer. They are treated as mere means to the deceiver's ends, seduced, humiliated on the stand, stripped of their just claims or defenses.[4] The deceiver not only betrays the trust of others, the bond between speech and truth itself is broken – truth is thus turned cuckold by a "cheating move in the language-game of truth telling."[5] Even perpetrators suffer. They lose credibility (at least when they are caught out), and even when deception works, they may lose themselves in their own lies.[6]

immunity rule for ordinary lawyers, see T. Leigh Anenson, "Absolute Immunity From Civil Liability," *Pepperdine Law Review* 31 (2004): 915.

[4] For a concise summary of Kantian and consequentialist accounts of the harm lies cause, see Alasdair MacIntyre, "Truthfulness, Lies, and Moral Philosophers," The Tanner Lectures on Human Values, April 6–7, 1994, at 314. See also, Thomas E. Hill, Jr., *Autonomy and Self-Respect* (Cambridge: Cambridge University Press, 1991), 25; Sissela Bok, *Lying: Moral Choice in Public and Private Life* (New York: Vintage Books, 1999).

[5] Id. at 312.

[6] Arthur Isak Applbaum, *Ethics for Adversaries* (New Jersey: Princeton, 1999), 15, 76.

Lawyers, the philosophers warn, become more deceptive in ordinary life as they acclimate to deception in the practice of law, and as importantly, they may lose sight of the line between permissible and impermissible deception in the role.[7] Finally, the integrity of the administration of justice and the rule of law are threatened insofar as people see deception prevail.[8] Even if "love's best habit is in seeming trust" (believing our lover's lies so that "in our faults by lies we flattered be") the law needs more than "seeming trust."[9] What Macbeth called "double trust," the very trust he betrays, is perhaps the more appropriate standard for sworn officers of the court.[10] Or so we are told.[11]

The philosopher's solution is to eliminate the duplicity. And it is obvious which aspect of the law's treatment of

[7] See Richard Wasserstrom, "Lawyers as Professionals," *Human Rights* 5 (1975–76): 1; David Luban, *Legal Ethics and Human Dignity* (Cambridge: Cambridge University Press, 2007).

[8] Courts and commentators commonly assert that: "Every branch and level of government relies upon sworn testimony. Therefore, the integrity of governmental processes depends in large part on the truthfulness of statements made under oath." Shamus Durac, "Perjury," *American Criminal Law Review* 50 (2013): 1343.

[9] Shakespeare Sonnet 138.

[10] William Shakespeare, The Tragedy of Macbeth, in *The Riverside Shakespeare*, ed. G. Blakemore Evans (Dallas: Houghton Mifflin, 1974), 1317.

[11] Maybe even triple trust. The Preamble to the American Bar Association's Model Rules of Professional Conduct insists that "[a] lawyer, as a member of the legal profession, is a representative of clients, and officer of the legal system, and a public citizen having special responsibility for the quality of justice."

deception must be excised. The legal system must be made more upright, more concerned with the truth – with what John Henry Wigmore, following Jeremy Bentham, called "rectitude of decision."[12] To accomplish this, lawyers must become more honest, must foster in law the double trust it deserves.

Lawyers, for the most part, blink in bemusement, both at the charge of duplicity and the naivety of philosophers. But when pressed to answer, an elaborate set of defensive pleas is offered. Most of the pleas are not new. The most shopworn were crafted in response to public criticisms leveled at lawyers and the legal system long before modern philosophers began spilling ink on ethics in the professions. The responses fall into roughly three categories. The first, and most shopworn of all, is the traverse, denying in various ways that deception accurately describes what lawyers do. Here are a few of the most common formulations:

- *Truth Wins Out*: What may seem like deception is actually adversary adjudication at work, and, appearances to the contrary notwithstanding, adversary techniques such as cross-examination are, as Wigmore claimed, "the greatest legal engine ever invented for the discovery of truth."[13]

[12] William Twining, *Theories of Evidence: Bentham and Wigmore* (Stanford: Stanford University Press 1986), 94–95. On the affinity between Bentham and Wigmore on this point, see id. at 117.

[13] John Henry Wigmore, *Evidence in Trials at Common Law* § 1367 (James H. Chadbourn ed., 1974): 32.

- *Role Differentiation 1*: Lawyers are not finders of fact. That job belongs to the jury, and to a lesser extent the judge, who rules on the admissibility of evidence. What lawyers do is present the strongest non-frivolous case for their clients to judge and jury.[14]
- *Radical Epistemological Doubt*: Truth can't be known; there is no fact of the matter until judge and jury say what it is. Asked by Boswell what he thought of "supporting a cause which you know to be bad," Samuel Johnson replied, "Sir, you do not know it to be good or bad until the judge determines it. An argument which does not convince yourself, may convince the Judge to which you urge it; and if it does convince him, why, then, Sir, you are wrong and he is right. It is his business to judge; and you are not to be confident in your own opinion that a cause is bad, but to say all you can for your client, and then hear the Judge's opinion."[15]
- *Role Differentiation 2*: Conduct required by the role poses no risk to the honesty or integrity of the person who plays it, certainly no risk to her honesty or integrity

[14] Monroe Freedman, *Lawyer's Ethics in an Adversary System* (Indianapolis: Bobbs-Merrill Co., 1975), 8, 9–24.

[15] Johnson's theory is discussed in Freedman, *Lawyer's Ethics* at 51. Courts have occasionally ratified this view. See *McCormick v. Kopmann*, 161 N.E.2d 720, 730 (1959) ("It has been aptly said that 'truth cannot be stated until known, and, for the purposes of the administration of justice, cannot be known until the trier of facts decides the fact issues.'") (quoting McCaskill, Illinois Civil Practice Act Annotated (1933)).

outside the role. Pressed by Boswell whether "affecting a warmth when you have no warmth, and appearing to be clearly of one opinion, when you are in reality of another opinion does not ... impair one's honesty," Johnson replied, "Why no, Sir. Everybody knows you are paid for affecting warmth from your client, and it is therefore properly no dissimulation: the moment you come from the bar you resume your usual behavior .... [A] man will no more carry the artifice of the bar into the common intercourse of society, than a man who is paid for tumbling upon his hands will continue to tumble on his hands when he should walk on his feet."[16]

The second set of responses take the form of demurrers, conceding that deception may occur in legal representation, but denying either its harmfulness or its moral and legal relevance.

- *Role Differentiation 3*: Deception may occur but the lawyer is not responsible for it. Either the client, for whom she is a mere agent, or the adversary, who fails to discover and counter the deception, is accountable.[17]
- *Pragmatism*: Deception occurs, and while the adversary system may not be the best method of eliciting the truth, it's what we have – no alternative is obviously superior.[18]

[16] James Boswell, *The Life of Samuel Johnson* (London: Wordsworth Editions, 1999): 278.

[17] See ABA Model Rule of Professional Conduct 1.2.

[18] Freedman refers derisively to Cuba and Bulgaria as examples of countries in which the criminal defense lawyer affirmatively

- *Prisoner's Dilemma / Consent*: Everyone knows there is some deception in litigation and negotiation, so (a) even upright lawyers working on behalf of upright clients feel compelled to use it to protect themselves and their clients against the deception of others, and (b) no one can claim to be harmed by deception, at least not those who voluntarily enter the legal process. As Judge Ray Finkelstein has conceded, "[l]awyers are just doing their job. Their approach is a rational response to a system which not only permits lawyers to take liberties with the truth, but actually encourages it .... Speaking personally, as counsel, I had no difficulty holding back information."[19]
- *Line Drawing*: The law tolerates certain strictly limited forms of deception and misleading conduct, but truly corrupt forms of deceit, such as perjury and fraud, are illegal and grounds for disbarment.[20]

cooperates with the state in convicting and punishing the accused. See Freedman, *Lawyer's Ethics* at 2. The examples are of course tendentious insofar as they obscure the uniqueness of the American system relative to other modern constitutional democracies and domestic procedural alternatives. For broader comparative insights, see Robert Kagan, *Adversarial Legalism: The American Way of Law* (Cambridge: Harvard University Press, 2001). For discussion of home-grown alternatives to adversary adjudication, See Jerry L. Mashaw, *Creating the Administrative Constitution: The Lost One Hundred Years of American Administrative Law* (New Haven: Yale University Press, 2012).

19 Finkelstein, "The Adversarial System and the Search for Truth," *Monash Law Review* 37 (2011): 137.

20 On the point of tolerance, the Supreme Court has long recognized that the government may use deception in criminal investigations.

- *Reasonable Epistemological Doubt*: Truth can be known, but it's the rare case in which there is a simple truth of the matter to reveal or suppress, and truth is not, in any event, the principal goal of the adversary system. Most cases (that do not settle) are rife with indeterminacies. As a prominent nineteenth century lawyer observed, "all matters of opinion are not capable of perfect mathematical demonstration [or] so obvious as to make it necessary that either party should prosecute his claim at the expense of integrity . . . the affairs of mankind are not so nicely adjusted as that one party in a law-suit should be entirely right and the other entirely wrong . . . . Consider the intricacies of contracts and commercial relations; the difficulty in many cases of ascertaining the true meaning of the will of testators; and above all, the nice distinctions to be made in determining the degree of criminality. It were palpably absurd for the advocate to prejudge

See *Sorrells v. United States*, 287 U.S. 435, 441 (1932) ("Artifice and stratagem may be employed to catch those engaged in criminal enterprises."). The standard practice of asking jurors to draw false inferences from true but misleading testimony is discussed in Stephen Gillers, "Taking L.A. Law more Seriously," *Yale Law Journal* 98 (1989): 1607. Broader arguments about the role of deception in law are covered in Larry Alexander and Emily Sherwin, "Deception in Morality and Law," *Law and Philosophy* 22 (2003): 393. And for examples of lawyers disciplined for making a deliberately false representation to a court, see *In re* Lightfoot, Lawyers Manual Professional Conduct 28 (2013) 225; *Maryland Attorney Grievance Comm'n v. Elmendorf, Lawyers Manual Professional Conduct* 24 (2008): 220.

the questions to which these and a thousand other subjects, equally complicated give rise."[21]

- *The Tragedy of "Necessary Offices"*: Conduct within the role may pose a risk of corrupting the person who plays it, but that is a "tragically necessary" cost of performing an important social function.[22]

A third response lays the blame at the feet of individual deviant lawyers and thus denies any meaningful connection between deception and the requirements of the role:

- *Hand Washing*: The rules of professional responsibility condemn dishonesty, demand that the lawyer disclose perjury, and permit the lawyer to refuse to engage in practices she reasonably believes to be dishonest. She may also refuse to represent clients she deems morally suspect.[23] That some lawyers persist in dissimulation is a reflection of their poor character, not duplicity in the law or the legal profession as a whole. As a mid-nineteenth-century disciple of Joseph Story once put it, "[w]e see unworthy members in every other profession, and therefore take no shame to ourselves that they are sometimes to be found in ours."[24]

[21] James Jackson, "Law and Lawyers: Is the Profession of the Advocate Consistent with Perfect Integrity," in Perry Miller, *The Legal Mind in America* (Garden City: Anchor Books, 1962), 278.

[22] W. Bradley Wendel, "Professional Roles and Moral Agency," *The Georgetown Law Journal* 89 (2001): 667, 709.

[23] See ABA Model Rules of Professional Conduct 1.16(b), 3.3 and 8.4.

[24] Timothy Walker, "Introductory Lecture on the Dignity of the Law as a Profession," in *The Legal Mind in America*, ed. Perry Miller

For ease of expression, consider the first set of responses variations on the "ideology of advocacy," as they depend heavily upon the view that the adversary system is a necessary and well justified social institution.[25] The second set gathers pleas by confession and avoidance, or just "avoidance." The third is a kind of "bad apples" theory. When public criticism reached a fever pitch during the Jacksonian populist movement of the mid-nineteenth century in America, these responses helped rebut and channel criticism into reforms closely supervised and controlled, for the most part, by the legal profession.[26] Still, these responses have never convinced philosophers, public ambivalence about the legal profession has remained acute, and more than a few lawyers reject some or all of the specific pleas in addition to sharing the ambivalence of the public.

(Garden City: Anchor Books, 1962), 255. The "hand-washing" argument has frequently been invoked by elite lawyers to locate the source of professional misconduct in lesser members of the bar.

25 The term is meant as no compliment by William Simon, but it captures the bar's frequently too casual use of this set of responses. See William Simon, "The Ideology of Advocacy: Procedural Justice and Professional Ethics," *Wisconsin Law Review* (1978): 30.

26 See Miller, *The Legal Mind*; Maxwell Bloomfield, *American Lawyers in a Changing Society, 1776–1876* (Cambridge: Harvard University, 2013); Charles M. Cook, *The American Codification Movement* (Westport: Greenwood Press 1981); Norman W. Spaulding, "The Privilege of Probity," *Georgetown Journal of Legal Ethics* 26 (2013): 301; Norman W. Spaulding, "The Myth of Civic Republicanism," *Fordham Law Review* 71 (2003): 1397.

On the latter point, there is a long tradition of morally activist professional idealism,[27] promoted for different reasons at different times by elite lawyers,[28] and a less well publicized tradition of simply abandoning the profession on grounds of its duplicity – or at least emphasizing duplicity and immorality even if other factors less flattering than intolerance for duplicity were responsible for the lawyer's decision to leave the bar.[29] Moreover, since the Watergate scandal and John Dean's famous exchange with Senator Herman Talmadge in the summer of 1973 revealing the number of lawyers involved in the Watergate burglary and cover-up,[30] some lawyers and legal scholars have made common cause with the philosophers and post-functionalist sociologists. Together they have expended considerable energy to expose the logical and moral bankruptcy of the Ideology of Advocacy – to reveal these pleas as an elaborate subterfuge deflecting attention from the

[27] Robert Gordon, "The Ideal and the Actual: Fantasies and Practices of New York Lawyers," in *The New High Priests: Lawyers in Post-Civil War America, 1870–1910*, ed. Gerald W. Gawalt (Westport, CT: Greenwood Press, 1984), 53.

[28] See Spaulding, "The Myth of Civic Republicanism"; Austin Sarat and Stuart Scheingold, *Cause Lawyering: Political Commitments and Professional Responsibilities* (Oxford: Oxford University Press, 1998).

[29] See Nicholas B. Wainwright, *A Philadelphia Perspective: The Diary of Sidney George Fisher, 1834–1871* (Philadelphia: Historical Society of Pennsylvania, 1967), 246–247, 553.

[30] Dean and Robenalt, "The Legacy of Watergate," *Litigation* 38 (2012): 19.

cupidity of the legal profession and the injustice of the adversary system, particularly its bias toward the wealthy.[31]

The Bad Apples theory is, on their view, mere subterfuge too. Drafting disciplinary rules that are almost never enforced and that confer discretion to engage in dissimulation rather than mandate candor does little, in their view, to counter the influence of competition and the Ideology of Advocacy on practice norms.[32] Some Avoidance pleas have received more critical attention than others, a point to which I'll return, but the same core objection is raised to this set of pleas as to the others. In sum, lawyers stand accused of duplicity about their role in the duplicity of the legal system.

Notably, criticism of the Ideology of Advocacy after the Watergate scandal coincided with a powerful conservative legal reform movement seeking to protect business interests from the vicissitudes of litigation brought on behalf of consumers, employees, the poor, civil rights advocates, and

[31] David Luban, *Lawyers and Justice* (Princeton, NJ: Princeton University Press, 1988); Simon, "The Ideology of Advocacy"; Deborah Rhode, ed., *Ethics in Practice* (Oxford: Oxford University Press, 2003); Richard Abel, *American Lawyers* (Oxford: Oxford University Press, 1989); Harry I. Subrin, "The Criminal Lawyer's 'Different Mission': Reflections on the Right to Present a False Case," *Georgetown Journal of Legal Ethics* 1 (1987): 125.

[32] Deborah L. Rhode, "Ethical Perspectives on Legal Practice," *Stanford Law Review* 37 (1985): 589, 647–648.

environmental activists.[33] So while the academic debate about duplicity in the legal system has more or less stalemated between "role critics" and defenders, at the political level, at the level of bar regulation, and at the level of the procedural mechanisms that govern litigation, two very different means of vindicating truth in the adversary system have been vying for dominance.

Neither side, it must be said, can be accused of any "foolish consistency." In pending litigation, for example, every advantage is generally sought by adversaries even as each side pursues legislative and judicial reforms designed to remove or dull the tools supposed to be most advantageous to their opponents. Liberals and plaintiffs' lawyers generally decry strict civil pleading standards and strict enforcement of Rule 11 as excessive constraints on advocacy, but blink at the charge that flexible pleading standards and permissive interpretations of what constitutes frivolous litigation invite false claims and strike suits.[34] Conservatives and corporate

[33] Thomas F. Burke, *Lawyers, Lawsuits, and Legal Rights: The Battle Over Litigation in American Society* (Berkeley: University of California Press, 2004).

[34] Compare, for example, Danielle Kie Hart, "And the Chill Goes On—Federal Civil Rights Plaintiffs Beware: Rule 11 Vis-à-Vis 28 U.S.C. §1927 and the Court's Inherent Power," *Loyola Law Review* 37 (2004): 645, 647, with Amendments to the Federal Rules of Civil Procedure, 146 F.R.D. 507 (1993) (Scalia, J., dissenting). With respect to the debate over strict pleading standards, compare the majority and dissenting opinions in *Bell Atlantic v. Twombly*, 550 U.S. 544 (2007) and *Iqbal v. Ashcroft*, 556 U.S. 662 (2009). Divided scholarly commentary on the new pleading rules is summarized in

defense lawyers invoke the Ideology of Advocacy when defending the duty of confidentiality and opposing the investigative powers of regulators, but assail the excesses of the adversary system when advocating limits on discovery and jury damage awards.[35] Something more than different *means* of vindicating the truth in litigation seems to be at issue. Indeed, one begins to suspect that very different

Raymond H. Brescia, "The Iqbal Effect," *Kentucky Law Review* 100 (2012): 256–257, n. 100–103.

[35] On the elite bar's opposition to exceptions to the duty of confidentiality imposed by Congress in securities practice following the financial accounting scandals in the early 2000s, see Roger C. Cramton, George M. Cohen, and Susan P. Koniak, "Legal and Ethical Duties of Lawyers After Sarbanes-Oxley," *Villanova Law Review* 49 (2004): 725, 728–729; Irma S. Russell, "Client Confidences and Public Confidence in the Legal Profession: Observations on the ABA House of Delegates Deliberations on the Duty of Confidentiality," *ABA Prof. Law* 13 (2002): 19; Susan P. Koniak, "When the Hurlyburly's Done: The Bar's Struggle with the SEC," *Columbia Law Review* 103 (2003): 1236. On the elite bar's opposition to regulatory policies that impinge upon the attorney-privilege, see Julie R. O'Sullivan, "Does DOJ's Privilege Waiver Policy Threaten the Rationales Underlying the Attorney-Client Privilege and Work Product Doctrine? A Preliminary 'No'," *American Criminal Law Review* 45 (2008): 1237, 1241. On the myths and realities of discovery abuse, see *Bell Atlantic v. Twombly*, fn.6; Linda S. Mullenix, "Discovery in Disarray: The Pervasive Myth of Pervasive Discovery Abuse and the Consequences for Unfounded Rulemaking," *Stanford Law Review* 46 (1994): 1393. On the debate about limiting jury damage awards in product liability cases, see Joanna M. Shepherd, "Products Liability and Economic Activity: An Empirical Analysis of Tort Reform's Impact on Businesses, Employment, and Production," *Vanderbilt Law Review* 66 (2013): 258.

meanings of truth are held, or that talk of reforming the adversary system to vindicate "truth" is but a duplicitous way of referring to "improvements" in the administration of justice that will assure consistent victories for one's favorite side. "I lie with her and she with me, And in our faults by lies we flattered be."[36]

My purpose here is not to enter either the stalemated academic debate, or the reform debate, at least not on their current terms. Rather, I am interested in why it is so difficult to talk candidly about the relationship between deception and the law. Obviously, as both the academic and reform debates suggest, the moral, political, and legal stakes are high. And high stakes can produce hyperbole. Even so, it is remarkable how distant these debates are from what we understand about the role of deception in ordinary life. Although it is sometimes conceded that ordinary people tell lies with some degree of frequency, that deception figures prominently in social roles other than the practice of law, perhaps especially politics, and that deceit may indeed be a pervasive feature of human interaction, the suggestion that deception plays a necessary, appropriate, or underappreciated, role in the rule of law and our system of rights definition remains anathema. If deception is not condemned, it is denied, and when it can't be denied it is framed either as a necessary evil or a deviant practice of bad lawyers.

Witness the outrage, saturated with anxiety, that greeted Monroe Freedman's claim that it may be appropriate

[36] Shakespeare, Sonnet 138.

for a criminal defense lawyer to assist her client in telling a lie. In January 1966, Freedman, then an assistant professor of law at George Washington University, gave a lecture to a group of lawyers preparing to enter criminal practice. Among other topics, he raised the question of what a criminal defense lawyer should do if her client wants to give false testimony. The ABA Canons of Professional Ethics, he argued, put the lawyer in an untenable situation, demanding, on the one hand, that a lawyer learn everything she can in aid of her client's defense and keep what she learns confidential, while on the other hand requiring the lawyer to divulge such confidences in court if doing so would avert or remedy perjury.[37]

Without denying the importance of the duty of candor, Freedman suggested that the client's constitutional right to assistance of counsel weighed in favor of permitting a client to testify falsely. The lawyer should remonstrate with the client and advise her "that the proposed testimony is unlawful."[38] However, if the client persists in testifying, the lawyer should "proceed in the normal fashion in presenting the testimony and arguing the case to the jury. Any other course would be a betrayal of the assurances of confidentiality given by the lawyer in order to induce the client to reveal everything, however damaging it might appear."[39]

[37] Monroe H. Freedman, "Getting Honest About Client Perjury," *Georgetown Journal of Legal Ethics* 21 (2008): 133, 137.

[38] Freedman, *Lawyer's Ethics* at 31.

[39] Id.

Warren E. Burger, then a judge on the D.C. Circuit Court of Appeals, learned of the lecture from a story in the *Washington Post* and promptly contacted the Committee on Admissions and Grievances of the federal bar in D.C. to insist that the Committee initiate disbarment proceedings against Freedman. The Committee sprang into action, informing Mr. Freedman just two days after the lecture that he was subject to disbarment proceedings on account of the views he had expressed.[40] Four months later, following a hearing and national media coverage, the charges were dismissed on an 8–1 vote, although both the Committee and ten judges of the United States District Court for the District of Columbia who reviewed the Committee's report made explicit their disagreement with Freedman's thesis.[41] The Committee stressed that although Freedman was free to express his viewpoint as an academic, "any lawyer carrying such views into practice would be guilty of professional misconduct."[42]

Time Magazine ran a story entitled *Professional Ethics: Lies and Lawyers*, in May, 1966, describing some of the intrigue. In the meantime, Burger pressed on other fronts, writing to the Dean of the law school at George Washington University in the hopes of convincing him to have

[40] Id. at 138.

[41] Id. See also Richard Corrigan, "Unit Rejects Action Against Freedman," May 15, 1966.

[42] Dana Bullen, "Should Lawyers Lie in Court?" *Boston Globe*, June 5, 1966, A5.

Freedman fired.[43] Burger also apparently had one of his law clerks "pose as a 'disinterested licensed' member of the American Civil Liberties Union" and write to the organization to "demand . . . that Freedman be removed as chair of its Washington, D.C., affiliate."[44] Only after a clerk for another judge threatened "to reveal the author's identity to Freedman" did the Burger clerk write to the ACLU to correct his earlier misrepresentation, noting "that candor compelled him to mention that he was, in fact, a clerk for Burger."[45]

The hypocrisy of using deception to advocate punishment for Freedman for having talked openly about the role of deception in the law apparently did not trouble Burger. But there was no shortage of hypocrisy to go around. Separately, Freedman reports, "a very liberal federal judge wrote to me, saying that I had done a disservice to the profession and to the rights of criminal defendants by publicly airing such issues."[46]

Freedman was not completely ostracized – more than a few elite lawyers came to his defense, he received tenure at George Washington, and the article he published based on the lecture has become one of the most cited articles in the

[43] Id. at viii; Jay Sterling Silver, "Truth, Justice, and the American Way: The Case Against the Client Perjury Rules," *Vanderbilt Law Review* 47 (1994): 339, 351.

[44] Silver, "Truth, Justice, and the American Way" at 353.

[45] Silver, "Truth, Justice, and the American Way" at 353, n.57.

[46] Freedman, *Lawyer's Ethics* at viii.

field of legal ethics.[47] Anthony Amsterdam defended Freedman's lecture as "a probing and responsible attempt to answer difficult and intensely practical problems created by our adversary system," and he criticized bar leaders for relying upon "vaporous platitudes called cannons of ethics which have somewhat less usefulness as guides to lawyers in the predicaments of the real world than do valentine cards as guides to heart surgeons in the operating room."[48] Other defenses tended to be more tepid, giving the impression that even Freedman's public supporters felt rather more like the "very liberal judge" who had chastised him for exhibiting candor about the role lawyers play in perjury.[49] On the merits of Freedman's position, even Amsterdam ultimately hedged, allowing that Freedman's "views ... were *probably* right judgments," but then shifting immediately

[47] Silver, "Truth, Justice, and the American Way" at 352, n.54. Fifteen years later, however, a Washington, D.C., trial judge resigned in protest from an organizing committee of the D.C. Judicial Conference upon learning that Freedman had been invited to speak on a legal ethics panel hosted by the Conference. Two other judges wrote protest letters, and the Chief Judge of the D.C. Appeals Court announced at the conference that Freedman's views were "appalling." Al Kamen and Benjamin Weber, "Freedman Uproar Renewed at Ethics Panel Address," *Washington Post*, June 15, 1981, WB 21.

[48] "Professional Ethics: Lies and Lawyers," *Time Magazine*, May 13, 1966.

[49] See, e.g., Samuel Dash, "Letters to the Editor: Lawyers and Lying," *Washington Post*, May 8, 1966; Anon., "Letters to the Editor: For the Defense," *Washington Post*, May 2, 1966; Alan Scheflin, "Letters to the Editor: Ethics in Law," *Washington Post*, May 13, 1966.

to a kind of plea in abatement: "supposing for a moment they were wrong, their wrongness hardly makes Professor Freedman censurable."[50] In a letter to the editor of the *Washington Post*, Amsterdam suggested that Freedman's views expressed in the lecture "were not put forward as his personal opinions," but rather as an advocate's legal opinion – "conclusions rationally deduced from the premises of our legal institutions."[51] Freedman the academic apparently may have been wearing the mask of a role-differentiated advocate.

After decades of debate, Freedman's position that a criminal lawyer may assist her client in presenting false testimony remains a deeply controversial, minority view among academic commentators; even more controversial is the view that a lawyer in civil practice may do the same, or that a lawyer of any kind may assist a non-party witness in presenting false testimony. The bar, for its part, has squarely rejected Freedman's position.[52] Or so it would

[50] Freedman, "Getting Honest About Client Perjury" at 138.

[51] Anthony Amsterdam, "Letters to the Editor: Brief for Freedman," *Washington Post*, May 1, 1966: E6.

[52] Model Rule 3.3 prohibits a lawyer from "knowingly" making a "false statement of fact or law," and from offering false evidence "that the lawyer knows to be false." A lawyer who makes a "material false statement" is obliged to correct it, and if a lawyer learns that she, her client, or a witness she has called has offered material evidence which "the lawyer comes to know [is] false," is obliged to "take reasonable remedial measures, including, if necessary, disclosure to the tribunal." Furthermore, a lawyer has a duty to prevent or rectify ("by disclosure to the tribunal," if necessary) criminal or fraudulent conduct by any person if she "knows" such

seem. In reality, as Freedman has delighted in pointing out, the bar has fashioned a feeble prohibition on deception. Provisions governing deception in litigation incorporate a strict *mens rea* element. Only "knowingly" making false statements or presenting false evidence is prohibited. And although the rules specify that what a lawyer knows "may be inferred from the circumstances," only "*actual* knowledge of the fact in question" triggers the duty of candor.[53] As Freedman emphasizes:

> By giving the "knowing" requirement a highly restrictive meaning, the ABA and the courts have permitted lawyers to avoid concluding that a client is lying, despite the fact that the client has told the lawyer inconsistent versions of the truth, and despite the fact that the client's testimony is far-fetched or preposterous, unsupported by other evidence, and dramatically contradicted by credible evidence.[54]

The bar and the courts have thus "enabled lawyers to preserve client confidences and to continue to present clients' false testimony to courts in the ordinary way."[55] A lawyer clumsy enough to make a false statement or present false

conduct has occurred or will occur. 3.3(b). See also ABA Model Rule of Professional Conduct 4.1. Model Rule 8.4's prohibition on engaging in conduct "involving dishonesty, fraud, deceit or misrepresentation" is broader, but discipline under this provision appears to be restricted to conduct consistent with the standards of Rules 3.3 and 4.1.

53 ABA Model Rule 1.0.

54 Freedman, "Getting Honest About Client Perjury" at 136.

55 Id. at 137.

testimony in a manner that leaves readily available evidence of her actual knowledge of its falsity will be disciplined as a Bad Apple. A lawyer who leaves readily available evidence of her clumsy efforts to *avoid* actual knowledge will also be disciplined as a Bad Apple (the legal term is "deliberate ignorance").[56] But any reasonably careful lawyer will rather easily avoid "actual knowledge" (or leave no clear record showing that she held it) even if she reasonably believes that what she has introduced in court is false.[57]

56 Examples can be found in the reports of bar discipline proceedings. See, e.g., *In re* Cardwell, 18 Lawyers Manual Professional Conduct 429 (2002) (attorney suspended for lying to judge and prosecutor that his client had no relevant prior offenses); *In re* Foley, 19 Lawyers Manual Professional Conduct 292 (2003) (attorney suspended for coaching client to offer false testimony).

57 Freedman, "Getting Honest About Client Perjury." Edward L. Wilkinson, "That's a Damned Lie!" *St. Mary's Law Journal* 31 (2000): 407, 413 (an attorney's "belief alone" is insufficient in some jurisdictions to meet threshold of actual knowledge; "Generally, courts have held that a criminal defense lawyer does not have a duty to investigate the truthfulness of his client's story."); Marvin E. Frankel, "Client's Perjury and Lawyers' Options," *Journal of the Institute for the Study of Legal Ethics* 1 (1996): 25, 32 ("Lawyers, by circumstance and by design, have been fortunate enough to avoid [the dilemma of knowing a client intends to commit perjury] almost always."); Norman Lefstein, "Client Perjury in Criminal Cases: Still in Search of an Answer," *Georgetown Journal of Legal Ethics* 1 (1988): 521, 531 (describing case in which attorney's knowledge that client had made "inconsistent representations to him about the possession of a gun" did not "support an inference that counsel knew that his client was going to commit perjury"). Cf. Subin, "The Criminal Lawyer's 'Different Mission'" at 138, n.58.

There is evidence that some lawyers take the duty of candor very seriously, respecting the spirit of its commitment to rectitude of decision and not just the "disingenuously manipulate[d]" letter of the knowledge requirement.[58] Regrettably, however, the evidence also suggests that, at least in criminal cases, lawyers who withdraw or inform the court that they "know" their client is lying are overwhelmingly court-appointed lawyers representing indigent and minority clients.[59] This "race- and class-based double standard" not only compounds the disingenuousness of prohibiting deception on terms that invite deceptive conduct, it suggests that deception is an element of the administration of justice reserved for the haves.[60] The bar can point to disciplinary action taken against Bad Apples and, blinking at the race and class double standard, it can point to Good Apples who have disclosed client perjury. All the while, "ordinary" lawyers are free to proceed in what Freedman calls "the ordinary way."

The crimes of perjury and subornation of perjury are also notoriously difficult to prove, and prosecutions are rare.[61] One

[58] Freedman, "Getting Honest About Client Perjury" at 135.

[59] Silver, "Truth, Justice, and the American Way"; Freedman, "Getting Honest About Client Perjury" at 148–149.

[60] Freedman, "Getting Honest About Client Perjury" at 148.

[61] On the difficulty of proving intent, falsity, and materiality, as well as other hurdles to successfully prosecuting perjury such as the two-witness rule, see Durac, "Perjury," at 1348–1361; Linda F. Harrison, "The Law of Lying: The Difficulty of Pursuing Perjury Under the Federal Perjury Statutes," *University of Toledo Law Review* 35 (2003): 397; Richard H. Underwood, "Perjury! The

prosecutor has observed that "[o]utside of income tax evasion, perjury is ... probably the most underprosecuted crime in America .... You can walk into court, take the oath, lie up a storm, and not have to worry about being punished for it."[62] Prosecutions of *lawyers* for perjury or subornation of perjury are particularly rare.[63] In many cases, perjury and lesser offenses involving deception are used as surrogates, providing a means of punishing individuals the government suspects, but cannot prove, have violated other criminal laws.[64]

If, as the Supreme Court insists, the "basic purpose of a trial is the determination of truth," why is it so hard to prove perjury and why is the crime so rarely charged? Why is the lawyer's duty of candor so weak if the Supreme Court is right that "the course of justice" must be kept "free from the pollution of perjury?"[65]

Charges and the Defenses," *Duquesne Law Review* 36 (1998): 715. With respect to the rarity of prosecutions for perjury, in 1997 just 87 of nearly 50,000 federal criminal cases were for perjury. Roberto Suro and Bill Miller, "Perjury: A Tough Case to Make," *Washington Post*, September 24, 1998, A14.

62 Mark Curriden, "'The Lies Have It,'" *ABA Journal*, May 1995, at 69–70 (quoting E. Michael McCann).

63 Of the nearly 500 federal cases involving subornation of perjury in the last 10 years, only a few dozen appear to involve claims of subornation of perjury against attorneys. Richard Underwood concurs that cases involving perjury or subornation of perjury against lawyers are "hard to find." Underwood, "Perjury!" at 240.

64 Durac, "Perjury," at 1344; Lisa Kern Griffin, "Criminal Lying, Prosecutorial Power, and Social Meaning," *California Law Review* 97 (2009): 1515.

65 *Bronston v. United States*, 409 U.S. 352, 357 (1973) (quoting *U.S. v. Williams*, 341 U.S. 58, 68 (1951)).

Enough has been said, I hope, to show that we are unlikely to arrive at compelling answers to these questions within the terms of the academic and litigation reform debates. Deception is both taken too seriously (solemnly condemned as an affront to common morality and the administration of justice) and not seriously enough (dismissed or defended as a practice of at best marginal relevance to the rule of law even though the law of perjury and the duty of candor are permissive).[66] In what follows I contend that it is difficult to talk about the relationship between truth and deception in the law because they are curiously interdependent. Indeed, they animate a culturally productive contradiction in the rule of law, a contradiction in what, to borrow from Samuel Johnson, might more precisely be called the "artifices of the law." Rather than trying to eliminate deception, as the philosophers and role critics advocate, or defending a right to lie in narrow circumstances, as Freedman has, we need to probe the sources of the interdependence and contradiction. We need, in short, to understand why clients struggle to be truthful, and how we arrived at evidentiary rules that permit individuals with so much at stake (and therefore so many reasons to lie) to testify at trial. As importantly, we need to understand why and how certain forms of deception, artful lies, if you will, support the various artifices of the

[66] A welcome exception in the literature is Larry Alexander and Emily Sherwin, "Deception in Morality and Law," *Law and Philosophy* 22 (2003): 393.

administration of justice, as well as how they affect our political culture and identity formation. Showing, as I intend to, that American law values principles other than truth and that certain forms of deception are deeply embedded in our politics and our self-conceptions will not establish that intentional misrepresentations are morally good. It should, however, provide reasons to support the rather narrow definition of perjury the law has long applied, and grounds to doubt the wisdom and feasibility of writing the philosophers' general objections to lying into law.

II. Perjury and the Right to Participate at Trial

Modern anxiety about deception cannot be disaggregated from the Enlightenment and the Protestant Reformation. In the law, this is most readily evident in the history of rules for determining truth and punishing lies. Medieval legal practice depended heavily upon divine sanction in assessing credibility. Trial by ordeal made determinations of truthfulness explicitly contingent on the will of God.

> In the ordeal of cold water, the accused was tossed in a pool with a rope tied around his hips. If he sank, he was hauled out an innocent person, for the purity of the water had accepted him; but if the water repelled him and he floated, he was condemned. In the ordeal of hot iron, the accused walked barehanded with a hot iron bar. Three days later, when her bandages were removed, her healing hands

revealed her fate; if the wounds were healing cleanly, she was absolved; if corruptly, condemned.[67]

Trial by jury gradually replaced trial by ordeal. As George Fisher explains, "when the Church decertified the ordeal, it wrecked it, for the system no longer could claim that God – and not some mere human authority – had decreed the accused's guilt and authorized punishment."[68] But truth remained, in the first instance, a sacred question. Elaborate rules governing oaths, the competence of witnesses, and the resolution of conflicts in sworn testimony operated to "reassure the public of God's continuing role in meting out human justice."[69]

Today an atheist can give sworn testimony, but for centuries this was not the case. Until the mid-nineteenth century, the purpose of the oath was to ensure the truthfulness of the testimony of a witness by inviting "divine vengeance" for perjury.[70] Perjury "was fully expected to bring its own punishment" in the afterlife.[71] With confidence equal to Wigmore's faith in cross-examination as the best means of eliciting the truth, a seventeenth-century commentator insisted that "an Oath is . . . [t]he greatest assurance, that a Man can give of the truth of his Testimony; the

[67] George Fisher, "The Jury's Rise as Lie Detector," *Yale Law Journal* 107 (1997): 575, at 585.

[68] Id. at 587.

[69] Id. at 587.

[70] Id. at 589.

[71] Id. at 589, n.36, 606 n. 104.

last result, the highest and utmost appeal that we can make; and the best means to find out the Matter of Fact, to determine Right and Wrong."[72] Accordingly, anyone who did not believe in the afterlife was disqualified from taking the oath.[73]

To protect the sanctity of the oath, and thus the divine sanction of human judgments made on the basis of assessing sworn testimony, early common law courts insulated sworn testimony in several ways. First, sworn testimony was presumed to be true.[74] Second, the crime of perjury was, for centuries, left exclusively to God to punish.[75] Prosecuting perjury, it was believed, would "broadcast the failure of an oath to secure truthful testimony,"[76] thus damaging "the public's confidence in the accuracy of jury verdicts."[77] Even after perjury was made criminal, prosecutions remained rare.[78] Third, the courts avoided conflicts

[72] Id. at 606, n.104.

[73] Wesley J. Campbell, "God, Hell, and Sworn Testimony in American Courts, 1800–1860," working paper.

[74] Fisher, "Jury as Lie Detector" at 606.

[75] Id.

[76] Id. at 606, n.104.

[77] Id. at 607.

[78] One study reports that in the latter decades of the twentieth century, perjury prosecutions constituted just 0.17 percent of all criminal cases. Winand Emons, "Perjury Versus Truth Revelation: Quantity or Quality of Testimony," *Journal of Institutional and Theoretical Economics* 161 (2005): 393. Another study reports that between 1966 and 1970, perjury cases in federal courts were just "two-tenths of one percent of the 166,664 cases commenced," and that only 11 defendants were sentenced to federal prison for the

between the sworn testimony of witnesses by rendering people who would be tempted to lie in court incompetent to give sworn testimony. Until the mid-nineteenth century, *all parties* to a proceeding were barred – "both plaintiff and defendant in a civil suit and all criminal defendants."[79] Also excluded were "spouses of parties, persons with financial interest in the case, convicted felons, irreligious persons, and various other classes of people."[80] Fisher asserts that "[t]here is no doubt as to the rules' rationale. All sources agree that they sought to keep from the witness stand anyone whose temptation or inclination to lie was greater than average."[81] As the eighteenth-century treatise writer Jeffrey Gilbert put it:

> Men are generally so short-sighted, as to look at their own private Benefit, which is nearer to them, rather than to the Good of the World that is more remote; therefore . . . the Law removes them from Testimony, to prevent their sliding into Perjury; and it can be no Injury to Truth, to remove those from the [hearing of the] Jury, whose Testimony may hurt themselves, and can never induce any rational belief.[82]

offense; in California in 1972, 53 charges were brought and less than half were convicted. Anon., "Perjury: The Forgotten Offense," *Journal of. Criminal Law and Criminology* 65 (1974): 361.

79 Id. at 624. Fisher observes that early on defendants could give unsworn testimony at trial but could not call *any* witnesses. Id. at 603.

80 Id. at 625.

81 Id.

82 Id.

"[B]y keeping likely liars from the witness stand," Fisher emphasizes, the competency rules "protected the presumption that all sworn evidence is truthful."[83]

Finally, should an apparent conflict nevertheless emerge in the sworn testimony of witnesses, the common law courts developed a rule to avoid the finding that either witness had committed perjury. In its most general formulation, jurors were instructed to "reconcile competing oaths ... by conclud[ing] that one witness was mistaken (or inattentive) before concluding that either had lied."[84] Thus, if one witness swore he saw "x" happen and another swore he did not see "x" happen, the witness swearing the affirmative would be credited over the witness swearing the negative on the theory that "witnesses who say something happened are much less likely to be mistaken."[85] In a frequently cited case the court instructed the jury that "one Affirmative was better than Forty Negative Oaths."[86] As Gilbert summarized the rule, "In contrary Proofs if Men's swearing can be reconciled, such Interpretation shall be put upon it as may make them agree, because every body shall be supposed to swear the Truth, and no Man shall be intended to swear a manifest Perjury."[87] Jurors were also instructed to accept the sworn testimony of an "unimpeached and uncontradicted witness," as well as to "give more credit to the side that produced the

83 Id.
84 Id. at 627–628.
85 Id. at 627.
86 Id. at 626.
87 Id. at 628 (quoting Gilbert).

greater number of witnesses."[88] Together, these rules not only protected the sanctity of the oath, they gave a powerful advantage to whichever party could produce competent, sworn witnesses.

Fisher and other scholars have detailed how this system, dependent on an integration of divine and human judgment, gradually gave way to the modern system, which relies on a non-denominational, indeed, secular, oath, sworn testimony by parties and other interested witnesses in both civil and criminal cases, cross-examination, the possibility of prosecution for perjury, and near complete power in the jury to assess credibility.[89] In the United States, witness competence rules barring parties from testifying in civil cases generally fell in the mid-nineteenth century.[90] Jud Campbell has shown that over roughly the same period, non-Christians and atheists were permitted to give sworn testimony.[91] In criminal cases, states first passed legislation allowing defendants to testify in the Civil War and Reconstruction period.[92]

There are several remarkable facts about the gradual diminution of the role of divine sanction in adjudication. First, even in trial by ordeal, human and divine judgment were mixed. As Fisher trenchantly observes,

[88] Id. at 653–652.
[89] Id. at 660–661.
[90] Id. at 669.
[91] Campbell, "God, Hell and Sworn Testimony in American Courts."
[92] Fisher, "Jury as Lie Detector" at 668.

> someone had to determine if the iron was hot enough and whether the wounds were clean enough or whether a partly submerged body had sunk or floated. ... Given that an omnipotent God surely could have spoken through a throw of the dice, we must assume that the system preferred an ordeal that left room for human discretion. The institutional brilliance of the ordeal was that it so neatly merged the appearance of divine judgment with the reality of a great measure of human control.[93]

In jury trials, the oath, evidentiary rules that insulate the presumption of truth given to sworn testimony, and of course the jury's "unbounded discretion to acquit ... reproduce[d] this very useful combination of traits."[94] In both trial by ordeal and the early jury trial, then, truth depended upon a carefully constructed artifice of divine supervision and intervention. A central effect, if not purpose, of the artifice, was to render opaque the role of fallible human memory, testimony, and judgment in the determination of truth.

In the modern system, there is no pretense of divine supervision or intervention – indeed, we prohibit displays of the Ten Commandments in courthouses as an unconstitutional establishment of religion[95] – but the artifice rendering human fallibility opaque remains. Rather than

[93] Id. at 600–601.

[94] Id. at 601; see also id. at 600, n.77.

[95] See *McCreary County v. American Civil Liberties Union*, 545 U.S. 844 (2005) (Ten Commandments display in county courthouse held unconstitutional).

regulate lying *ex ante* through the oath and witness competence rules, it is regulated *ex post* by the jury, and to a far lesser extent, by the possibility of prosecution for perjury.[96] The capacity of jurors to distinguish truthful from perjured testimony was regularly invoked by opponents of the competency rules.[97] In civil cases, where the standard of proof is a mere preponderance of the evidence, the jury's task is arguably simplified by the fact that it need only decide "which witness was the *more* truthful."[98] However, in criminal cases, as Fisher emphasized, the temptation of the defendant to lie is nearly irresistible and the standard of evidence precludes jurors from evading genuinely conflicting evidence.[99] Reformers nevertheless prevailed in dramatically expanding the participatory rights of parties to both civil and criminal litigation.

This democratic expansion of participatory rights was no small achievement. After centuries of presuming interested witnesses would be likely to lie, there was no naivety among courts or reformers about the consequences of including their sworn testimony.[100] In criminal cases, "even moderate observers predicted 'perjury on every occasion,' a 'fearful and overpowering temptation to perjury' . . . 'perjury on a gigantic scale.'"[101] Equally striking, in light of these predictions, is

[96] Id. at 582, 681.
[97] Id. at 698 n.570, 659.
[98] Id.
[99] Id. at 582.
[100] Id. at 659.
[101] Id. at 663.

that in the century and a half since the floodgates to perjury were opened with the dismantling of competency rules the legal definition of perjury has remained narrow.[102] Nor has there been any significant effort to increase perjury prosecutions to supplement the lie-detecting function of the jury. Truth now rests almost exclusively in the hands of the jury to determine even though "most of the evidence we have suggests that juries have no particular talent for spotting lies."[103] Thus for the artifice of divine intervention and supervision we have substituted the dubious lie-detecting

[102] There has been some drift. For instance, the two-witness rule in many jurisdictions is now satisfied by one witness and circumstantial evidence, falsity can now be proven by circumstantial rather than direct evidence, and 18 U.S.C. § 1623, which permits conviction where the defendant has made inconsistent statements even if the prosecution cannot prove either is false, uses a "knowing" rather than a "willful" *mens rea* standard, and dispenses with the two witness rule, was added in 1970. See Durac, "Perjury"; Charles Doyle, "Perjury Under Federal Law," Congressional Research Service, January 28, 2014. Commentators nevertheless appear to be in agreement that the drift is modest, see id., and the federal courts have narrowly construed the elements of perjury. See, e.g., *Bronston v. United States*, 409 U.S. 352, 358–59 (1973) (a literally true but patently misleading statement is not "false"). For discussion of lower federal court precedent, see Doyle, "Perjury Under." For trenchant criticism of prosecutorial expansion of the "false statements" statute, 18 U.S.C. § 1001, see Griffin (2009).

[103] Not only do experimental subjects rarely perform much better than chance at distinguishing truth from falsehood, but they think they are better lie detectors than they are." Id. at 707. See also Jill Donner Kagle, "Are We Lying to Ourselves About Deception," *Social Service Review* 72 (1998): 234, 242.

capacities of jurors, complemented by the opacity of the jury deliberation room,[104] and, by the end of the twentieth century, an increasingly elaborate framework of judicial preemption, supervision, and intervention that prevents the vast majority of cases from ever reaching a jury.[105] The artifice here is that the law itself, in the form of jury instructions and close judicial oversight (at both the trial and appellate level), will ensure rectitude of decision. Divine supervision now wears the mask of reason.[106]

III. Democracy, Pluralism, and Hypocrisy

Deception has a long, complex, and arguably constitutive history in politics as well. For present purposes, the role of deception in both revolutionary and ordinary democratic politics is most salient. We learn from Gordon Wood that

[104] Fisher, "Jury as Lie Detector" 706.

[105] On the disappearance of jury trials, see Marc Galanter, "The Vanishing Trial: An Examination of Trials and Related Matters in Federal and State Courts," *Journal of Empirical Legal Studies* 1 (2004): 459.

[106] The standards for a judge to take a case away from a jury or overturn the verdict of a jury turn on determinations of what a reasonable jury could find based on the evidence. See Fed. R. Civ. Proc. 50; Fed. R. Crim. Proc. 29, 33; *Jackson v. Virginia*, 443 U.S. 307 (1979); *Galloway v. United States*, 319 U.S. 372 (1943). See also Norman W. Spaulding, "The Enclosure of Justice: Courthouse Architecture, Due Process, and the Dead Metaphor of Trial," *Yale Journal of Law and Humanities* 24 (2012): 311. On deception in the ordinary operation of legal interpretation, see Alexander and Sherwin (2003).

"[m]asquerades and hidden designs formed the grammar and vocabulary for much of the thought of the age" leading up to the American Revolution.[107] The morality of deception was much debated, but it was widely understood that certain forms of deception were necessary. As Lord Chesterfield admonished his son in 1749, "[n]othing in Courts is exactly as it appears to be. Interest, which is the real spring of everything there, equally creates and dissolves friendships, produces and reconciles enemies."[108] The best strategy, therefore, is to "observe ... such a degree of reserve with your friends, as not to put yourself in their power, if they should become your enemies, and such a degree of moderation with your enemies, as not to make it impossible for them to become your friends."[109] Chesterfield counseled dissimulation not simply as a convention, but because it provided a rational substitute to violence.

> Courts are unquestionably seats of politeness and good-breeding; were they not so they would be the seats of slaughter and desolation. Those who now smile upon, and embrace, would affront and stab each other if manners did not interpose: but ambition and avarice, the two prevailing

[107] Gordon S. Wood, "Conspiracy and the Paranoid Style: Causality and Deceit in the Eighteenth Century," *William and Mary Quarterly* 39 (1982): 401, 421.

[108] Wood quotes part of this letter, id. at 422. The full text appears at Philip Dormer Stanhope Earl of Chesterfield, *The Works of Lord Chesterfield* (New York: Harper and Brothers, 1838), 269.

[109] Id. at 268.

> passions at Courts, found dissimulation more effective than violence; and dissimulation introduced that habit of politeness which distinguishes the courtier from the country gentleman. In the former case the strongest body would prevail; in the latter, the strongest mind.[110]

At least in letters to his son, Chesterfield carefully distinguished dissimulation (deception aimed at concealing one's thoughts and feelings) from "simulation" (the more affirmative form of misrepresentation entailed in pretending). With Bacon and Bolingbroke, he criticized "simulation" as "false, mean, and criminal ... crooked ... a *stiletto*; not only an unjust but an unlawful weapon ... the use of it very rarely to be excused, never justified."[111]

Of course the intricacies of this distinction between different techniques of deception were quite often lost on others, and even for those who accepted it in principle, the distinction was often lost in practice. As Wood describes, "what was prudence and sociability to some became deceit and flattery to others."[112] This "in turn encouraged an

[110] Id. at 269.

[111] Id. at 256–257. In advising his son about relations with women, however, Chesterfield wrote: "Here dissimulation is very often necessary, and even simulation sometimes allowable; which, as it pleases them, may be useful to you, and is injurious to nobody." Id. at 258. And in foreign relations, no holds were barred: "Both simulation and dissimulation are absolutely necessary for a foreign Minister; and yet they must stop short of falsehood and perfidy." Id. at 623.

[112] Wood, "Conspiracy and the Paranoid Style" at 422.

opposition politics dedicated to the umasking of hypocrisy."[113] In an increasingly profane world in which all effects were assumed to have rationally identifiable causes, "[t]he idea of deception" provided an explanation for "the gaps that often seemed to exist between causes and effects, between men's proclaimed intentions and their contrary actions."[114] It is no accident, as Wood emphasizes, that in the opposition politics developed by American colonists to support revolutionary violence, the idea of deception was central. "The British government's claim to have the interests of the colonies at heart, while its actions seemed clearly harmful to those interests, only confirmed its duplicity in colonial eyes."[115]

Not surprisingly, a literature and "politics of sincerity" emerged and quickly became associated with republican

[113] Id. at 423. Lionel Trilling describes a more general "intellectual tendency," or "disposition of mind, salient in Europe for some centuries," which Henri Ellenberger dubbed the "unmasking trend." Lionel Trilling, *Sincerity and Authenticity* (Cambridge: Harvard University Press, 1978), 141. Ellenberger defined this trend as "the systematic search for deception and self-deception and the uncovering of underlying truth (currently known in France as demystification). This trend seems to have started with the French moralists of the seventeenth century. La Rochefoucauld in his *Maxims*, unmasked virtuous attitudes and acts as disguised manifestations of amour-propre (in today's language narcissism)." Ellenberger, *The Discovery of the Unconscious* (1970), 537, quoted in Trilling, *Sincerity and Authenticity* at 141.

[114] Wood, "Conspiracy and the Paranoid Style" at 425.

[115] Id.

virtue.[116] This new politics of sincerity drew upon a long Christian tradition of sincerity in faith and an equally long tradition of castigating those who either profess a faith they do not genuinely hold or betray in action beliefs they genuinely do hold.[117] As Judith Shklar has argued, our "[h]abits of ideological combat were inherited from religious controversy. The art of unmasking one's opponent has always been a favorite weapon in religious warfare."[118]

Whatever hope victorious American revolutionaries may have had about replacing the deception of court politics with republican virtue and sincerity were of course quickly dashed.

> As soon as democracy became a working political system, it was damned as a sham. . . . . Democracy was just hypocrisy at large to those who had suffered an intense erosion of faith when the actual republic replaced the city of their hopes. American representative democracy was meant to be unlike other governments in all ways, not only in some. The difference proved to be insufficiently great and the actuality was perceived as fraudulent.[119]

The disappointment was grounded not merely in comparison to other political systems, but in the very structure of political competition and representation that defines democratic

116 Id. at 426–427.

117 Judith Shklar, *Ordinary Vices* (Cambridge: Harvard University Press, 1984), 47–49.

118 Id. at 48.

119 Id. at 68–69.

engagement. There is a "built-in tension" because "the disparity between what is said and what is done is great."[120] The effects of contingency and compromise on policy choices can never match the high rhetoric regarding first principles necessary to win elections. Shklar notes that the "gap" between promises and policy "exists in every association, not only in political units. No one lives up to a collective ideal. This is the fatality on which Machiavelli capitalized, and on which his political honesty thrived."[121]

For every democratic position, interest group, and party, the charge of hypocrisy is always ready to hand. The charge can be made internally, by those who wish to replace existing leaders because they have purportedly betrayed the founding principles of the group or the country, and externally, by competing interest groups. Shklar emphasizes that the latter practice is inescapable and indeed most acute under conditions of value pluralism – the very conditions liberal democratic politics are supposed to suit. "When political actors disagree about right and wrong, and everything else, they can only undermine each other with the revelation that their opponent is not living up to his own professed ideal. . . . It is . . . easier to dispose of an opponent's character by exposing his hypocrisy than to show that his political convictions are wrong."[122] Paradoxically, those who are most eager to make

[120] Id. 69.
[121] Id.
[122] Id. at 48.

democracy work under conditions of value pluralism, those willing to compromise, "are particularly liable to be charged with hypocrisy."[123] Indeed, even as the exposure of and anxiety about hypocrisy feeds a "demand for sincerity," expediency and the "politics of persuasion" continue to "require . . . a certain amount of dissimulation."[124] Democracy thus "generates disappointment, and a sense of always being deceived" not only when the political process becomes dysfunctional, but also when it appears to work.[125] As Shklar succinctly puts it, "[w]hat we have to live with is a morally pluralistic world in which hypocrisy and antihypocrisy are joined to form a discrete political system."[126] In this volume, William Eskridge details some of the more pathological legal consequences of this system.

The first deception, the first and perennial source of dissimulation, is the pretense that the people are sovereign.[127] Non-revolutionary democratic politics always disappoint in relation to this false promise regarding the location of sovereignty, and various sleights of hand are constantly employed to mobilize, or at least mitigate, that disappointment. These new deceptions fuel opposition politics and the demand for sincerity, which, in exposing hypocrisy, deepens disappointment. That is the system.

[123] Id.
[124] Id.
[125] Id. at 75.
[126] Id. at 62.
[127] Id. at 70.

Both the literature and politics of the Jacksonian period, Shklar observes, struggled mightily with the disappointments of democracy as a "working political system." Of particular concern was the realization that "claims for post-Revolutionary republican government were exaggerated,"[128] and that the political sphere could so easily be monopolized by elites. The "current quarrel between those who seek to ground democratic legitimacy in active citizen participation," and those who "are content with it as a system of leadership selection" are replaying "the Jacksonian script. And it is as evident now as it was then that 'the people' so ardently championed is not an actual but an invented entity."[129] On this view, the foundation of democratic legitimacy is itself an artifice.

Shklar is quick to point out, however, that we can scarcely do without this artifice and the other forms of dissimulation it invites. "It is not at all clear that zealous candor would serve liberal politics particularly well."[130] This is so for at least two reasons. First, excessive sincerity is the enemy of civility. Hypocrisy, Shklar provocatively asserts,

> may be indispensable if we are ever going to fully accept human diversity in all its individual manifestations. The democracy of everyday life ... does not arise from sincerity. It is based on the pretense that we must speak to each other

[128] Id.
[129] Id. at 71–72.
[130] Id. at 48.

> as if social standings were a matter of indifference in our views of each other. This is, of course, not true. Not all of us are even convinced that all men are entitled to a certain minimum of social respect.[131]

Freedom of thought, of conscience, and democratic dialogue in a pluralistic society thus depend in no small degree upon dissimulation. Knowing the legacy of slavery, Jim Crow, and white supremacy, "[w]ould any egalitarian prefer more public frankness? . . . Often our public manners are better than our personal laxities. That 'sugary grin' is . . . a very necessary pretense, a witness to our moral efforts no less than to our failures."[132] Shklar's point is not that silence or outright lies are preferred modes of political expression, but rather that pluralistic democratic societies avert violence (and disorder nearing violence) by the same means Lord Chesterfield identified as essential to peace at court.

The point should not be overstated. As African-Americans and other minorities know all too well, dissimulation has too long been a condition of mere safety in public life. In his famous poem, *We Wear the Mask*, Paul Laurence Dunbar wrote of the "mask that grins and lies," of the "myriad subtleties" covering "torn and bleeding hearts," and of the "debt" blacks pay "to human guile."[133] The poem is a

[131] Id. at 77.

[132] Id. at 78.

[133] "We Wear The Mask," in Joanne M. Braxton, ed., *The Collected Poetry of Paul Laurence Dunbar* (University of Virginia Press, 1993), 71.

chilling reminder that dissimulation can become more costly to personal and political integrity than candor or even violence. Pluralistic societies not only need respectful tolerance for different viewpoints but a certain level of toleration for expressions of outrage regarding moral and political failure. Nonetheless, Shklar's point holds: even these moments of candor must be carefully orchestrated to resonate beyond the group lodging the complaint. Outrage in particular must be very carefully orchestrated. Dunbar's poem, for instance, ingeniously plays upon the reader's desire for sincerity, questioning whether the world should ever "be overwise," and concluding "let the world dream otherwise / We wear the mask!"[134] The poem thus publishes a secret about deception even as it insists that the deception be maintained. In addition to showing that not all masking is voluntary, Dunbar dares the reader to doubt that even candor wears a mask.

As our contemporary political culture draws into vivid relief, the second reason to doubt the virtue of zealous candor, is that "a stiff-necked refusal to compromise" can make governing impossible.[135] Along with "[h]onesties that humiliate," zealous candor in the name of reform can "ruin democratic civility."[136] If a new consensus fails to emerge from the disruption caused by zealous candor, the political

[134] Id.
[135] Shklar, *Ordinary Vices* at 78.
[136] Id.

process can be paralyzed by ideological factionalization. The risk of failure is great because "[o]ur sense of public ends is so wavering and elusive ... we often do not even see the same social scene before us. We do not agree on the facts and figures of social life, and we heartily dislike one another's religious, sexual, intellectual, and political commitments – not to mention one another's ethnic, racial, and class character."[137] In light of these basic differences, "one might well argue that liberal democracy cannot afford public sincerity."[138]

If these claims seem distant from the problem of deception in the practice of law, they are not. If Shklar is right that "we do not even see the same social scene before us," that "we do not agree on the facts and figures of social life," the adversarial space in which our most ordinary and acute social, political, and economic disputes are adjudicated will often seem rife with hypocrisy, dissimulation, and perfidy. It could not be otherwise. Adjudication provides one of the principal sites in which people of divergent viewpoints seek authoritative disposition of their charges of discrepancy between an adversary's words and actions, her interests and legal duties. Sincerity is thus always on trial. And "once the possibility of falsehood or of hidden or oblique meanings is broached, it becomes difficult to return to straightforward speech (assuming there is such a thing) because that utterance will be subjected to the same

[137] Id.
[138] Id.

suspicious interpretation as all the others."[139] Litigants must instead, as Macbeth put it, "lie . . . like truth."[140]

Trial is also one of the principal sites where the artifice of popular sovereignty is staged. While wearing the mask of candor litigants, jurors, and spectators practice the lie that "the people" are law-givers. It is no insult to democracy or the rule of law that we feel the need to believe the lie even as we repeat it, or that we delight in ripping off the mask. There are far worse lies to live by.[141]

None of this yet provides a theory of the level of deception that is appropriate in litigation. However, placed alongside the history of perjury (which teaches us that only the most crystalline of lies under oath have ever been treated as criminal), the inclusion of interested-witness testimony in the nineteenth century (which amplifies participation in the legal process by those with the greatest incentive to lie), and the jury's dominant role in credibility assessment (notwithstanding evidence that juries make poor lie detectors), it becomes difficult to entertain the assumption that the adversary system is designed to vindicate the same concept of "truth" that moral philosophers invoke when they condemn deception. Indeed, the assumption begins to look rather facile, and the Avoidance pleas – particularly the plea of Reasonable Epistemological Doubt – somewhat more convincing.

139 William O. Scott, "Macbeth's – And Our – Self-Equivocations," *Shakespeare Quarterly* 37 (1986): 160, 162.

140 Id. at 174.

141 The phrase is turned from Shklar, *Ordinary Vices* at 86.

Nor is it clear that reforms, such as expanding the definition of perjury, would draw the system any closer to the philosopher's concept of truth. The likely outcome is that as the risk of prosecution increased, fewer witnesses (both dishonest *and* honest) would be willing to testify, diminishing not only participation but the quality and reliability of testimony.[142] And as pressure to prosecute cases of possible, but not crystalline, perjury increased, the risk of contested ideologies and stereotypes informing decisions about whether to prosecute would increase.[143] Resurrecting witness competence rules and expanding the already broad powers of judges to preempt, supervise, and intervene in the decision-making of juries would only make the law less democratic, the mask of reason in adjudication all the more intricate and cumbersome.[144]

IV. Self-Deception

> "I am not what I am"
> – *Iago, William Shakespeare's* Othello

142 Underwood, "Perjury!" at 722, 735.

143 Fisher documents the rank political abuse of perjury prosecutions in late seventeenth century England: "in the rash of treason trials that marked the reigns of the Stuarts, the government ... shamefully ... employed sworn perjurers to defeat the unsworn but truthful witnesses of the unhappy defendants." Fisher, "Jury as Lie Detector," at 617.

144 On the intricacies of the law's reliance on legal fictions and the deceptiveness of ordinary legal rules, see Larry Alexander and Emily Sherwin, "Deception in Law and Morality," at 422–430.

Lawyers often represent clients who have been deceived by others, but the duty of confidentiality forestalls open discussion about the fact that clients consistently deceive themselves, that they come to lawyers under all manner of spells they themselves have cast, and that they cling to liberal fantasies about what the possession or recognition of a right will do. No small part of a lawyer's task is identifying and either piercing or redirecting these self-deceptions to advantage in the legal process. As Elihu Root once observed, "About half the practice of a decent lawyer consists in telling would-be clients that they are damned fools and should stop."[145] But the problem of self-deception does not end there. Clients are divided against themselves, want conflicting things from the law, and hence expect conflicting things from the representation lawyers provide. And of course lawyers are self-deceiving and divided subjects as well.

Social, cognitive, and Freudian psychologists have made much greater headway than the legal profession in understanding the self-deceptions and divisions of the modern subject. The once dominant association of mental health with accurate perception of reality – the view that "perception of reality is . . . mentally healthy when what the individual sees corresponds to what is actually there" – has been disrupted.[146] "[A] certain degree of contact with

[145] Quoted in Richard Hofstadter, *The Age of Reform* (New York: Vintage Books, 1955), 162.

[146] Shelley E. Taylor and Jonathan D. Brown, "Illusion and Well-Being: A Social-Psychological Perspective on Mental Health," *Psychological Bulletin* 103 (1988): 193; Timothy D. Wilson,

reality seems to be essential to accomplish the tasks of everyday life," but rigorous examination of social cognition has revealed that "information processing is full of incomplete data gathering, shortcuts, errors, and biases. In particular, prior expectations and self-serving interpretations weigh heavily in the social judgment process."[147] Regarding the traditional assumption that "the social perceiver monitors and interacts with the world like a naïve scientist ... gather[ing] data in an unbiased manner, combin[ing] it in some logical, identifiable fashion; and reach[ing] generally good, accurate inferences and decisions," one study has pointedly observed:

> Instead of a naïve scientist entering the environment in search of truth, we find the rather unflattering picture of a charlatan trying to make the data come out in a manner most advantageous to his or her already-held theories.[148]

Findings of error and bias have been sufficiently robust that some psychologists have adopted the term "illusion" to

Strangers to Ourselves: Discovering the Adaptive Unconscious (Cambridge: Belknap Press, 2002); Shelley E. Taylor, *Positive Illusions: Creative Self-Deception and the Healthy Mind* (New York: Basic Books, 1989).

147 Taylor and Brown, "Illusion and Well-Being" at 194, 200.

148 Id. at 194. See also David Dunning, Chip Heath, and Jerry Suls, "Flawed Self-Assessment: Implications for Health, Education, and the Workplace," *Psychological Science in the Public Interest* 5 (2004): 69; Simine Vazire and Erika N. Carson, "Self-Knowledge of Personality: Do People Know Themselves?" *Social and Personality Psychology* 4 (2010): 605.

reflect the "pervasive, enduring, and systematic" nature of these cognitive processes and to avoid the implication that inaccurate perceptions of reality "might be caused by careless oversight or other temporary negligences."[149]

Ironically, research shows that people suffering from depression and low self-esteem tend to have a more realistic perception of themselves and their environment as compared to "well-adjusted" individuals.[150] "[N]ormal individuals possess, unrealistically positive views of themselves, an exaggerated belief in their ability to control their environment, and a view of the future that maintains that their future will be far better than the average person's."[151] Part of the reason happy people are happy, in short, is that they systematically misjudge reality in self-serving ways, falsely attribute outcomes to their agency, and cling to optimism. They also remember the past in self-serving ways.[152] Indeed, "individuals who are most apt to engage in self-deception . . . score lowest on measures of psychopathology."[153] By contrast, high levels of "private self-consciousness" – i.e., "detailed and accurate self-knowledge" – are "positively correlated with depression," and experimental research is suggestive of a causal relationship ("focusing attention on the self may engender negative emotional states").[154]

149 Id. at 194.
150 Id. at 197.
151 Id.
152 Id. at 202.
153 Id. at 197.
154 Id.

As Nietzsche, himself a perceptive and quintessentially unhappy modernist, famously observed about Hamlet's depression and paralysis, Hamlet had

> penetrated into the true nature of things . . . *perceived*, but it is irksome for [him] to act; for [his] action cannot change the eternal nature of things; the time is out of joint and [he] regard[s] it as shameful or ridiculous that [he] should be required to set it right. Knowledge kills action, action requires the veil of illusion.[155]

Clinical and psychiatric research has further shown that people with serious mental disorders are unable "to monitor reality effectively."[156] Self-deception thus figures in both normal and abnormal psychic states.

There is more. For in order to preserve positive illusions of themselves, and to preserve the positive illusions others have about themselves, people regularly deceive each other.[157] This begins very early on and appears to be associated with identity formation. "Intentional deceit and secrecy are essential to psychic development, emerging during the period of separation-individuation as the child begins to establish the

[155] Friedrich Nietzsche, *The Birth of Tragedy* (Mineola: Dover, 1995), 23.

[156] Taylor and Brown, "Illusion and Well-Being" at 200.

[157] We avoid giving feedback to others or mute our criticism, and when receiving feedback we discount negative comments as mistaken or less credible than positive comments. Id. at 201–202. See also Michael Lewis and Carolyn Saarni, *Lying and Deception in Everyday Life* (New York: Guilford Press, 1993).

self and create an inner world."[158] Nor is the association trivial. "By inventing deceptions and withholding information, children establish boundaries between self and others, test the limits of adult power and control, and move toward independent thought and action."[159] Even "children with a reputation for honesty enter adolescence and adulthood with a repertoire of deceptive behavior."[160]

Deception is not only adaptive for a proper level of self-esteem, privacy, and individuation, it is also "frequently used to establish control or redress real or perceived imbalances in power among individuals and groups."[161] Truthfulness on this view is a kind of luxury good. "In general, those in power have greater access to resources and are not as reliant on deception to gain advantage and exert control as are those with less power."[162] However, those in power may nevertheless withhold the truth for both benign and opprobrious reasons. For example, professionals who have skills a client cannot effectively assess may use deception "paternalistically to save clients from painful truths ... [or selfishly,] to strengthen their authority, avoid unpleasantness, or expedite decisions."[163]

[158] Kagle, "Are We Lying to Ourselves About Deception" at 237.

[159] Id. at 238.

[160] Id.; see also Lewis and Saarni, *Lying and Deception in Everyday Life*.

[161] Kagle, "Are We Lying to Ourselves About Deception" at 240.

[162] Id. at 241.

[163] Id. On the use of deception by lawyers with their clients, see Lisa Lerman, "Lying to Clients," *University of Pennsylvania Law Review* 138 (1990): 659. Lerman quotes a lawyer who admits

The beneficial effects of maintaining positive illusions (happiness, increased cooperation with and care for others, improved productivity and capacity for creative work, and ability to overcome adversity) must of course be weighed against the risk of inviting pathological behavior.[164] One study speculates that "[a] chief value of [positive] illusions may be that they can create self-fulfilling prophecies. They may help people try harder in situations with objectively poor probabilities of success."[165] The authors note that it would be "maladaptive" for an individual to persist "endlessly at a task that is truly intractable," but that is just one of the downside risks.[166] The more serious risk is that positive illusions may lead to or exacerbate morally condemnable ideation and behavior. Combined with indifference to futility, the consequences can be most pernicious. Macbeth's vice is not wanting more power ("Vaulting ambition, which o'erleaps itself") but rather his compulsively disguised belief, reached and affirmed by a tour de force of self-deception, that he can make the witches' prophesies come true. His seeming indifference (until it is too late) to the witches' admonition regarding Banquo's heirs compounds the tragedy.[167]

he lies to his clients about settlement values. "You know what is a good settlement and what he should take. If it is necessary to lie and cheat him to get him to accept what's good for him you do it." Id. at 701.

164 Taylor and Brown, "Illusions and Well-Being," at 198–199.

165 Id. at 199.

166 Id. at 199, n.4.

167 Scott, "Self-Equivocations" at 165.

Cognitive and social psychologists have attempted to define an "optimal margin of illusion" to check the pathological risks of positive self-deception.[168] Macbeth nevertheless remains a vexing case precisely because he is not, at least not initially, delusional. On the contrary, the audience witnesses his self-deception emerge precisely from self-awareness, from sustained efforts to closely scrutinize his intentions in light of events and what others have said to him. As the critic William Scott has aptly described, "Macbeth wants *consciously* to deceive himself; and if such a wish cannot be articulated without an artificial dramatic convention, cannot even be expressed without undermining itself and thereby *rending the self*, we see all the more the extremity of his situation."[169]

Scott notes that Freud detailed the inner workings of this divided subject, a subject for whom "unconscious impulses can become conscious only on condition of their being denied (a denial which ... actually reinforces their validity)."[170] Similarly, Scott contends, "Macbeth brings to mind his impulses perhaps also on the equivocal condition of their being denounced and shown futile, again without invalidating them."[171] Not only is Macbeth "not finally dissuaded from bloodshed against Duncan by his misgivings, he even goes on self-taught to other bloody instructions: the guards,

[168] Roy F. Baumeister, "The Optimal Margin of Illusion," *Journal of Social and Clinical Psychology* 8 (1989): 176, 182.

[169] Scott, "Self-Equivocations" at 164 (emphasis added).

[170] Id. at 165.

[171] Id.

Banquo, Macduff's family."[172] Over and over, Macbeth "beguiles himself" into committing murder "with a fully intended resistance .... His imaginings impel him onward, yet he must refuse their actuality as they lead him."[173] Wearing the mask of candor, Macbeth lies to almost everyone in the play, but it is the evolution of his "conscious" self-deception that drives the plot. "Though he had once been honest with himself about the consequences of evil while self-deceiving about his motives for thinking of them," by the end of the banquet scene "he ... is fully aware of his purposes but unwilling to give the foretelling of consequences a proper scrutiny."[174]

Scott insists that, as the audience of the play, we are drawn to "join in understanding" Macbeth's plight "though we would not or dare not" join him in action.[175] In Freud's theory of the unconscious, however, particularly as expressed in his later work, we are all Macbeth before the deed.[176] Even when we manage to resist the deed, as

[172] Id. at 166. On Freud's interest in Macbeth, see Peter Gay, *Reading Freud* (Yale University Press, 1990).

[173] Scott, "Self-Equivocations" at 166–167.

[174] Id. at 170. Diminishing consequences of misconduct fits the model of self-deception offered by cognitive psychologists. See Sandra T. Sigmon and C.R. Snyder, "Looking at Oneself in a Rose-Colored Mirror: The Role of Excuses in the Negotiation of a Personal Reality," in Lewis and Saarni *Lying and Deception in Everyday Life* at 148; Roy F. Baumeister, "Lying to Yourself: The Enigma of Self-Deception, in Lewis and Saarni," *Lying and Deception in Everyday Life* at 166.

[175] Id. at 174.

[176] See also Kermode, "Macbeth Is an Everyman" at 1309.

Macbeth does not, our self-restraint amplifies internal divisions. As Lionel Trilling has put it, "although the superego demands renunciation on the part of the ego, every renunciation which the ego makes at its behest, so far from appeasing it, actually increases its severity. . . . The more the ego submits to the superego, the more the superego demands in the way of submission."[177] Worse still, our speech is crooked. The truth about our self-deception and our deception of others comes out not in direct speech, but in dreams, jokes, hesitations, and slips of the tongue.[178] Direct speech looks "like th'innocent flower," but the serpent is *ever* "under't."[179]

If pluralism leaves us with what Shklar called "a discrete political system" of hypocrisy and anti-hypocrisy, Freud's theory of the unconscious suggests a psychic system at war with itself – and the war is total, a system in which self-deception is not only constitutive and unavoidable, but always at risk of expressing itself pathologically. The concept of a "supreme" or "pure inner self" upon which the politics of sincerity and the philosopher's concept of truthfulness depend, is, on this view, a romantic fiction.[180] Not only fragile, but false.

Must we believe the lie? Are there better lies to live by?

177 Trilling, "Sincerity and Authenticity" at 153–154.

178 Jacques Lacan, *Ecrits* (New York: W.W. Norton, 2006), 209. See id. at 66–67, 250.

179 Lady Macbeth to Macbeth, *Riverside Shakespeare* at 1317.

180 Shklar, *Ordinary Vices* at 76.

V. Lying Like Truth

If psychologists are right about the divided subject, and Shklar is right about the divisiveness and dissimulation in our political culture, it is perhaps wise that the law does not attempt to eliminate deception from litigation. The effort to broaden the definition of perjury would not only be self-defeating – by diminishing incentives to testify and raising doubts about the motives of perjury prosecutions – but futile. If people are systematically self-deceiving, excessive expectations of candor toward others, particularly adversaries, are bound to disappoint.

As it stands, the law allows deception in the very mechanisms by which it is purportedly excluded. The temptation is ever to resolve this contradiction or deny that it exists – to swear that the law is made of truth and to insist that the law and lawyers be made to fulfill this promise. However, the narrow definition of perjury and competence rules suggest that the contradiction may be culturally productive by providing an artifice of truth that accommodates the fallibility of human memory, testimony, and judgment. The accommodation is not perfect, and of course causes disappointment, indeed, failures of justice. But as with other features of the space in which American adversarial adjudication occurs, the rules governing testimony have the virtue of promoting direct participation in the process of rights definition on terms that engage rather than suppress the anxiety of parties, witnesses, jurors, and the public about the meaning of justice.[181]

Engagement with anxiety about the meaning of justice occurs most vividly when witnesses don the mask of candor in order to testify. The witness must decide in those moments what she is willing to say to vindicate her view of justice as against the views of others. Allowing the witness this choice about what to say without allowing the witness to lie is not possible. And as the choice itself depends on the existence of multiple ways to characterize the experience one reports, it is fraught with the perils of self-deception even for the witness who believes she wears the mask of candor sincerely.

We are now in a better position to appreciate the delicacy of the lawyer's task. The lawyer must help the client understand how to wear the mask of candor, and she must be equally adept at piercing the mask (not only of the client, but of opposing witnesses, opposing counsel, the judge, and even herself). The lawyer must perceive, as Hamlet perceives, but without allowing understanding to kill action. And she must act as much as possible without illusion while using illusions held by others. Truth for the lawyer cannot be the truth of the "naïve" or even the sophisticated scientist. It is rather a "value that (cor)responds to the

[181] On the connection between these anxieties, participation, and the democratic legitimacy of adversary adjudication, see Spaulding, "Enclosure" (2012). On the role of participation in conceptions of democratic legitimacy, see Tom Tyler, *Why People Obey the Law* (Princeton, NJ: Princeton University Press, 2006).

uncertainty with which man's lived experience is phenomenologically marked."[182]

None of this provides an unfettered license to deceive. Blindly feeding the client's base desires and manipulating his illusions, as Lady Macbeth does with her husband upon learning of the witches' prophesies, meets neither the duty of competence nor the duty of candor.[183] The assumption that a client's base desires are identical to his best interests is usually false, reflecting a dangerous union of self-deception on the part of the lawyer and client. When that assumption arrests or distorts inquiry into the client's conduct, the surrounding circumstances, and the client's internal divisions, the lawyer betrays both the law and the client in the name of loyalty to the client. That loyalty is hollow – certainly no "double trust." As psychologists understand, the subject who initially speaks may not even be the client to whom one owes

[182] Lacan, *Ecrits* at 63.

[183] Lawyers are quite properly sanctioned for engaging in misconduct of this kind. See, e.g., *Garlow v. State Bar*, 640 P.2d 1106 (1982) (attorney was suspended for counseling his client to give false testimony, as well as forging his clients' signatures on documents and submitting them to the court as valid); *In re* Conduct of Jones, 951 P.2d 149 (1997) (attorney suspended for perjury after he had his client sign blank documents which the attorney then filled in with false information); *Kentucky Bar Ass'n v. Lyon*, 181 S.W.3d 554 (2005) (an attorney was suspended for almost five years for forging changes and signatures on a will to give an inheritance to a disinherited family member); *In re* Lynch, 840 So.2d 508 (2003) (an attorney was disbarred after helping a client cover up a child pornography ring and attempting to suborn perjury and obstruct justice after investigations began).

a duty of fidelity. The network of divisions in and through which the client constitutes herself can only be discovered through genuine due diligence. There is no serving the client without this diligence and the trust that flows from communication grounded in what the diligence discloses.

Nor is either duty met by hastily abandoning the client upon his expression of base desires or the discovery of inconsistencies in his representation of events. Here Freedman is spot on: candor is not served because the client learns to be more deceptive from such encounters, not less, and competence is not served because the client is abandoned.[184] Evidence that poor and minority clients are more frequently abandoned draws the risk of incompetence into even sharper relief. It also highlights the ways that pluralism complicates judgments regarding deceptiveness. All subjects are divided, their speech and memory is divided, and the lawyer must ever be aware that she does not stand at an Archimedean point in relation to the client. The task is rather to help the client become more conscious of his internal divisions as the lawyer learns of them, to help the client understand the legal consequences of adopting alternative positions, and to settle on a felicitous network of representations. All the while the lawyer must be alert to her own divisions, and not just on the ordinary levels regulated by the law of conflicts of interest.

The art is determining what networks of representations are indeed felicitous – threading the warp and weft of law

[184] Freedman *Lawyer's Ethics* at 33–34.

and fact into an appropriately fine weave. That is as much an aesthetic and rhetorical as a legal or moral skill. Macbeth intends an insult to the witches when at the end of the play he complains that the apparitions they conjured "lie ... like truth."[185] But that phrase, irksome as it must be to philosophers and role critics, nicely captures the problem of deception in litigation. The purpose of the prohibition on perjury and the lawyer's duty of candor is not to eliminate lying, but to place deception in a productive relationship to the artifice of truth.

185 Act V, Scene V, *Riverside Shakespeare* at 1338.

3

Lies to Manipulate, Misappropriate, and Acquire Governmental Power

Helen Norton*

Often we focus on the ways in which lies harm individual victims: the target fleeced by the fraudulent lie, the spouse betrayed by the deceitful lie, the adversary disparaged by the defamatory lie. However, a variety of lies threaten harm to the public in general because they involve the government in some way. One category of such lies seeks to manipulate governmental decision-makers; another seeks to misappropriate the government's power through false claims that one is a government official; and a third involves lies to acquire public power by influencing

* Thanks to Rachel Arnow-Richman, Bill Eskridge, Mary Anne Franks, Stuart Green, Paul Horwitz, Beto Juarez, Nantiya Ruan, Austin Sarat, Catherine Smith, and Norm Spaulding for their thoughtful comments, and to Austin Sarat and the members and staff of the *Alabama Law Review* for their generosity in hosting the "Law and Lies" conference. Thanks too to Cassady Adams and Adam Kutniewski for very helpful research assistance.

voters' decisions. Although such lies can inflict harms both tangible and intangible upon their individual targets, they also pose substantial (if often less tangible) harm to the collective public precisely because of their governmental nexus. Drawing from Frederick Schauer's counsel that thoughtful First Amendment analysis requires that we consider the harms posed by contested expression not only to second parties (the listeners) but also to third parties (those other than the speakers and listeners),[1] we can understand lies to manipulate, misappropriate, or acquire governmental power as inflicting not only second-party harms upon their targets but also third-party harms upon the general public as well.

In response, a variety of laws regulate lies in at least three contexts that threaten harm because they involve the government in some way: the first category of laws punishes lies to a certain audience (the government), the second punishes lies about the source of speech (as governmental), and the third punishes lies to influence specific decisions (about who will become the government). In other words, a wide range of federal and state statutes prohibit an array of lies *to* the government; a large number of federal and state laws prohibit lies *about being* the government; and some state laws prohibit lies told in efforts *to become* the government – i.e., political candidates' lies to influence voters. These laws share some resemblance to laws punishing public corruption

[1] Frederick Schauer, "Harm(s) and the First Amendment," *Supreme Court Review* 2011 (2012): 81, 107.

in their efforts to protect the general public from wrongful efforts to influence or exercise public power for private advantage.[2]

Because laws prohibiting lies to, about being, and to become the government punish speech, they trigger important First Amendment questions. Consider, more specifically, the following deliberate falsehoods told in different settings by a speaker who has never been a law enforcement officer nor in the military:

1) "I am a decorated military veteran and a former police officer" (told to the government with the intent or capacity to affect its decision-making);
2) "I am a decorated military veteran and police officer" (told to anyone with the intent or capacity to change their course of conduct); and
3) "I am a decorated military veteran and former police officer" (told by a political candidate with the intent or capacity to influence listeners' voting decisions).

Laws punishing lies in the third category (i.e., campaign lies) currently generate considerably more First Amendment controversy than laws prohibiting lies in either of the first two.

[2] Teddy Roosevelt described the collective public harms of corruption in similar terms. See Zephyr Teachout, *Corruption in America* (Cambridge, MA: Harvard University Press, 2014), 185. ("Roosevelt's 1903 address to Congress condemned bribery and named corruption the central sin against democracy .... The 'bribe giver' is 'worse than the thief, for the thief robs the individual, while the corrupt official plunders an entire city or State.' ")

In this chapter, I seek to identify recurring themes and consistencies in, as well as to expose some tensions and challenge some assumptions about, the law's treatment of these lies. More specifically, I explore whether and when the First Amendment should be understood to permit the government to regulate lies to, about being, and to become the government.[3] I suggest that the differences among these categories of lies (and the laws regulating them) are matters more of degree than of kind, and that any differences in assessing their First Amendment treatment should be similarly nuanced. In short, although the harms of lies to, about being, and to become the government track those of other lies in some ways (e.g., in their assault on listeners' autonomy), such lies' governmental nexus at times threaten additional and distinct collective harm to the public that warrants legislatures' (and courts') attention. Indeed, lies to, about being, and to become the government can frustrate key First Amendment interests in enlightenment and democratic self-governance. Government efforts to regulate them, on the other hand, can threaten free speech harms of their own, especially when such laws are not narrowly

[3] Lies *by* the government represent another significant set of lies with a governmental nexus. Unlike lies (and other speech) by nongovernmental speakers, however, the government's own lies are not protected by the First Amendment and in fact may be constrained by the Constitution. I address the very different constitutional issues raised by the government's own lies elsewhere. See Helen Norton, "The Government's Lies and the Constitution," 91 Ind. L.J. (forthcoming 2015).

tailored to capture those lies that truly threaten the harms of wrongful manipulation, misappropriation, or acquisition of public power.

Although the Supreme Court has yet to identify a majority approach for assessing whether and when the First Amendment protects certain lies from government regulation, its various opinions require that we carefully attend to the harms of such lies. More specifically, the great variety of lies' potential effects – sometimes harmful, sometimes harmless, and occasionally even beneficial – led the Supreme Court in *United States v. Alvarez* to find a First Amendment right to lie in many, but by no means all, contexts.[4] In *Alvarez,* the Court considered the constitutionality of the Stolen Valor Act, a federal law that made it a crime for any person falsely to claim that he or she had received certain military honors. A divided Court struck the statute down on First Amendment grounds, with no majority agreement on a test for determining when the Constitution protects certain lies from governmental regulation.[5] Justice Kennedy's plurality opinion concluded, first, that only harm-causing lies have historically been treated as unprotected by the First Amendment and, second, that the Act impermissibly punished lies that did not actually cause harm and that were thus entitled to First Amendment protection. Justice Breyer's concurrence

[4] *United States v. Alvarez*, 132 S. Ct. 2537 (2012).

[5] For a more extensive discussion of *Alvarez*, see Helen Norton, "Lies and the Constitution," *Supreme Court Review* 2012 (2013): 161.

balanced the harms threatened by the targeted lies against the harms to free speech values posed by the Act's enforcement and found that the latter outweighed the former. Justice Alito's dissent concluded that lies have been historically unprotected apart from any harm they cause, but nevertheless also found that the Act permissibly punished harmful lies without threatening to chill any valuable (and thus protected) speech.

In short, each opinion wrestled in different ways with the potential harms of such lies, as well as with the potential harms posed by governmental efforts to regulate them. This chapter thus considers more precisely when, how, and to whom lies to, about being, and to become the government cause harm, as well as whether and when the government's efforts to regulate them inflict free speech harms of their own.

I. Manipulating Public Power: Lies to the Government

The harms of lies in particular[6] – and deception in general – center on the potential manipulation of the listener and the resulting injury to her autonomy. Lies to the government may manipulate not only the second-party governmental

[6] In this discussion, I use the term "lie" (or "deliberate falsehood") to mean a speaker's factual assertion made with the knowledge that it is false and with the intent that the listener understands it to be true. I thus put aside for now the many other ways in which speakers may deceive or mislead their audiences.

listener but also the third-party public (and its resources) as represented by that listener. Although, to be sure, lies to the government can harm their individual targets, government seeks to punish such lies in great part to protect the public from harm to its collective interests. A wide variety of laws thus punish lies to the government, sometimes to specific government decision-makers in particular settings, and sometimes to government audiences more generally.

Perjury laws exemplify laws prohibiting lies to specific government decision-makers in particular settings (e.g., judges and juries) by prohibiting "false statement[s] willfully made as to facts material to the hearing" under an oath authorized by law and taken before a competent tribunal, officer, or person.[7] Not only do such lies inflict very specific harms to individual parties when they lead to erroneous verdicts, but they also threaten more generalized harms to the public's ability to trust in the integrity of the justice system. As the *Alvarez* plurality explained,

> Perjury undermines the function and province of the law and threatens the integrity of judgments that are the basis of the legal system. Unlike speech in other contexts, testimony under oath has the formality and gravity necessary to remind the witness that his or her statements will be the basis for official governmental action, action that often affects the rights and liberties of others. Sworn testimony

[7] See *United States v. Debrow*, 346 U.S. 374, 376 (1953) (describing federal perjury law).

is quite distinct from lies not spoken under oath and simply intended to puff up oneself.[8]

By targeting lies that are material to high-stakes decisions in circumscribed settings, perjury laws punish lies that are potentially very harmful with little likelihood of chilling valuable speech.

A few examples of the many other setting-specific prohibitions on lies to the government include federal statutes that prohibit, inter alia, false statements in tax returns and related documents, false statements of material fact knowingly made to obtain unemployment compensation for federal service, knowing and willful false statements of material fact in applications for special agricultural worker status, and knowingly false material statements in compliance documents required of hazardous waste management and medical waste tracking programs.[9] These too target lies intended to influence government decisions in very particular settings.

Other statutes are substantially more comprehensive in scope, punishing lies (and sometimes misrepresentations and other deceptive communications more broadly) to the government in general. Consider, for instance, the Federal

[8] *Alvarez*, 132 S. Ct. at 2546 (plurality) (internal citations omitted).

[9] See 26 U.S.C.A. § 7206 (prohibiting a wide range of false statements in federal tax returns and related communications); *United States v. Wells*, 519 U.S. 482, 505–507 and notes 8–10 (1997) (Stevens, J. dissenting) (listing more than 100 federal statutes prohibiting false statements to the government in various settings).

False Statements Act, which imposes criminal penalties upon an individual who

> in any matter within the jurisdiction of the executive, legislative, or judicial branch of the Government of the United States ... knowingly and willfully (1) falsifies, conceals, or covers up by any trick, scheme, or device a material fact; (2) makes any materially false, fictitious, or fraudulent statement or representation; or (3) makes or uses any false writing or document knowing the same to contain any materially false, fictitious, or fraudulent statement or entry.[10]

The Act's precursor – enacted during the Civil War – criminalized certain lies to the federal government that furthered military contractors' monetary scams, and Congress amended the law during World War I to prohibit any lie made with the intent to defraud the federal government of money or property.[11] Congress significantly expanded the Act's scope yet again during the New Deal to prohibit any material lie made to the federal government; as Justice Ginsburg more recently explained, "The new regulatory agencies relied heavily on self-reporting to assure compliance; if regulated entities could file false reports with impunity, significant Government interests would

10 18 U.S.C. §1001.

11 See Steven R. Morrison, "When Is Lying Illegal? When Should It Be? A Critical Analysis of the Federal False Statements Act," *John Marshall Law Review* 43 (2009): 111, 125–126.

be subverted even though the Government would not be deprived of any property or money."[12]

The Act now prohibits lies to the federal government without regard to whether the liar intended to obtain a monetary benefit or whether the lie caused any financial harm to the government. To be sure, the scope of the Act (and similar statutes) includes lies that can cause quite tangible harms by skewing government decisions that have financial or other easily measurable consequences: examples include lies that may influence governmental decisions about disability benefits, immigration status, and Medicare reimbursements.[13] However, the Act is not limited to lies that cause tangible harm, and thus sweeps even more broadly in light of Congress's "intent to protect the authorized functions of governmental departments and agencies from the perversion which might result from the deceptive practices described."[14] Examples include lies that affect the government's decisions about whether and how to deploy its investigative efforts. As the Court has explained, any false statement to investigators may potentially "pervert" governmental functions given the possibility that investigators will be deceived;[15] such lies inflict collective public harm in that

[12] *Brogan v. United States*, 522 U.S. 398, 412 (1998) (Ginsburg, J., concurring).

[13] See *U.S. v. Kappes*, 936 F.2d 227 (6th Cir. 1991); *U.S. v. Phoeun Lang*, 672 F.3d 17 (1st Cir. 2012); *U.S. v. Kraude*, 467 F.2d 37 (9th Cir. 1972).

[14] *United States v. Gilliland*, 312 U.S. 86, 93 (1941).

[15] *Brogan*, 522 U.S. at 402.

the public suffers from the wasteful diversion or depletion of its government's enforcement resources. Consider, as an illustration, a defendant's false reports to the FBI that his wife had been kidnapped when she had instead left him – lies told in hopes that they would spur the agency to find her.[16] The statute's broad scope thus recognizes that lies to the government can manipulate public power to private advantage in damaging ways that sometimes have little, if anything, to do with financial harm.

The many lies prosecuted under the Act also include false denials in response to queries by federal officials about possible wrongdoing, also known as "exculpatory nos." Prominent but by no means infrequent examples include Marion Jones' lies to federal investigators about her use of performance-enhancing drugs[17] and Martha Stewart's lies about her stock trading activity.[18] A number of states and localities have enacted similarly broad laws prohibiting lies to their investigators and other law enforcement officials.[19]

The Supreme Court has interpreted the Federal False Statements Act broadly in other ways as well. For example, although the government must prove that the speaker knew that her assertion was false, the Court has ruled

[16] *U.S. v. Rodgers*, 466 U.S. 475 (1984).

[17] See Michael Schmidt and Lynn Zinser, "Jones Pleads Guilty to Lying About Drugs," *New York Times*, October 5, 2007.

[18] See *U.S. v. Stewart*, 433 F.3d 273 (2nd Cir. 2006).

[19] See, e.g., Texas Penal Code § 37.08 (criminalizing lies to state or local law enforcement officers).

that the Act does not require the government to prove that she knew that her lie concerned a matter involving the federal government. It identified the primary purpose of the statute's jurisdictional language as instead simply "to identify the factor that makes the false statement an appropriate subject for federal concern"; as it emphasized, "Noticeably lacking from this enactment is any requirement that the prohibited conduct be undertaken with specific intent to deceive the Federal Government, or with actual knowledge that false statements were made in a matter within federal agency jurisdiction."[20]

Some laws sweep even more broadly than the Federal False Statements Act in prohibiting lies to the government. For example, although the Act includes a textual requirement that the lie be "material" (that the Court has interpreted to mean being capable of influencing the decision-maker to whom the lie was addressed), not all federal statutes that punish lies to the government include, or have been interpreted to include, such a materiality requirement. As just one example, the Court declined to interpret 18 U.S.C. § 1014 (which criminalizes knowingly false statements made for the purpose of influencing the decision of a federally insured bank) to include an implied materiality element.[21] In other words, some

[20] *United States v. Yermian*, 468 U.S. 63, 68–73 (1984).

[21] *Wells*, 519 U.S. at 484 (majority opinion). Justice Stevens documented at least fifty federal statutes prohibiting lies to the government that did not include an express materiality requirement. See id. at 505 (Stevens, J., dissenting).

federal laws prohibit lies to governmental audiences that are intended to influence government decision-making even if they are not material to – i.e., not likely to affect – such decision-making. Examples include flattering lies intended to influence the decision-maker even if they are not (or should not be) material to his decision.[22]

Under this approach, the government need not show that the lie actually influenced the government decision-maker's behavior nor even that it was likely to – but instead simply that the lie was told with that intent. Perjury laws and the Federal False Statements Act, to name other laws prohibiting lies to the government, do not require that the government prove that the perjurer's lie actually influenced the fact-finder (although some of these laws require such lies to be material). Contrast legislatures' and courts' focus in commercial settings on the listener's actual and justifiable reliance on a lie as an element of fraud.[23] In other words, legislatures may choose to punish only lies on which the decision-maker has actually relied, thus requiring not just the risk but also the certainty of manipulation; or they may choose more broadly to punish lies that increase the risk of manipulation (regardless of reliance) because they are material to the listener's decision-making; or they may choose

[22] See id. at 502.

[23] See Restatement (Second) of Torts § 546 (1977) ("The maker of a fraudulent misrepresentation is subject to liability for pecuniary loss suffered by one who justifiably relies upon the truth of the matter misrepresented, if his reliance is a substantial factor in determining the course of conduct that results in his loss.").

more broadly still to punish lies intended to manipulate governmental decisions (regardless of materiality or reliance) because such intent creates the initial risk of manipulation. Legislatures' (and courts') reluctance to insist uniformly on a materiality (much less a reliance) requirement with respect to lies to the government suggests their view that such lies' moral culpability and their instrumental threat to the public interest rest in large part on the liar's efforts to *try* to manipulate the government's decisions for her own purposes – i.e., to bend its (and our) will to her own – regardless of whether the effort is, or is likely to be, successful in so doing.

In short, legislatures often quite broadly draft (and courts quite broadly interpret) statutes prohibiting lies to manipulate the government. None of the three *Alvarez* opinions cast doubt on the constitutionality of such laws, although they varied in their descriptions of such laws' scope as well as in the strength of their endorsement. More specifically, the dissent underscored such statutes' breadth as support for its sweeping contention (rejected by the plurality and concurrence) that false statements of fact have long been understood as entirely unprotected by the First Amendment, emphasizing its understanding that such laws do not require a showing of pecuniary harm or other specific harm of any type and that, unlike perjury laws, they are not limited to specific settings. Justice Breyer's concurrence emphasized such statutes' focus on collective harm to the public as evidence that they are appropriately tailored to survive constitutional scrutiny: "Statutes forbidding lying to a government official (not under oath) are typically limited to circumstances where a lie is likely to work particular and specific harm by interfering with the functioning of a government department, and those statutes also require a showing of materiality."[24] As discussed above, however, not all such statutes require specificity or materiality, so perhaps some of them apply more broadly than Justice Breyer would find constitutionally comfortable. The plurality simply observed that courts had generally found such laws to be permissible, and noted that their "prohibition on false statements made to Government officials, in communications concerning official matters, does not lead to the broader proposition that false statements are unprotected when made to any person, at any time, in any context."[25]

Not all lies to the government, however, may threaten to manipulate the government. A number of commentators and courts, for example, have vigorously questioned the breadth of these statutes on policy (rather than constitutional) grounds, urging that a narrower sweep more appropriately captures those lies to the government that truly threaten wrongfully to influence governmental power and that are thus sufficiently morally culpable and instrumentally dangerous to the public's collective interests to justify punishment. As Stuart Green has explained elsewhere,

[24] *Alvarez*, 132 S. Ct. at 2554 (Breyer, J., concurring).
[25] Id. at 2546 (plurality).

defensive or self-protective lies (like the "exculpatory no") strike many as morally excusable (even if not morally justifiable) because they are motivated by our natural human tendency toward self-preservation. Such lies thus offer another specific illustration of the thesis of Bill Eskridge's contribution to this volume, in which he explores a number of ways in which law itself can encourage, and in fact produce, deceit. What's more, as Lisa Kern Griffin has observed, in many cases the government questioner often already knows the answer to her question so is unlikely to be deceived by the speaker's lie; government's prosecution of a speaker's defensive lies in such contexts thus does not protect governmental law enforcement efforts from wasteful diversion and related instrumental harm but instead simply furthers law enforcement's efficiency interests, as it can be easier for prosecutors to prove a lie than the elements of a substantive crime.[26]

For related reasons, Justice Ginsburg expressed concern that, as written, the Federal False Statement Act would be employed unfairly to punish spontaneous and unconsidered lies:

> Because the questioning occurs in a noncustodial setting, the suspect is not informed of the right to remain silent. Unlike proceedings in which a false statement can be prosecuted as perjury, there may be no oath, no pause to concentrate the speaker's mind on the importance of his or her

[26] Lisa Kern Griffin, "Criminal Lying, Prosecutorial Power, and Social Meaning," *California Law Review* 97 (2009): 1515.

> answers. As in Brogan's case, the target may not be informed that a false "No" is a criminal offense until *after* he speaks.[27]

She further cautioned that that sweeping statutory prohibitions on lies to the government invite prosecutorial abuse by permitting law enforcement officials essentially to manufacture crimes where none otherwise could be proved – e.g., because the statute of limitations has run or because all of the elements of a crime could not otherwise be established. More specifically, she expressed concern that, as written, the Federal False Statements Act permits "an overzealous prosecutor or investigator – aware that a person has committed some suspicious acts, but unable to make a criminal case – [to] create a crime by surprising the suspect, asking about those acts, and receiving a false denial."[28] Such concerns can extend to other laws prohibiting lies to the government; other commentators have warned, for example, that some prosecutors may similarly abuse perjury laws by calling a target before a grand jury with the deliberate aim of securing perjured and thus prosecutable testimony when otherwise unable to prove the elements of a substantive crime.[29]

For these reasons, Justice Ginsburg is among those to urge Congress to adopt a more circumscribed focus for the

27 *Brogan*, 522 U.S. at 411 (Ginsburg, J., concurring).

28 Id. at 416.

29 Bennett L. Gershman, "The 'Perjury Trap,'" *University of Pennsylvania Law Review* 129 (1981): 624–625.

Federal False Statements Act by targeting "aggressive" lies (i.e., lies to the government made with the knowledge of their unlawfulness or where the liar initiated the interaction with the government or in other circumstances that do not suggest unfair surprise) and not "defensive" lies (i.e., those in response to queries initiated by the government). Years earlier, the Fifth Circuit suggested a similar distinction, characterizing the purpose of the Federal False Statements Act as "to protect the Government from the affirmative, aggressive, and voluntary actions of persons who take the initiative; and to protect the Government from being the victim of some positive statement which has the tendency and effect of perverting normal and proper governmental activities and functions."[30]

While Justice Ginsburg has taken the position that Congress has drafted the Act broadly but unwisely (thus identifying the legislature as the appropriate source of the Act's potential reform), in a number of concurring and dissenting opinions Justice Stevens urged instead that courts could, and should, address such concerns by interpreting such laws' existing text more narrowly. To this end, he argued that unnecessarily broad interpretations of laws punishing lies to the government not only threaten unfair and unwise criminalization of relatively minor lies but also run afoul of principled statutory analysis. For example, he urged courts to "distinguish the trivial from

[30] *Paternostro v. United States*, 311 F.2d 298, 303 (5th Cir. 1962).

the substantive" by interpreting such laws to require a materiality requirement even if the statutory text does not expressly include one.[31] More specifically, he characterized flattering but immaterial lies intended to curry favor with a government decision-maker as both common and relatively harmless, and thus undeserving of criminal penalty.[32] Along the same lines, Justice Rehnquist warned courts to be slow to interpret such laws to punish what he felt to be unconsidered and relatively trivial lies in dissenting from the majority's conclusion that the Federal False Statements Act did not require the government to prove that the speaker knew that her lie related to matters with which the federal government was involved:

> It seems to me highly unlikely that, without so much as a hint of explanation, Congress would have changed the statute from one intended to deter the perpetration of deliberate deceit on the Federal Government, to one intended to criminalize the making of even the most casual false statements so long as they turned out, unbeknownst to their maker, to be material to some federal agency function.[33]

These disagreements illustrate the trade-offs inherent when seeking to craft legal distinctions that are both

[31] *Kungys v. United States*, 485 U.S. 759, 786–787 (1988) (Stevens, J., concurring in the judgment).

[32] *Wells*, 519 U.S. at 512–513 (Stevens, J., dissenting).

[33] *Yermian*, 468 U.S. at 82.

conceptually coherent and normatively attractive.[34] A legislature's choice to prohibit all lies to the government – or none – is conceptually intelligible, as we can readily ascertain what is and is not prohibited. As we have seen, however, a number of courts and commentators find such an approach normatively unappealing because it punishes self-protective or casual lies that do not significantly threaten to influence governmental power in morally culpable or instrumentally dangerous ways (and that in fact may sometimes reflect natural, rather than aberrant and wrongful, human behavior). In other words, the challenge here is to target lies to the government that wrongfully seek to manipulate public power – and some self-protective or unconsidered lies to the government may not fall within this category.

As a final area of disagreement, lower courts are currently split on the constitutionality of certain laws prohibiting lies to the government that distinguish on the basis of viewpoint. Consider the large number of laws that punish lies about the presence or absence of police misconduct to government decision-makers in the specific context of police misconduct proceedings. Such lies can inflict relatively specific harms in terms of inaccurate outcomes and wasted investigative and administrative resources. Some of these laws, however,

[34] See Pierre Schlag, "The Legal Argument Toolkit" at *13–18 (unpublished manuscript on file with the author) (identifying conceptual intelligibility and normative appeal as among the criteria for "sound" legal distinctions). As Schlag points out, these criteria stand in some tension with each other, which makes ideal legal distinctions elusive. Id. at *19–20.

prohibit only knowingly false reports of police misconduct – and not knowingly false statements in support of the police – in such proceedings. Such viewpoint-based distinctions invite First Amendment challenges under *R.A.V. v. City of St. Paul*,[35] in which the Court held that government generally may not make viewpoint-based distinctions when regulating otherwise proscribable speech. In other words, even though lies in police misconduct proceedings may be generally regulable because they threaten significant individual and collective harm, *R.A.V.* counsels that the First Amendment does not permit governments to make viewpoint-based distinctions in choosing which of those lies to regulate.

At least one state Supreme Court, however, has rejected such a challenge and held that such viewpoint-specific laws do not violate the First Amendment because they simply regulate defamation in a particular setting. More specifically, the Minnesota Supreme Court concluded that only lies that incriminate police officers in these settings (and not lies that might exonerate them) are potentially defamatory: "Speech that is supportive of peace officer conduct fails to satisfy the elements of defamation because it does not tend to harm the plaintiff's reputation and to lower the plaintiff in the estimation of the community."[36]

[35] 505 U.S. 377, 386–387 (1992).

[36] *Minnesota v. Crawley*, 819 N.W.2d 94, 109 (Minn. 2012); see also id. at 113 ("[T]he secondary effects of knowingly false accusations of peace officer misconduct – the expenditure of public resources to conduct investigations and the diversion of those resources away from other matters – justify the regulation. . . .").

Surely, however, some exonerating lies can be defamatory: consider, for example, lies that the complaining witness, rather than the police officer, engaged in violent or illegal behavior. Moreover, exonerating lies in this context threaten substantial harm to public integrity and trust. As the Ninth Circuit explained when striking down such a viewpoint-specific statute on First Amendment grounds, "[A] knowingly false assertion made by a peace officer or witness in support of a peace officer during the course of a misconduct investigation, like a knowingly false complaint of misconduct, is equally 'at odds with the premises of democratic government.'"[37] Such lies thus threaten collective third-party harms by undermining the public's trust in, and willingness to cooperate with, law enforcement more generally if individuals cannot be confident in the process for disciplining police officers alleged to have engaged in misconduct.

Perhaps a viewpoint-specific approach can be better justified as reflecting the common moral intuition that an exonerating lie (like the "exculpatory no") is less morally culpable than an incriminating lie. However, both kinds of lies in this setting threaten substantial third-party harm to the public: law enforcement's effectiveness is severely compromised when the public cannot trust the outcome of police

[37] *Chaker v. Crogan*, 428 F.3d 1215, 1226 (9th Cir. 2004) (quoting *Garrison v. Louisiana*, 379 U.S. 64, 75 (1964)); id. at 1226 ("[A] peace officer or witness who lies during an investigation is equally to blame for wasting public resources by interfering with the expeditious resolution of an investigation.").

misconduct proceedings. In short, laws prohibiting such lies to the government effectively address collective public harms while remaining attentive to First Amendment concerns when they are viewpoint-neutral – i.e., when they prohibit both lies that exonerate as well as those that incriminate government officers (and others) charged with misconduct.

II. Misappropriating Public Power: Lies About Being the Government

Consider next the wide range of laws that prohibit lies about being the government – i.e., laws that punish an individual's false claims to be a government official or that she speaks on behalf of the government. For example, a number of state and local laws specifically punish lies that one is a law enforcement officer.[38] Moreover, 18 U.S.C. § 709 prohibits a speaker's unauthorized use of federal agencies' names in a manner reasonably calculated to convey the impression that the speaker's message was approved or endorsed by the agency, and 18 U.S.C. § 912 punishes various lies and misrepresentations that one is "an officer or employee acting under the authority of the United States."

Lies about being the government are a type of lie about the quality of the source of speech – i.e., whether the speaker

[38] E.g., Kan. Stat. § 21–5917 (criminalizing falsely "represent[ing] oneself" as an officer); Virginia Code § 18.2–174 (criminalizing "falsely assum[ing] or pretend[ing] to be" a law enforcement officer).

is sufficiently trustworthy or powerful to influence the listener to do what the speaker asks (or demands). Such lies threaten significant harm to individual (second-party) listeners who may make very different decisions in response to speech that they attribute to a government official. Indeed, many such lies are told to secure very tangible advantages, such as those told by persons claiming to be Social Security employees and demanding return of alleged "overpayments," those told by persons claiming to be Immigration and Naturalization Service employees offering to expedite immigration applications in exchange for money, or those told by persons claiming to be law enforcement officers told to avoid traffic tickets or other enforcement action.[39]

Moreover, such lies told by those who purport to wield coercive government power may be especially worthy of punishment because they threaten the autonomy of their targets not only through deception (i.e., bending another's will to one's own by manipulating information) but also through coercion (i.e., bending another's will to one's own by exerting force or power). Such intuitions are similarly reflected in tort law, where courts treat lies that seek to misappropriate power as satisfying the outrageousness element of an intentional infliction of emotional distress claim. The Second Restatement of Torts, for example, identifies

[39] See *Wilkes v. U.S.*, 469 U.S. 964 (1984); *U.S. v. Romero*, 293 F.3d 1120 (9th Cir. 2002); *U.S. v. Gilbert*, 143 F.3d 397 (8th Cir. 1998); *U.S. v. Rippee*, 961 F.2d 677 (7th Cir. 1992); *U.S. v. Bryant*, 117 F.3d 1464 (D.C. Cir 1997).

specific examples of outrageous, and thus tortious, conduct to include lies that one is a police officer told to coerce the target's behavior.[40] There courts consider, among other factors, whether the actor abused a position of authority and whether the target was known to the actor to be especially vulnerable – i.e., they identify certain lies as especially worthy of punishment when the manipulative harms of deception are accompanied, and exacerbated, by the harms of coercion and breach of trust.

Lies about being the government also threaten more collective third-party harms to the public by creating doubt in the public's mind about who speaks for the government and thus whether purported government officials can be trusted. As the Supreme Court observed a century ago, lies about being the government endanger the government's reputation and thus its legitimacy and effectiveness:

> In order that the vast and complicated operations of the government of the United States shall be carried on successfully and with a minimum of friction and obstruction, it is important – or, at least, Congress reasonably might so consider it – not only that the authority of the governmental officers and employees be respected in particular cases, but that a spirit of respect and good will for the government and its officers shall generally prevail. And what could more directly impair this spirit than to permit unauthorized and unscrupulous persons to go about the country falsely assuming, for fraudulent purposes, to be entitled to the

[40] See Restatement (Second) of Tort, § 46, cmt. d-f (1965).

> respect and credit due to an officer of the government? ... It is the aim of the [statute prohibiting lies about being the government] not merely to protect innocent persons from actual loss through reliance upon false assumptions of Federal authority, but to maintain the general good repute and dignity of the service itself.[41]

Lies about being a law enforcement officer illustrate these points. Such lies are often told in an effort to manipulate the listener's behavior – i.e., to extort money or to avoid a speeding ticket. Such lies can also threaten substantial collective harms to the public's trust in law enforcement. If the public cannot be confident that police officers are who they claim to be, they will be less likely to cooperate with the police, and the police, in turn will be less effective – and the public will suffer harm as a result. Just as lies to the government can inflict collective public harm when they wrongfully manipulate the deployment of public resources to personal advantage, so too can we understand lies about being the government as inflicting collective harm when they wrongfully misappropriate public power to private benefit. In other words, we might understand lies about being the government as inflicting collective public harm by "stealing" the government's power and trustworthiness. Indeed, for these reasons, the Fourth Circuit has described such lies about being a law enforcement officer as a form of "identity theft."[42]

41 *United States v. Barnow*, 239 U.S. 74, 78, 80 (1915).
42 *United States v. Chappell*, 691 F.3d 388, 395 (4th Cir. 2012).

Recognizing the gravity of such harms to both the second-party listener and third-party government and public, legislatures often quite broadly draft (and courts quite broadly interpret) statutes punishing lies about being the government. These laws thus prohibit a wide range of deliberate falsehoods that seek to shape the public's interaction with purported government officials, regardless of the lies' connection to tangible benefit or detriment. Recall, for example, 18 U.S.C. § 912, which punishes an individual who either "falsely assumes or pretends to be an officer or employee acting under the authority of the United States or any department, agency, or officer thereof, and acts as such" or who "in such pretended character demands or obtains any money, chapter, document, or thing of value." The Court has broadly interpreted the statute's first clause to punish lies about being the government that seek "to cause the deceived person to follow some course he would not have pursued but for the deceitful conduct"[43] without any connection to the receipt of something of value. As it explained,

> While more than mere deceitful attempt to affect the course of action of another is required under the second clause of the statute, which speaks of an intent to obtain a "valuable thing," the very absence of these words of limitation in the first portion of the act persuade us that under it, a person may be defrauded although he parts with something of no measurable value at all.[44]

[43] *United States v. Lepowitch*, 318 U.S. 702, 704 (1943).
[44] Id. at 704–705.

As an example, the Court has held that a lie about one's law enforcement status told to convince a listener to share information (that she was otherwise unwilling to divulge) about another person's whereabouts constituted a prohibited lie about being the government because it sought to cause the target to change her course of conduct even if she was not deprived of anything of value.[45]

In short, lies about being the government told to influence listeners' decision-making (broadly understood) justify punishment because they reflect the liar's efforts to misappropriate public power to private advantage, just as public corruption laws relatedly punish extortion by public officials who wrongfully seek to exercise public power for personal gain. Moreover, because laws about being the government almost always target aggressive rather than defensive lies, they seem unlikely to trap unwary speakers unfairly and are less likely to trigger concerns about prosecutorial abuse. In other words, falsely claiming that one is a police officer or some other government representative requires more forethought than a spontaneous "no" when surprised by a question about one's misconduct: the former is hard to characterize as defensive and thus strikes many as more morally blameworthy. Such laws thus remain largely uncontroversial as a First Amendment matter in great part because they address real (if often intangible) harm to the

[45] Id. at 705 (interpreting the statute to prohibit the defendant's lie about being an FBI agent that led his listener to divulge information about another person's location).

public as well as to the individual target. Indeed, none of the *Alvarez* opinions cast doubt on the constitutionality of laws prohibiting lies about being the government, and the *Alvarez* plurality emphasized such lies' collective third-party harms, observing that "statutes that prohibit falsely representing that one is speaking on behalf of the Government, or that prohibit impersonating a Government officer, also protect the integrity of Government processes, quite apart from merely restricting false speech."[46]

Again, contrast legislatures' (and courts') relatively capacious understanding of harm in these contexts with their focus in commercial settings and other areas only on lies that pose economic (and thus more easily measurable) harm. A choice to punish lies only when they threaten economic harm provides conceptual coherence yet normative discomfort because it ignores the many other ways in which lies can cause significant – if intangible – harm. This is especially the case of lies that seek to influence or misappropriate public power in important, yet nonfinancial, ways. For this reason, legislatures' (and courts') focus on lies to and about being the government intended to manipulate their targets' behavioral choices (defined broadly) may add to the challenges of conceptual coherence, at least at the margins (which, of course, is where conceptual coherence generally breaks down). At the same time, however, a broader focus offers considerable normative appeal because it captures the wider range of significant – even when nonfinancial – harms

[46] *Alvarez*, 132 S. Ct. at 2546 (plurality opinion).

threatened by the manipulation and misappropriation of public power.

Not all lies about being the government, however, may threaten to misappropriate public power. Lies about being the government that constitute mere bragging or puffery, for example, may be relatively harmless and thus undeserving of punishment. Along these lines, some federal judges have invoked *Alvarez* to cast doubt on statutes that punish lies about being the government that fail to require a connection of some sort to the target's course of conduct, questioning whether lies about one's police officer status should be treated any differently for First Amendment purposes from lies about one's status as a Congressional Medal of Honor winner. More specifically, the Fourth Circuit's Judge Wynn objected in dissent to a Virginia law punishing false claims that one is a law enforcement officer that "does not require any act, does not require that the individual obtain anything of value, and does not include any showing of actual deception or harm," and that in his opinion thus prohibits "children playing cops and robbers on the front lawn; trainees at a police academy role-playing; and actors in plays in which peace officers are characters" from "falsely pretending" to be a law enforcement officer.[47]

To be sure, Judge Wynn's specific examples did not apply to the defendant in that particular case, who lied about being a law enforcement officer in an effort to avoid a speeding ticket. Nor are his examples "lies" as I have defined them for

[47] *Chappell*, 691 F.3d at 408 (Wynn, J., dissenting).

purposes of this discussion, as they are not uttered with the intent that the listener understand them to be true. Indeed, courts generally take pains to interpret laws prohibiting false statements to require the speaker's intent to deceive her listeners, an intent lacking in actors or others playing governmental roles for educational or entertainment purposes.[48]

However, we can anticipate that lies about being the government may indeed sometimes occur in situations where they have little, if any, connection to any listener decision-making, and where we might thus be reluctant to view them as threatening to misappropriate governmental power. Consider, for example, such lies when told in purely social and private conversation, such as those invoked by Justice Breyer's mention of "barstool braggadocio" in *Alvarez*.[49] In other words, sometimes speakers falsely brag about their credentials or otherwise engage in puffery without any intent to manipulate their listeners' decisions and thus to abuse power, nor with any likelihood of doing so. Such lies may strike many of us as neither terribly morally blameworthy nor instrumentally dangerous.

Legislatures and courts can screen such lies from punishment by requiring that the regulated lie about being the government be accompanied by the intent or capacity to manipulate targets' behavioral choices in some way. To this

[48] See, e.g., *United States v. Perelman*, 695 F.3d 866 (9th Cir. 2012), cert. denied, 133 S. Ct. 2383 (2013).

[49] *Alvarez*, 132 S. Ct. at 2555 (Breyer, J., concurring).

end, recall the Stolen Valor Act at issue in *Alvarez*, which also regulated a type of lie about the speaker's credentials and thus his stature and credibility. More specifically, the Act punished false claims that the speaker had received military awards signaling the government's endorsement of his honor and courage. However, the Act criminalized false claims that one had received certain military honors, without more: it did not require proof of the liar's intent to manipulate listeners' choices in some way, much less proof that the lie actually influenced listeners' decisions or was predictably capable of doing so.[50] Although the Stolen Valor Act's very title indicates Congress' conclusion that these sorts of lies constitute a type of identity theft that warrants punishment, the Court's response in *Alvarez* required some connection between the speaker's lie and the listener's decision-making to consider the lie sufficiently harmful to justify regulation consistent with the First Amendment.

More specifically, Justice Breyer's concurring opinion suggested that "a more finely tailored statute might, as other kinds of statutes prohibiting false factual statements have done, insist upon a showing that the false statement

[50] Lies about being the government also may inflict different third-party harms than those threatened by lies about being honored by the government. The former can inflict harms of coercion and breach of trust in addition to those of deception. For example, depending on the context, a request or demand by a (purported) Medal of Honor winner does not necessarily carry the same coercive potential as that by a (purported) FBI agent or immigration officer.

caused specific harm or at least was material, or focus its coverage on lies most likely to be harmful or on contexts where such lies are most likely to cause harm."[51] Although Justice Breyer did not explain more specifically what he meant by "harm" in these contexts, we might understand "specific harm" to mean the listener's actual reliance on the lie for decision-making purposes (where the harm of manipulation has actually occurred); we might understand "material" harm to refer to those lies that carry an increased risk of manipulating listeners' behavioral choices; and we might understand "lies most likely to be harmful or [i]n contexts where such lies are most likely to cause harm" as lies that have the intent to manipulate, and thus create the initial risk of manipulating, listeners' decisions.

In response to the Court's decision in *Alvarez*, Congress amended the Stolen Valor Act to punish only those false claims about receiving certain military honors made "with intent to obtain money, property, or other tangible benefit."[52] By requiring a connection to relatively measurable harm, this response likely cures any constitutional violation. At the same time, however, it may be narrower than constitutionally required (a policy choice that Congress, of course, is entirely free to make). In other words, the *Alvarez* opinions' comfort with laws broadly punishing lies about being the government suggests that the Justices might be similarly willing to uphold statutes

[51] *Alvarez*, 132 S. Ct. at 2555–2556.
[52] Stolen Valor Act of 2013, 18 U.S.C. §704(b) (2014).

punishing related lies about the speaker's credentials (e.g., military honors conferred by the government) that threaten wrongfully to manipulate their targets – as signaled by their intent to change the listeners' course of conduct or to deprive the target of something of value (broadly defined) – even when they are not directed to decisions with particularly tangible consequences.

III. Acquiring Public Power: Lies to Become the Government

Some state laws prohibit political candidates' deliberate falsehoods told to influence voters' choices in contested electoral campaigns – i.e., they punish lies to become the government.[53] Manipulative lies of this sort endanger not only individual voters' autonomy but also threaten collective harms to the public. Such harms include skewing election outcomes, deterring quality candidates, and lowering the quality of campaign discourse – which, in turn, contributes to voter cynicism, distrust, and disengagement.[54] At the same time, however, governmental efforts to regulate such

[53] E.g., Fla. Stat. § 104. 271; Mass. Gen. Law. Ch. 56 § 42; Minn. Stat. § 211B.06; Oh. Rev. Code § 3517.21; W. Va. Code § 3-8-11(c); Wis. Stat. § 12.05.

[54] See, e.g., Gerald G. Ashdown, "Distorting Democracy: Campaign Lies in the 21st Century," *William & Mary Bill of Rights Journal* 20 (2012): 1085; William P. Marshall, "False Campaign Speech and the First Amendment," *University of Pennsylvania Law Review* 153 (2004): 285.

lies threaten to chill core political speech and raise the specter of selective enforcement and partisan abuse. These competing concerns invite the question whether the harms caused by efforts to regulate such lies are greater than the harms of the lies themselves; for these reasons, laws punishing lies to be the government have triggered substantially more First Amendment controversy than the laws discussed in Parts I and II.[55]

The differences among these laws for constitutional purposes may be smaller than often assumed. Indeed, as the Supreme Court has previously recognized, intentionally false political speech can harm key First Amendment interests in democratic self-governance and enlightenment:

> Although honest utterance, even if inaccurate, may further the fruitful exercise of the right of free speech, it does not follow that the lie, knowingly and deliberately published about a public official, should enjoy a like immunity.... That speech is used as a tool for political ends does not automatically bring it under the protective mantle of the

[55] See, e.g., *281 Care Committee v. Arneson*, 766 F.3d 774 (8th Cir. 2014) (striking down Minnesota law that prohibited paid political advertisements or campaign materials that make recklessly or intentionally false statements about ballot questions and are intended to promote or defeat the ballot question); *Susan B. Anthony List v. Ohio Elections Comm'n*, 2014 WL 4472634 (S.D. Ohio 2014) (striking down Ohio law that prohibited knowingly or intentionally false statements concerning candidates that are intended to influence the election of such candidates as well as false statements "concerning the voting record of a candidate or public official").

> Constitution. For the use of the known lie as a tool is at once at odds with the premises of democratic government and with the orderly manner in which economic, social, or political change is to be effectuated.[56]

The question is thus not whether the Constitution ever permits the regulation of campaign lies, but instead when, how, and why, as the Court already understands the First Amendment to permit the government to punish some campaign lies.

For example, the Court has interpreted the free speech clause to permit the punishment of campaign lies about individual candidates that satisfy the elements of defamation, so long as the defamatory falsehood is accompanied by the speaker's malice (i.e., when she makes a statement that she knows to be false, or where she is recklessly indifferent as to its truth or falsity).[57] Defamation law thus permits the punishment of reputation-damaging campaign lies consistent with the First Amendment so long as accompanied by *mens rea* safeguards to prevent the chilling of truthful speech.[58]

[56] *Garrison v. Louisiana*, 379 U.S. 64, 75 (1964); see also *McIntyre v. Ohio Elections Comm'n*, 514 U.S. 334, 349 (1995) (characterizing the state's interest in preventing election fraud as carrying "special weight during election campaigns when false statements, if credited, may have serious adverse consequences for the public at large").

[57] *New York Times, Inc. v. Sullivan*, 376 U.S. 254, 264 (1964); see also *Harte-Hanks Communications, Inc. v. Connaughton*, 491 U.S. 657 (1989) (upholding defamation claim by candidate for elected judicial office).

[58] In addition to establishing the speaker's malice, a plaintiff in such a defamation action must generally prove "a false and defamatory

The Court has also interpreted the First Amendment to permit the punishment of some campaign lies about the source of political speech. More specifically, campaign disclosure and disclaimer laws require the truthful identification of the source of certain political contributions and communications because such information is often of great interest and value to listeners. As the Court explained in *Citizens United v. Federal Election Commission,* "The First Amendment protects political speech, and disclosure permits citizens and shareholders to react to the speech of corporate entities in a proper way. This transparency enables the electorate to make informed decisions and give proper weight to different speakers and messages."[59] Indeed, a significant body of evidence suggests that knowing the identity of a candidate's supporters (or opposition) helps comparatively uninformed voters to vote as "competently" – i.e., to vote in a way consistent with their own policy preferences – as comparatively well-informed voters.[60] As a constitutional matter, the Court has generally upheld campaign disclosure and disclaimer laws, concluding that the informational benefits of requiring such truthful speech to

statement concerning another," "an unprivileged publication to a third party," and "either actionability of the statement irrespective of special harm or the existence of special harm caused by the publication." Restatement (Second) of Torts § 558 (1977).

59 *Citizens United v. Federal Election Commission*, 558 U.S. 310, 371 (2010).

60 See, e.g., Michael S. Kang, "Democratizing Direct Democracy: Restoring Voter Competence Through Heuristic Cues and 'Disclosure Plus,'" *UCLA Law Review* 50 (2003): 1141, 1161.

listeners outweigh the expressive costs to speakers who seek to conceal themselves as the source of such expression.[61]

In short, the Court already interprets the First Amendment to permit government to punish not only campaign lies that harm their targets by damaging their reputation, but also campaign lies about the source of certain political contributions or communications that harm listeners by frustrating their ability to evaluate that speech. As discussed in Part II, the Court also interprets the First Amendment to permit government to punish a type of lie about the source of speech – i.e., lies about being the government – that harm both second-party listeners and the third-party public when they misappropriate public power to private advantage. Taken together, these developments suggest the possibility that the First Amendment can be understood to permit the government to regulate other campaign lies about the source of speech that harm both individual listeners and the public – e.g., lies about whether the speaker is sufficiently trustworthy or competent such that the listener should do what the speaker asks by voting to confer her with public power.

For purposes of this discussion, I will focus on a candidate's reputation-enhancing lies about objectively verifiable matters relevant to her competence, stature, and credibility. Examples include lies that she received a certain degree or honor, that she held certain jobs or served in

[61] See, e.g., *Doe v. Reed*, 561 U.S. 186, 197 (2010); *Buckley v. Valeo*, 424 U.S. 1, 67 (1976).

the military, or even that she is the incumbent (indeed, candidates' false representations that they are the incumbent are not uncommon since voters often consider incumbency a relevant factor when making voting decisions[62]). To be sure, candidates' reputation-enhancing lies represent only a small fraction of the universe of potential campaign lies. I focus on them largely because they parallel the often-regulated lies discussed in Parts I and II, which suggests the possibility that the lessons learned from governmental efforts to regulate lies that seek to manipulate and misappropriate governmental power may shed light on whether and when the First Amendment should be understood to permit the regulation of certain lies that seek to acquire public power.

Campaign lies seek to manipulate listeners' decisions about matters that are at least as important as decisions about how to spend time and money, whether to give a speeding ticket, or whether to share information that one would otherwise prefer not to divulge – decisions, as we have seen, that the law protects from lies in other contexts with little First Amendment controversy. A focus on lies intended to manipulate voting decisions is thus no less conceptually

[62] See, e.g., *Ohio Democratic Party v. OEC*, 2008 WL 3878364 (Ohio Ct. App. 2008) (concluding that campaign advertisements misrepresented candidates as already holding the office that they sought); *Treasurer of the Committee to Elect Gerald D. Lostracco v. Fox*, 150 Mich. App. 617 (1986) (rejecting First Amendment challenge to injunction against defendant's misrepresentations that he was the incumbent).

coherent than a focus on lies intended to manipulate many other sorts of decisions.

Whether one finds such a focus normatively appealing, however, depends on one's cost-benefit analysis – i.e., the assessment of the harms of campaign lies compared to the First Amendment harms of regulating them. And to be sure, as discussed below, the free speech harms of laws punishing lies to become the government may be different from the others in a number of ways that may suggest greater First Amendment difficulties. Such concerns are substantial but not, however, necessarily irrefutable.

First, we may be reluctant to find that a candidate's reputation-enhancing lies about herself are harmful (and thus worthy of punishment) because the multitude of reasons that inform voters' choices complicates our ability to establish a causal connection between any particular lie and listeners' voting decisions. In other words, we might feel that decisions about for whom to vote are no less important than decisions about whether and how to spend one's money, but that we should nevertheless be slower to conclude that lies about the former are harmful and thus worthy of punishment because the causal influences on those sorts of decisions can be so complex.

But of course many important decisions – including those about very tangible things, such as whether to buy a certain house or car or take a certain job or go to a certain school – have complex causal chains, with multiple factors in play. We often consider lies intended to manipulate those decisions (e.g., a university's lies about its graduates' employment rates, a job applicant's lies about her experience, or a car dealer's lies about a vehicle's accident history) to threaten punishable harm even if other factors also influenced their targets' choices. For example, a number of states specifically prohibit certain lies about the speaker's credentials told to secure employment, educational, or business opportunities – i.e., résumé fraud – and these decisions' causal complexity does not insulate such lies from punishment.[63] Relatedly, recall that legislatures and courts often decline to insist on materiality in the context of lies to and about being the government, again focusing on the speaker's manipulative intent – and not just her manipulative success – as harmful and thus worthy of punishment in and of itself. In other words, decisions' causal complexity in other contexts does not necessarily undermine our assessment that lies intended to manipulate those decisions are morally blameworthy and instrumentally costly, especially when the liar seeks wrongfully to influence or exercise public power.

Similarly, we may be reluctant to find that lies to become the government are harmful (and thus worthy of

[63] See, e.g., Iowa Code Ann. § 715A.6A (prohibiting knowingly false claims of certain academic degrees to secure employment or certain other benefits); Tenn. Code. Ann. § 39-17-112 (same); see also *Baker v. Dorfman*, 239 F.3d 415, 424–425 (2nd Cir. 2000) (upholding client's fraud verdict against attorney for attorney's resume lies about his length of practice, employment history, and academic credentials).

punishment) because they occur in campaign contexts where the audience may be especially skeptical and thus less easily fooled and manipulated. As a threshold matter, however, this premise is contested, as a growing body of social science evidence indicates that many voters are not terribly skeptical of campaign speech and instead often rely uncritically on the assertions of favored sources.[64]

In any event, audience skepticism in other contexts does not necessarily undermine our assessment that lies intended to manipulate that audience remain morally blameworthy or instrumentally damaging. As we have already seen, the law frequently punishes lies to law enforcement (and other government officials) even though such audiences are professionally trained to be skeptical: again, in those contexts the law treats a liar's efforts to manipulate her targets' decisions – and not just her manipulative success – as harmful and thus worthy of punishment. Moreover, even if many voters have low expectations of political candidates' truthfulness, perhaps the law can and should shape norms in this area by enforcing higher expectations of those who seek to become the government. This may be especially important in light of emerging social science evidence that tolerance for lies begets more lies: in other words, so long as we expect lies,

[64] See, e.g., Daniel R. Ortiz, "The Engaged and the Inert: Theorizing Political Personality under the First Amendment," *Virginia Law Review* 81 (1995): 1, 14.

we can expect to get more of them.[65] Treating campaign lies as inevitable fuels our cynicism and inability to talk with each other to productive political ends. Law is one – but by no means the only – way to shape behavioral expectations about the appropriate use of, and means of acquiring, public power.[66]

Next, we might think that counterspeech, rather than regulation, offers the more appropriate remedy for campaign lies. As a number of commentators have observed, however, the effectiveness of counterspeech is often more assumed than proven.[67] For this reason, for example, counterspeech is not considered a sufficient remedy for perjury, even though opportunities for rebuttal abound there. As Geof Stone observed, "[W]e recognize that it takes time and energy to respond to false statements and that disputes over such evidence can distract and confuse jurors, even if they eventually discern the falsehood. And, of course, there

65 See Dan Ariely, *The (Honest) Truth About Dishonesty* (New York: HarperCollins, 2012), 137, 207 (concluding that observing acts of dishonesty often encourages additional acts of dishonesty).

66 See, e.g., Cass Sunstein, *Simpler: The Future of Government* (New York: Simon & Schuster, 2013), 68 (explaining that "[b]oth enacted laws and regulations can provide important signals; they have expressive functions" that signal social norms and public expectations).

67 See, e.g., Frederick Schauer, "Facts and the First Amendment," *UCLA Law Review* 57 (2010): 897, 910–911 ("Indeed, the persistence of the belief that a good remedy for false speech is more speech, or that truth will prevail in the long run, may itself be an example of the resistance of false factual propositions to argument and counterexample.").

is always the possibility that they will not discern the falsehood and that they therefore will reach an erroneous conclusion on the basis of knowingly false testimony."[68] Indeed, counterspeech may itself be counterproductive, as a body of social science evidence suggests that efforts to refute a lie can instead actively reinforce it in listener memory.[69]

Barriers to effective counterspeech in the campaign context more specifically include time and money. First, the targets of lies told in the waning hours or days before an election may not have the opportunity to respond effectively. Second, counterspeech may not be a realistic option for less wealthy candidates or causes, who may not have the resources to match lies with rebuttals of equal volume or frequency, or in the same (expensive) setting (e.g., print rebuttals to lies initially disseminated via television advertisements may not reach those who encountered the original lie). As Daniel Kahneman has observed, "a reliable way to make people believe in falsehoods is frequent repetition, because familiarity is not easily distinguished from truth."[70] These concerns are exacerbated in a post-*Citizens United* world in which the amount and source of campaign speech are largely unregulated.

[68] Geoffrey R. Stone, "A Free and Responsible Press," *University of Chicago Legal Forum* 1993 (1993): 127, 139–140.

[69] Ian Skurnik, Carolyn Yoon, Denise C. Park, and Norbert Schwarz, "How Warnings About False Claims Become Recommendations," *Journal of Consumer Research* 31 (2005): 713.

[70] Daniel Kahneman, *Thinking, Fast and Slow* (New York: Farrar, Strauss, and Giroux, 2011), 62.

An unfettered right to lie – and lie repeatedly – combined with an unfettered right to spend on political speech works to the great disadvantage of comparatively underfinanced speakers seeking to rebut such lies. Opportunities for refuting lies in the campaign context thus may be limited and do not necessarily provide an effective remedy for the harms of such lies.

Finally, even if we believe that a candidate's reputation-enhancing lies about her credentials threaten significant harm, we may still remain concerned that efforts to regulate them threaten even greater harms of their own by chilling valuable political speech or inviting selective governmental enforcement. As Mary Anne Franks' contributions to this volume suggests, however, any concerns about partisan enforcement should extend beyond campaign lies to laws prohibiting lies to the government – such as perjury laws – that similarly invite selective prosecution by those in power.

In any event, narrowly tailored – i.e., nuanced – regulatory responses may help ameliorate these concerns. More specifically, Justice Breyer's concurrence in *Alvarez* signaled the possibility that certain narrowly tailored approaches to campaign lies might survive First Amendment scrutiny:

> I recognize that in some contexts, particularly political contexts, such a narrowing will not always be easy to achieve. In the political arena a false statement is more likely to make a behavioral difference (say, by leading the listeners to vote for the speaker) but at the same time criminal prosecution is particularly dangerous (say, by radically

> changing a potential election result) and consequently can more easily result in censorship of speakers and their ideas. Thus, the statute may have to be significantly narrowed in its applications. Some lower courts have upheld the constitutionality of roughly comparable but narrowly tailored statutes in political contexts.[71]

Legislatures can try to address these concerns in a number of ways. For example, as Justice Breyer observed in *Alvarez,* prohibiting "only knowing and intentional acts of deception about readily verifiable facts within the personal knowledge of the speaker" reduces the risk of chilling valuable speech.[72] Regulating a candidate's (or campaign's) reputation-enhancing lies similarly targets a specific set of verifiable matters to which the speaker has excellent informational access and within the speaker's control to confirm. Relatedly, such laws target aggressive, rather than defensive, lies, and thus seem particularly unlikely to trap unwary speakers unfairly and are less likely to trigger concerns about prosecutorial abuse. Moreover, laws prohibiting lies about matters that are provably true or false raise fewer concerns about institutional competence (i.e., the decision-maker's ability to determine what is and is not a lie). Indeed, a speaker's lies about her credentials that seek to shape

[71] *Alvarez,* 132 S. Ct. at 2556.

[72] Id. at 2553 (Breyer, J., concurring) ("[T]he Court emphasizes *mens rea* requirements that provide 'breathing room' for more valuable speech by reducing an honest speaker's fear that he may accidentally incur liability for speaking.").

listener decision-making are the sorts of lies that are typically prosecuted in the contexts described in Parts I and II; perjury law, for example, generally targets false and material assertions, "the truth or falsity of which can be ascertained by relatively uncontroversial methods."[73] In contrast, some of the current state laws prohibiting campaign lies sweep considerably more broadly, and thus potentially unwisely, to punish, inter alia, "any false statement concerning a candidate" or any "false statement" concerning a ballot proposition or issue.[74]

Legislatures' choice of penalty can also play a role in appropriate statutory design, as statutes that provide for softer or more flexible remedies may ameliorate the dangers of enforcement.[75] More specifically, the penalties for campaign lies may more appropriately be confined to declaratory relief or limited civil penalties. Richard Hasen, for example, has suggested the possibility of "a government 'truth commission' with the power to declare, before the election but subject to judicial review, that campaign speech is false" (while also expressing concern that such an approach, even if constitutional, may not be desirable as a policy matter).[76]

[73] Green, "Lying, Misleading, and Falsely Denying" at 175.

[74] See, e.g., Oh. Rev. Code §§ 3517.21; 3517.22.

[75] See Michael Coenen, "Of Speech and Sanctions: Toward a Penalty-Sensitive Approach to the First Amendment," *Columbia Law Review* 112 (2012): 991, 1003 (noting the connection "between the severity of a law's penalty and the intensity of its deterrent effect on valuable speech").

[76] Richard L. Hasen, "A Constitutional Right to Lie in Campaigns and Elections?" *Montana Law Review* 74 (2013): 53, 75–76.

In contrast, many of the laws punishing lies to or about being the government described earlier imposed criminal penalties, as do some of the state laws that currently regulate campaign lies. In short, appropriate tailoring may help legislatures limit the potential for government overreaching posed by laws punishing lies to become the government.

On the other hand, however, more narrowly tailored approaches may strike some as incompletely capturing the universe of harmful campaign lies. The United Kingdom, for example, casts a somewhat wider net by prohibiting campaign lies about a candidate's "personal character or conduct."[77] This approach recognizes that lies about one's opponent may be deeply damaging even if they fall short of defamation. Consider, for example, lies that one's opponent is gay or lesbian, or was born in Africa. Such lies are not (or should not be) considered defamatory in that they should not damage one's reputation if true; nevertheless they are often told to damage an opponent's candidacy by exploiting the audience's bigotry. In sum, the normative appeal of a narrow approach to campaign lies depends on one's assessment of the harms of such lies compared to the harms of efforts to regulate them.

Conclusion

We lie frequently and for an impressively wide range of reasons. We lie to be cruel, we lie to be kind, we lie to advance

[77] Representation of the People Act, 1983, c. 2 § 106 (UK).

our interests, we lie to protect ourselves, we lie because we are humanly flawed. Our lies can be shattering and destructive. Sometimes, however, our lies are relatively innocuous or even helpful. This is no less true of lies to, about being, and to become the government. Exploring our intuitions about – and the law's treatment of – these lies and their harms expose some common themes as well as some inconsistencies.

Laws punishing lies to the government often broadly target lies that wrongfully seek to manipulate governmental power to personal benefit, akin to public corruption laws that punish bribes that wrongfully seek to manipulate public power to private advantage. Some self-protective or unconsidered lies to the government, however, may not threaten actual manipulation of the government's decisions in morally culpable and/or instrumentally dangerous ways. In other words, most – but not all – lies to the government threaten to manipulate public power in ways that justify their regulation consistent with the First Amendment.

Laws prohibiting lies about being the government often broadly target lies that seek to misappropriate public power for private benefit, again akin to public corruption laws that punish government officials who abuse their power for personal gain. Some lies about being the government, however, that take the form of mere bragging and puffery without any effort to shape listeners' decisions may not threaten harm to second-party listeners nor the third-party public. In other words, most – but not all – lies about being the government threaten to misappropriate public power in ways that are sufficiently morally culpable and instrumentally dangerous to justify their regulation consistent with the First Amendment.

Lies to become the government seek to acquire public power by influencing voters' decisions, and thus threaten collective harm in ways reminiscent of lies to manipulate or misappropriate government power. Indeed, the law punishes manipulative lies about objectively verifiable facts in other contexts (to or about being the government) to prevent the wrongful influence or exercise of public power even when the regulated lies involve skeptical audiences, abundant opportunities for counterspeech, and causally complex listener decision-making about matters no more (and often much less) important than voting. Lies to become the government, on the other hand, are told in campaign contexts that invite greater concerns that regulatory efforts may chill core political speech or encourage selective enforcement. There thus may be good reason to treat lies to acquire governmental power differently from lies to manipulate or misappropriate governmental power for First Amendment purposes – but the differences may be smaller than originally supposed. Treating these laws differently for constitutional purposes, moreover, leads to an uncomfortable view of the First Amendment that bars legislatures from requiring the same honesty of those who seek to become the government as they do of those speaking to or about being the government.

The great variety of reasons for which we tell lies and the wide range of our lies' effects prevents us from describing all – or none – of them as protected by the First Amendment. Indeed, I do not pretend that that there are easy answers to the hard First Amendment controversies about the regulation of lies to, about being, or to become the government. This requires us to make some hard choices. Ideally, legislatures and courts will grapple transparently with these concerns to identify narrowly tailored – i.e., nuanced – regulatory responses that minimize neither the harms of such lies nor the challenges of efforts to regulate them.

4

Lies, Rape, and Statutory Rape

Stuart P. Green*

When a defendant lies or uses other forms of deception to induce an adult partner into sex, the law only rarely treats that as rape, even if the partner would not have engaged in the act absent the deception. But when the defendant himself is deceived into having sex with a partner who is underage, such deception is normally no defense to charges of *statutory* rape, even if, once again, it was a "but-for" cause of the act. To put it another way, in the case of rape, the lie-perpetrator normally escapes liability, while in statutory rape, the lie-victim is punished. At first

* An earlier version of this chapter was presented at the University of Alabama Law School conference on "Law and Lies" and at a faculty workshop at Cornell Law School, and I am grateful for the many helpful questions and comments I received. Special thanks to Sherry Colb, Bill Eskridge, Mary Anne Franks, Stephen Garvey, Helen Norton, Jens Ohlin, Austin Sarat, Ken Simons, and Norman Spaulding.

glance, this seems reversed. Why does deception play what seems to be a morally inverted role in these two contexts? Can such a regime be justified?

As the analysis below suggests, there is no neat answer to these questions. The law of rape and of statutory rape each developed according to their own logic, in their own historical contexts, in response to distinctive policy concerns. Still, it is worth considering the two offenses in relation to each other, since both are ultimately concerned with questions of sexual autonomy and consent to sexual relations, and both are key components in a larger system of sexual offenses. On the view that I present here (and which will be developed in much greater detail in a book I am writing[1]), the law of sexual offenses is understood as protecting a wide range of "sticks" that comprise the "bundle" of sexual autonomy rights. Under this view, individual sexual offenses like rape and statutory rape are understood as protecting specific collections of sticks within that bundle, rather than sexual autonomy *in toto*.

Given that rape is the most serious of the sexual offenses, one would expect it to protect the most serious of the sexual autonomy rights. These would include, at the least, the right to decide whether or not to have sexual intercourse or other penetrative sex, and the right to decide *whom* one will have it with. Thus, where *D* induced *V* into sex by lying about the fact that they were having sex (say, in the course of a

[1] Tentatively titled *Criminalizing Sex: A Unified Theory* (under contract with Oxford University Press).

fraudulent medical procedure), or about his identity (by impersonating her regular lover), that *would* constitute rape on my view. More difficult are cases in which *D* obtained sex from *V* by lying about matters, such as whether he was married, using birth control, carrying a sexually transmitted disease, or interested in a long-term romantic relationship. While I shall not attempt to resolve all of these issues in this brief chapter, I believe that the beginning of an answer lies in determining – as we do in other legal contexts, such as perjury and fraud – which kinds of deception are more wrongful or harmful than others.

Thinking more broadly about the sexual offenses can also shed light on the role that deception plays, or ought to play, in the context of statutory rape. Like the law of rape, the law of statutory rape is concerned with protecting potential victims' sexual autonomy – but it does so in a quite convoluted manner. Unlike adults, juveniles are not recognized as having sexual autonomy in those cases in which they genuinely wish to have sex; in such cases, lack of consent to sex is said to be "presumed." Paradoxically, it is only when juveniles are subject to truly unwanted sex – as in the case of forcible rape – that their ability to consent is implicitly recognized. To avoid this paradox, I suggest that we abandon the idea of statutory rape as involving a presumption of nonconsent, and instead simply view it as analogous to other offenses that are intended to prevent the exploitation of potentially vulnerable members of society. Where the "victim" herself has used deception to induce the offender into having sex, however, the prevention-of-exploitation model breaks down – indeed, is turned on its head – and the rationale for imposing liability is thrown into doubt.

I. Deception and the Law of Rape and Statutory Rape

I begin with a brief description of how deception-induced sex is currently treated in the law of rape and of statutory rape.

A. Rape

At common law, a successful prosecution for rape normally required proof not only that the victim did not consent to intercourse but also that such intercourse was obtained by "force." Indeed, the issues of nonconsent and force were essentially merged: the only way to prove lack of consent was by presenting evidence of force. This meant that nonconsensual sex obtained by means other than force, such as deception or coercion, was generally not subject to prosecution as rape. Sex induced by deception was treated, if at all, under the law governing the tort (and, later, the lesser crime) of seduction.[2] Thus, it was not rape if a man obtained a woman's consent to sex by falsely claiming, for example, that he loved her, was single, would marry her, was a famous movie director, was using birth control, was sterile, or did

[2] See Jane E. Larson, "Women Understand So Little, They Call My Good Nature 'Deceit': A Feminist Rethinking of Seduction," *Columbia Law Review* 93 (1993): 374.

not have a venereal disease.[3] And this was true even if it could be proved that the victim would not have had sex with the defendant but for his lie.

There were, however, two important exceptions to the general rule: Courts generally held that it *was* rape if the man obtained consent to sex by deceiving his victim into believing that she was (1) undergoing a medical procedure, rather than intercourse, or (2) having sex with her spouse. In so doing, the courts relied on a distinction, borrowed from commercial law, between "fraud in the factum" and "fraud in the inducement." Fraud in the factum was said to occur when the victim was unaware of the "true nature" of the transaction into which she was entering.[4] For example, if *X* was tricked into signing a document not knowing that it was, say, a contract or deed, that would be regarded as fraud in the factum, and the document would have no legal effect. This was to be contrasted to cases of fraud in the inducement, in which *X* was deceived not about whether she was signing a will or deed as such, but rather about the specific rights and obligations created by the documents. In such cases, the deception was said to be "collateral," and the agreement would be enforceable.[5]

Applying the factum/inducement distinction in the context of sexual relations, courts held that it was rape if the

[3] See generally Patricia J. Falk, "Rape by Fraud and Rape by Coercion," *Brooklyn Law Review* 64 (1998): 39.

[4] *People v. Morales*, 212 Cal.App.4th 583, 594 (2013).

[5] *McArthur v. Johnson*, 61 N.C. 317, 319 (1867).

victim was unaware that the act to which she was consenting was sexual intercourse. This could happen, most commonly, when the woman was tricked by a doctor (or someone posing as a doctor) into believing that she was undergoing a vaginal examination or surgical operation, rather than having intercourse.[6] By contrast, when the victim understood the basic nature of the act, but was mistaken about certain material facts, her consent would not be vitiated. For example, it would not be rape if the victim understood that she was having sexual intercourse, but was misled into believing that such intercourse was a medical necessity.[7]

Many courts held that it was also rape if the defendant obtained sex by impersonating the victim's spouse. For example, in the Irish case of *Dee*, the defendant had sex with the victim after sneaking into her darkened bedroom and pretending to be her husband.[8] Reasoning that the victim had consented only to *marital* intercourse, not adultery, the court held that the defendant's act constituted fraud in the factum rather than merely fraud in the inducement.[9]

[6] E.g., *People v. Minkowski*, 23 Cal. Rptr. 92, 105 (Cal. Ct. App. 1962) (victims believed they were being penetrated with medical instrument for medical purposes).

[7] E.g., *Boro v. Superior Court*, 210 Cal. Rptr. 122 (Cal. Ct. App. 1985) (victims believed that intercourse was medically necessary).

[8] *Regina v. Dee*, 15 Cox 579 (1884).

[9] For a contrary rule, see *Lewis v. State*, 30 Ala. 54 (1857) (holding that there was no rape where the defendant, a slave, climbed into bed and had sexual relations with a white woman who believed she was having sex with her husband, as the defendant did not use force and the woman "consented" to the act).

This traditional common law rule (now largely codified), which recognizes rape by deception only in cases of fraudulent medical procedures and spousal impersonation, continues to be the law in most Anglo-American jurisdictions, including England, Canada, and a majority of U.S. states.[10] But the broader law of rape has undergone tremendous change in the last generation or two, ranging from an expansion in the definition of penetration, to the softening or repeal of the resistance requirement and the abolition of the marital rape exemption.[11] And so it is not surprising that there has been some movement to expand the scope of rape by deception as well.

A handful of jurisdictions have done so. Under a recently enacted Idaho law, a man commits rape if he has sex with a woman who, because of his "artifice, pretense or concealment," believes him to be "someone other than" who he is.[12] Tennessee, similarly, has defined rape to include "sexual penetration . . . accomplished by fraud."[13] And a law was recently proposed (though never enacted) in Massachusetts that would have made it rape to have sexual intercourse with another person after "having obtained

[10] For a helpful survey, see Falk, "Rape by Fraud." See also English Sexual Offences Act 2003 s. 76(2)(a) (identifying two sets of circumstances in which lack of consent is presumed: where *D* (1) deceived *V* as to the nature or purpose of the relevant act, or (2) induced *V* to consent by impersonating a person known personally to *V*).

[11] For a helpful summary, see David P. Bryden, "Redefining Rape," *Buffalo Criminal Law Review* 3 (2000): 317.

[12] Idaho Code Ann. § 39-13-503(a)(4).

[13] Tenn. Code Ann. § 39-13-503(a)(4).

that person's consent by the use of fraud, concealment or artifice."[14] Sometimes the sex-obtained-by-fraud cases are treated as rape, and other times as a lesser offense, as in the Model Penal Code's sexual intercourse by imposition.[15]

Perhaps the most prominent, and controversial, example of the broadened approach to rape by deception can be seen in the Israeli district court decision in *State of Israel v. Kashur*.[16] The defendant misrepresented himself to a prospective sexual partner as unmarried, Jewish, and interested in a serious romantic relationship. Relying on these misrepresentations, the partner consented to sex. After his lies were discovered, the defendant was charged with rape under Israeli Penal Law, which is defined to include "intercourse with a woman ... with the woman's consent, which was obtained by deceit in respect of the identity of the person *or the nature of the act*."[17]

The court's task on appeal was to determine whether lies about marital status and romantic intentions constitute lies

[14] Massachusetts Legislature, House Docket No. 631 (filed January 9, 2009), https://malegislature.gov/Bills/BillHtml/642?generalCourtId=2.

[15] See text accompanying notes below for a discussion of the original Model Penal Code approach, creating the lesser offenses of deviate sexual intercourse by imposition (Section 213.2(c)) and seduction (Section 213.3(d)).

[16] CrimA 5734/10 (Jerusalem District Court) (published in Takdin, January 25, 2012) (Israel) (English translation obtained from VolokhConspiracy blog, http://www.unz.org/Pub/VolokhConspiracy-2010oct-00078).

[17] Penal Law, 5737-1977, Special volume LSI 1, § 345(a)(2)(1977)(Israel) (emphasis added).

about the "nature of the act" within the meaning of the statute.[18] In upholding the conviction, the court reasoned that the:

> defendant interfered with [the victim's] ability to object by means of misrepresenting the facts of his personal situation – that he was a single man interested in a serious relationship. Consequently, the defendant exploited the accuser's desire for a deep emotional connection, for only on account of this did she agree to have intercourse with him.[19]

In holding that rape by deception can exist in contexts well beyond cases of fraudulent medical procedures and spousal impersonation, the *Kashur* decision thus marks a significant departure from the prevailing rule in Anglo-American jurisdictions.

B. Statutory rape

Deception plays a quite different role in the context of statutory rape. The focus here is not on the defendant's lies, but

[18] The procedural posture of the case is a bit obscure, but it appears that the defendant was originally charged with forcible rape, and pled guilty to rape by deception, while preserving for appeal the right to have the court decide whether the facts as alleged established a case of rape by deception.

[19] *Kashur*, above. See also *Saliman v. State*, CrimA 2411/06 (Israel) (August 17, 2008) Israeli Supreme Court (2008) (upholding conviction of rape by fraud where defendant procured sex from *V* by falsely claiming to be a Housing Department who could help her obtain an affordable apartment).

on the lies of the supposed "victim."[20] The clear majority rule in Anglo-American jurisdictions is that a defendant who is deceived into believing, even reasonably and in good faith, that an underage sexual partner has reached the age of consent has no defense. The traditional rule, creating strict liability as to the victim's age, can be traced to the 1875 English case of *Prince*.[21] The defendant was convicted of eloping with a minor without her father's permission. Despite the jury's finding that the defendant did not know the girl was underage, the court denied a defense. It reasoned that, though the defendant lacked the intent to commit statutory rape, he did have an intent to do something wrong (namely, eloping with a young woman without her father's permission), and this intent to do a "lesser wrong" was sufficient to establish the mental element necessary for statutory rape.

The rule in *Prince* has led to very harsh results, perhaps most notably in the Maryland case of *State v. Garnett*, in which a twenty-year-old man with an IQ of 52 and social skills of an eleven-year-old was seduced by a girl just shy of her fourteenth birthday, who became pregnant as a result of the intercourse.[22] Garnett's conviction for statutory rape was upheld by the state Supreme Court, less on policy grounds than on the basis of strict statutory construction.

[20] I use scare quotes here to indicate my skepticism that mature juveniles who deceive adults into having sex should necessarily be regarded as victims.

[21] [1875] 2 L.R.C.C.R. 138.

[22] 632 A.2d 797 (Md. 1993).

Although *Garnett* reflects the clear majority rule, that rule is not universal. In 1964, the California Supreme Court held in *People v. Hernandez* that an honest and reasonable belief regarding the defendant's age would constitute a defense to charges of statutory rape.[23] The court reasoned that, "if [the defendant] participates in a mutual act of sexual intercourse, believing his partner to be beyond the age of consent, with reasonable grounds for such belief," criminal intent is lacking.[24] Only a handful of states have followed the approach in *Hernandez*, though honest mistakes about age do now provide a defense to charges of statutory rape in most European jurisdictions (the UK, Ireland, Italy, and Norway excepted).[25]

II. Conceptual Framework

Before we can begin to critique the legal rules described above, it will be helpful to have some basic conceptual tools with which to work. The framework offered here will be developed in much greater detail in my book.

23 393 P.2d 673 (Cal. 1964).

24 Id. at 676.

25 Belinda Carpenter et al., "Harm, Responsibility, Age, and Consent," *New Criminal Law Review* 17 (2014): 23, 35 (on European jurisdictions); Catherine L. Carpenter, "On Statutory Rape, Strict Liability, and the Public Welfare Offense Model," *American University Law Review* 53 (2003): 313, 316–317 (2003) (on minority U.S. jurisdictions).

A. Criminalization, blameworthiness, and sexual autonomy

Under liberal retributive principles, only conduct that is blameworthy can legitimately be subject to state punishment. Elsewhere, I have argued that blameworthiness should be analyzed in terms of at least two overlapping types of moral content: harmfulness and wrongfulness.[26] Harmfulness reflects the degree to which an act causes, or risks causing, what Feinberg called a "significant setback to another's interests."[27] Wrongfulness reflects the extent to which a criminal act involves the violation of a moral norm, rule, or right.[28]

[26] I addressed this issue in Stuart P. Green, *Thirteen Ways to Steal a Bicycle: Theft Law in the Information Age* (Cambridge, MA: Harvard University Press, 2012), 72–73. Intent, knowledge, and other forms of culpability constitute a third type of moral content under my scheme, but they are not directly relevant here.

[27] Joel Feinberg, *The Moral Limits of the Criminal Law: Harm to Others* (New York: Oxford University Press, 1984), 31–36.

[28] Some examples will be helpful in explaining the distinction. Imagine a case in which *X* and *Y* engage in consensual sexual intercourse. Despite good intentions and reasonable precautions on *X*'s part, *Y* nevertheless finds herself with an unwanted pregnancy or a sexually transmitted disease brought on by the sexual act. To the extent that *X* has caused *Y* to suffer a setback to her interests, we should say that *X* has caused *Y* harm. We should not, however, conclude that *Y* has been wronged by *X*, since *X* committed no violation of a norm, rule, right, or duty. To put it another way, the harm caused to *Y* by *X* was not unjustified. We can think of what *Y* has to done *X* as a "wrongless harm."

Finding an instance of harmless wrongdoing in this context is a bit more difficult. Consider a hypothetical case originally described in John Gardner and Stephen Shute, "The Wrongness of Rape," in

For present purposes, I shall assume that the wrongfulness in nonconsensual sexual offenses like rape and sexual assault comes from violations of a victim's sexual autonomy. But to make this assumption is only to begin the analysis, not to end it. What remains to be determined is what sexual autonomy means in particular circumstances and how particular offense provisions should protect it.

Sexual autonomy is often characterized as a kind of undifferentiated "self-determination in matters of sexual life."[29] This aggregative approach, however, is at odds with both how sexual autonomy is dealt with in law and how it is thought about by people in their normal lives. A better way to think about sexual autonomy is in terms of its component parts. I suggest that we conceive of sexual autonomy as loosely analogous to the concept of property. Property is often characterized as a "bundle" of rights organized around the idea of securing, for the right of the holder, exclusive possession or use or access to, or control of, a

Jeremy Horder (ed.), *Oxford Essays in Jurisprudence: Fourth Series* (Oxford: Oxford University Press, 2000), 193. *X* has sexual intercourse with *Y* while she is unconscious. *X* wears a condom and causes no physical injury to *Y*, and neither *Y* nor anyone else ever becomes aware that the act has occurred. Such an act undoubtedly involves a serious and unjustified violation of *Y*'s rights, and is therefore wrongful. But, as Gardner and Shute argue, it seems that *Y* has not been harmed, in the sense described above.

29 Stephen J. Schulhofer, *Unwanted Sex: The Culture of Intimidation and the Failure of Law* (Cambridge, MA: Harvard University Press, 1998), passim.

resource.[30] Sexual autonomy, similarly, can be thought of as a bundle of rights organized around the idea of securing for its possessor various forms of sexual self-determination.

Sexual autonomy, on this view, is not a single, monolithic right to choose one's own sexual path, but rather a complex, multifarious collection of rights to engage in, or refrain from, various forms of sexual activity and sex-related conduct. Such autonomy can be negative or positive in its form.[31] Negative autonomy is essentially freedom from interference by external bodies. The law of forcible rape epitomizes the protection of negative liberty in the sense that it protects people from being forced to have penetrative sex they do not wish to have, while having no separate effect on their freedom to engage in sex they do desire. Positive autonomy, by contrast, involves not just freedom *from* restraints, but the freedom to achieve self-realization. The law of marriage arguably provides a legal framework for achieving one form of positive autonomy in the sexual sphere.[32]

So what rights are, or should be, contained in the bundle of rights that comprise sexual autonomy (at least in the case

[30] For a useful discussion, see Joseph William Singer, *Introduction to Property*, 2nd ed. (Boston: Aspen, 2005), 2; A. M. Honoré, "Ownership," in Anthony G. Guest (ed.), *Oxford Essays in Jurisprudence* (Oxford: Clarendon Press, 1961), 107.

[31] See, most famously, Isaiah Berlin, "Two Concepts of Liberty" (originally published in 1958), in Berlin, *Four Essays on Liberty* (Oxford: Oxford University Press, 1969).

[32] See Carlos A. Ball, "The Positive in the Fundamental Right to Marry: Same-Sex Marriage in the Aftermath of *Lawrence v. Texas*," *Minnesota Law Review* 88 (2004): 1184, 1203–1207.

of adults – I defer until later the question of sexual rights for juveniles)? Obviously, the list will be subject to debate, but I would suggest, for starters, the right to engage in (or forgo) activities such as vaginal intercourse, anal intercourse, oral sex, kissing, fondling, foreplay, masturbation, preserving or giving up one's virginity, inflicting or receiving sexual pain, viewing sexual images and performances, using sex toys, displaying (or concealing) one's sexual identity and history, cross-dressing, changing one's gender identity, mutilating or modifying one's genitals, becoming pregnant, undergoing fertility treatments, having an abortion, using contraception, being protected from or allowing oneself to be exposed to sexually transmitted diseases, selling sex, buying sex, and thinking, talking, reading, or writing about sex. Having sexual autonomy means not only the right to decide whether to engage in such activities, but also the right to decide whom one will have sexual activity with, where and when one will have it, and under what additional circumstances.

There are, of course, significant limitations on such autonomy. In a liberal society that respects the harm principle, almost all of these rights will be circumscribed in some way by the potentially conflicting rights of others. Thus, *A*'s right to have sex with *B* – at a particular time, in a particular manner, under particular conditions – will be circumscribed by *B*'s willingness to have sex with *A*, under those conditions. Similarly, *C*'s right to observe *D* having sex will be circumscribed by *D*'s willingness to display her sexual behavior to *C*; *E*'s right to display his sexuality to the public will be circumscribed, in some way, by the public's right not to be offended by such activity; *F*'s right to inflict sexual pain on *G* will be limited by *G*'s willingness to receive sexual pain from *G*; and so on.

B. How the law of sexual offenses protects (and sometimes undermines) sexual autonomy

Assuming it is helpful to think about property *rights* as a model for understanding sexual autonomy rights, I would suggest that we also think about the property *offenses* as a model for understanding the sexual offenses. Different property offenses protect different sticks in the bundle of property rights in different ways.[33] Laws regarding trespass, joyriding, and unauthorized use of a movable, for example, prohibit offenders from temporarily using others' property without permission; laws regarding vandalism and criminal damage prohibit offenders from causing damage to an owner's property, but without dispossession; the law of theft applies to cases involving more substantial and permanent kinds of interference with an owner's property rights. Such offenses are graded depending on the seriousness of the infringement. Theft, for example, is normally treated as a more serious offense than joyriding, since it involves a more serious infringement of the property owner's rights.

The law of sexual offenses affects different sticks in the bundle of sexual rights in an analogous manner. In the main,

[33] The discussion here is drawn from Green, *Thirteen Ways to Steal a Bicycle* at 74–75.

it protects people's sexual autonomy by preventing others from forcing them to engage in conduct in which they do not wish to engage. For example, laws against groping and sexual assault protect people from being sexually touched when they do not wish to be touched; statutes prohibiting indecent exposure, public lewdness, and public nudity protect people from having to witness the sexuality of others whose conduct they do not wish to witness; laws against voyeurism protect people from having their sexual activity observed when they do not wish it to be observed; and so on. As in the case of the property offenses, the sexual offenses are graded in a manner that is supposed to reflect the seriousness of the infringement. For example, touching someone sexually on the subway who does not wish to be touched is punished less severely than subjecting another to unwanted sexual intercourse.

Some sexual offenses, however, rather than *protecting* people's rights to sexual autonomy, have the effect of *infringing* those rights, by preventing them from engaging in sexual conduct that, in some significant number of instances, does no wrong or harm to others. This is true most obviously in the case of prohibitions on fornication, sodomy, consensual adult incest, and consensual sadomasochistic sex. But it can also occur in the context of offenses that are otherwise consistent with the harm principle. As we shall see below, the law of statutory rape, though protecting juveniles from unwanted sex in at least some cases, also chills juveniles' sexual freedom by subjecting their potential sexual partners to the prospect of criminal prosecution.

C. Sexual autonomy and consent

One of the principal indicators for determining whether an individual's sexual autonomy is respected is consent. Consent, of course, is a highly complex concept, and it will be impossible to probe all of that complexity here. Nevertheless, several key issues can be identified.

First, there is a debate in the literature about whether consent should be understood primarily as a subjective mental or psychological state, or instead as a communicative or performative act.[34] To say that consent is a mental state is to say that when *A* consents to *B*'s touching her, she has a particular attitude toward *B*'s act. But what kind of attitude? One possibility is preference: when *A* consents to *B*'s touching her, *A* prefers the state of *B*'s touching her to his not touching her; all things considered, she wishes to acquiesce in the desired conduct.[35] Another possibility is that *A*'s consent is a means of expressing a decision that *B* should touch her. Obviously, *A* can consent to *B*'s touching her without expressing that wish. She can also express consent when she does not really mean it (say, if she feels pressured to do so).

[34] For an excellent account, see Alan Wertheimer, *Consent to Sexual Relations* (Cambridge: Cambridge University Press, 2003), 144–162. Among those who take the subjective view are Heidi Hurd, "The Moral Magic of Consent," *Legal Theory* 2 (1996): 121; Larry Alexander, "The Moral Magic of Consent II," *Legal Theory* 2 (1996): 165.

[35] See Peter Westen, *The Logic of Consent* (Farnham, Surrey: Ashgate, 2004), 30.

We also need to distinguish between consent in its communicative or factual sense and consent in its prescriptive or normative sense. Simply because consent has been given in a factual sense does not necessarily mean that it will be regarded as effective in a moral or legal context. Consent has prescriptive force in morality or law only if (among other things) it is made voluntarily, knowingly, and competently. There are also cases where consent is presumed, and therefore has prescriptive force, even if it has not been communicated (e.g., as in the case of some organ donor regimes).

Consent is normally deemed to be invalid when one or more of three kinds of condition exists. The first is incapacity. A person must be capable of understanding what she is consenting to and what the effects of her consent will be. A person who is unconscious or heavily intoxicated is presumed to be incapable of giving consent.[36] People who have very low intelligence or mental illness are also sometimes deemed to be incapable of giving consent. Juveniles are also sometimes said to be *per se* incapable of consenting – to sex, to contracts, to a waiver of constitutional rights – though, as we shall see below, this claim is problematic in at least some cases of statutory rape.

The second circumstance in which consent is said to be invalid is when it is obtained under coercion. For example,

[36] This is true at least contemporaneously; it's an open question whether a person could give consent to sex prospectively, so that it would apply even after one is incapacitated in the future, as in the case of advance directives or living wills.

if *A* threatened to disclose embarrassing information about *B* unless *B* agreed to have sex or give up some piece of property, *B*'s consent would be coerced and therefore invalid. A good example of the difference between descriptive and prescriptive consent in this context can be found in the Hobbs Act, which defines extortion as "the obtaining of property from another, *with his consent*, induced by wrongful use of actual or threatened force, violence, or fear."[37] The kind of consent being referred to here is expressive consent. Valid prescriptive consent would still be lacking, since expressive consent was given under the force of coercion.

Third, there is consent made invalid by deception, which is of course the main concern of this chapter. If *A* obtains *B*'s (factual) consent to some action by lying to *B* about the circumstances surrounding such action, and *B*'s consequent mistaken belief was a but-for cause of his consent – a "deal breaker," in Tom Dougherty's phrase[38] – the consent will be deemed normatively invalid, even if it was effectively communicated or felt. An example of the difference between descriptive and prescriptive consent here can be found in Section 345(a) of Israeli Penal Law, which says that a person commits rape if the person "had intercourse with a woman . . . (2) *with the woman's consent*, which was obtained by deceit in respect of the identity of the person or the nature of the act."[39] The consent referred to here is once

[37] 18 U.S.C. § 1951(b)(2) (emphasis added).

[38] Tom Dougherty, "Sex, Lies, and Consent," *Ethics* 123 (2013): 717, 719.

[39] Israeli Penal Law, Section 45(a)(2) (emphasis added).

again expressive. Consent in the prescriptive sense would be lacking.

Finally, it has been said that consent is "transformative," in the sense that *B*'s consent has the potential to make *A*'s action morally or legally permissible in circumstances in which it otherwise would not be. In an oft-quoted phrase, consent is said to be capable of transforming "a rape into love-making, a kidnapping into a Sunday drive, a battery into a football tackle, a theft into a gift, and a trespass into a dinner party."[40] Likewise, the withdrawal of consent is said to be capable of turning a "fond embrace" into "assault and battery."[41]

As stated, however, this last set of claims is misleading. As we saw above, not all descriptive consent (or nonconsent) constitutes prescriptive consent (or nonconsent).[42] Consider

[40] Hurd, *Moral Magic* at 123.

[41] See Rollin M. Perkins and Ronald Boyce, *Criminal Law*, 3rd ed. (Mineola, NY: Foundation Press, 1982), 1075. The fact that consent was refused will not always make *A*'s action criminal, however. For example, *A*'s embrace of *B* without *B*'s consent might be a justified exercise of *A*'s police powers (though it is admittedly hard to imagine any circumstance in which sexual intercourse could be justified without the consent of both parties). But if *B* does consent to *A*'s embrace, then we can say unequivocally that *A*'s conduct did not constitute a battery. This is not to say that *A*'s conduct will necessarily be right or justified. There might be some other reason that *A*'s act is deemed wrongful; for example, it might reflect his bad temper or meanness. But if *B* did consent, and such consent was valid, then we can at least say that *A*'s act is exempt from criminal liability.

[42] Cf. William Eskridge, "The Many Faces of Sexual Consent," *William and Mary Law Review* 37 (1985): 47 (arguing that consent is "contextual and status-based").

a case in which a corporate raider threatens to take over a target company unless his shares in its stock are bought out at a premium price. Descriptively, it appears that the target's sale of stock was nonconsensual. But, prescriptively, it is less clear that we should regard this as the kind of nonconsent that should give rise to extortion liability. Most people would regard this kind of coercion as less serious than a case in which *D* threatened to defame *V* or expose a secret of *V*'s, and such a distinction might be relevant to decisions about criminalization. Similarly, consider a case in which *V* consents to sex with her longtime partner, *D*, only after *D* threatens to break off their relationship unless *V* does so. Once again, we *could* treat this as rape, because the partner's consent was arguably invalid in a moral sense, but it's unclear whether we should we want to treat it as a crime. Much more analysis remains to be done before it can be determined exactly which nonconsensual acts should be criminalized (whether as rape or as some other offense), and which should not.

III. When Should Sex Obtained by Deception Be a Crime?

Having considered some of the basic concepts that inform the law of sexual offenses, we can now return to where we left off, with the question of how the law of sexual offenses should treat deception-induced sex. We first consider deception used by the defendant (in the case of rape) and then deception used by the victim (in the case of statutory rape).

A. The argument for expanding the offense of rape by deception

Scholars who have considered the so-called "riddle" of rape by deception have tended to take one of two main positions: One is that the law of rape should be expanded to include every, or almost every, instance in which deception plays a but-for role in securing consent to sex. The argument for this position consists of three steps: First is the idea, embraced by most contemporary criminal law theorists, that rape should be understood as involving a violation of a victim's sexual autonomy.[43] Second is the notion that *V*'s sexual autonomy is violated, and rape is therefore committed, when she is subject to sex without her consent. Third is the claim that deception negates consent just as thoroughly as force.[44] If all these statements were true, it would seem to follow that all sex obtained by deception should constitute rape, at least so

[43] As one scholar has put it, "the moral wrongness of rape consists in violating an individual's ... sexual self-determination and the seriousness of rape derives from the special importance we attach to sexual autonomy." Joan McGregor, "Force, Consent, and the Reasonable Woman," in *Harm's Way: Essays in Honor of Joel Feinberg*, eds. Jules Coleman and Allen Buchanan (Cambridge: Cambridge University Press, 1994), 231, 236.

[44] See Jonathan Herring, "Mistaken Sex," *Criminal Law Review* (2005): 511 ("Deceit, as much as force and threats, can 'negate consent.' Deceit, like violence, manipulates people into acting against their will. Like threats, deceit restricts the options available to another. It does this by making the other unaware of the options the other has available.... Restricting the information on which a person makes a choice can be as inhibiting of a free choice as making an option unattractive through a threat.").

long as the deception was a but-for cause of the consent. And, indeed, based on reasoning of this sort, a number of leading scholars – including, Susan Estrich and Jonathan Herring – have argued for a dramatic expansion in the scope of rape by deception, akin to that endorsed by the Israeli Supreme Court in *Kashur*.[45] Similarly, Tom Dougherty, while careful to avoid arguing that such conduct should be treated as rape as such, nevertheless believes that it involves a "serious wrong" that is comparable to other serious wrongs that *are* treated as rape.[46]

Other scholars have resisted the notion that we should criminalize every case in which *D*'s deception of *V* is a but-for cause of *V*'s consent, arguing instead for a more selective list of circumstances in which rape by deception (or perhaps a lesser offense) is said to occur.[47] They have argued, for example, that almost everyone, at some point in their lives, has engaged in, or been the target of, some form of deception in the context of sex. As Sherry Colb has put it, "[p]eople routinely wear perfume and deodorants that disguise their body odor; they wear makeup that disguises facial flaws or

[45] See Susan Estrich, "Rape," *Yale Law Journal* 95 (1986): 1087, 1095–1096; Herring, "Mistaken Sex" at 511, 517 (rape is committed whenever V is "mistaken as to a fact" and "had s/he known the truth about that fact would not have consented to it").

[46] Dougherty, "Sex, Lies, and Consent" at 721.

[47] See, e.g., Rebecca Williams, "Deception, Mistake and Vitiation of the Victim's Consent," *Law Quarterly Review* (2008): 132; Hyman Gross, "Rape, Moralism, and Human Rights," *Criminal Law Review* (2007): 220; Wertheimer, *Consent to Sexual Relations* at 209.

install hair plugs that disguise baldness; some color, straighten or curl their hair or undergo cosmetic surgery."[48] Any of these deceptions could serve as a but-for cause of *V*'s consent to sex. But, these scholars say, to treat all such cases as rape would trivialize the offense, and chill private, socially positive or neutral behavior.[49]

I am inclined to agree with those scholars who have expressed concerns about the policy implications of over-criminalizing rape by deception. I am also skeptical about the ability of courts to determine when a defendant's deception should be considered a but-for cause of the victim's decision to have sex. Such a determination will inevitably be based on the consideration of a complex counterfactual: *how would the victim have behaved differently had she*

48 Sherry Colb, "Rape by Deception, Rape by Impersonation, and a New California Bill," Justia.com, http://verdict.justia.com/2013/05/01/rape-by-deception-rape-by-impersonation-and-a-new-california-bill#sthash.N0uIxiPS.dpuf (May 1, 2013).

49 There is also a third position. Apparently out of concern with the practical effects of wholesale expansion, on the one hand, and frustration with the supposed ad hoc-ness and inconsistency of selective incorporation, on the other, Jeb Rubenfeld has written a controversial article urging a rejection of the view that rape should be understood as involving a violation of sexual autonomy. Jeb Rubenfeld, "The Riddle of Rape-by-Deception and the Myth of Sexual Autonomy," *Yale Law Journal* 122 (2013): 1372. Because this argument seems to me based on a non sequitur, and because it has already generated numerous responses from others – see http://www.yalelawjournal.org/forum – I shall not be concerned with it further here: As explained in the text, merely because we view the law of rape as concerned with protecting sexual autonomy does not mean that all deception-induced sex must be treated as rape.

known the truth – a determination that will have to be made on the basis of the victim's testimony, which in some cases will be tinged with regret and the distorting lens of hindsight.

I hope to consider these policy and evidentiary issues in my book. For present purposes, however, I would like to focus instead on what I perceive to be a *conceptual* error that underlies much of the analysis on this issue. That error, as I shall explain in the next section, is to think of "sexual autonomy" and "consent to sex" as undifferentiated, all-or-nothing concepts that are either respected, and therefore legal, or disregarded, and therefore criminal. As I will explain, things are actually more complicated than such an account would suggest.

B. Grading moral blameworthiness

As suggested above, many scholars have approached the sexual offenses in what we can think of as either/or terms: Intercourse is either "lovemaking" (if consensual) or "rape" (if not); consent is either valid (if voluntary, knowing, and competent) or invalid (if one of these conditions is lacking); sexual autonomy is either respected (and therefore exempt from criminal sanctions) or violated (and therefore criminal).

I believe that this binary approach lacks the flexibility and nuance that a liberal society should demand of its system of sexual offenses. My alternative approach is motivated by three basic premises: The first is that sexual autonomy is a highly variegated concept. Not every stick in the bundle of sexual autonomy rights is equally important; some will be valued more highly than others. The second is that, in a liberal society, we need to be wary of the potential for overcriminalization, especially in an area as personal and intimate as that involving sexual conduct. Third, we need to abide by the principle of "fair labeling" – the idea that "widely felt distinctions between kinds of offences and degrees of wrongdoing are respected and signaled by the law, and that offences should be divided and labeled so as to represent fairly the nature and magnitude of the law-breaking."[50] Rape, in particular, should be viewed as just one weapon in a diversified arsenal, reserved for a small collection of very serious, "core" violations of sexual autonomy.

If this view of the criminal law is correct, it raises the possibility that not all nonconsensual "lovemaking" should be viewed as morally or legally equivalent. Some deception- or coercion-induced sex might be more or less blameworthy than other deception- or coercion-induced sex. Obviously, moral judgments will need to be made: we will have to ask, for example, whether obtaining sex by lying to one's sexual partner about the use of birth control or the fact that one has a sexually transmitted disease is more or less wrongful or

[50] The *locus classicus* is Andrew Ashworth, *Principles of Criminal Law*, 4th ed. (Oxford: Oxford University Press, 2003), 89–90; see also James Chalmers and Fiona Leverick, "Fair Labelling in Criminal Law," *Modern Law Review* 71 (2008): 217, 239.

harmful than obtaining sex by lying to one's partner about whether one is married or is interested in a serious romantic relationship.

Tom Dougherty has rejected a moral line-drawing approach of this sort. He argues that, "[o]ne of the key achievements of waves of sexual liberation has been the promotion of a sexual pluralism that allows each individual to pursue his or her own conception of the sexual good, so to speak.... [I]t is up to each individual to determine which features of a sexual encounter are particularly important to her."[51] According to Dougherty, one person might think that a person's false claim about his marital status or romantic intentions is a "deal breaker" in terms of deciding whether to have sex, while another person may view it as basically inconsequential. To attempt to distinguish between more and less serious forms of deception, he says, constitutes a kind of "sexual moralism."[52]

I believe that Dougherty is mistaken. As properly understood, moralism, at least in the context of law, refers to criminalizing or otherwise prohibiting conduct that may be immoral or wrongful, *but is not harmful*, and therefore fails to satisfy the harm principle.[53] In the case of the sexual offenses, criminal law moralism arguably occurs when we criminalize acts like adultery and adult incest. But moralism

51 Dougherty, "Sex, Lies, and Consent" at 730.

52 Id. at 727.

53 See generally Joel Feinberg, *Moral Limits of the Criminal Law: Harmless Wrongdoing* (New York: Oxford University Press, 1988).

has never been understood to refer to the making of judgments about which kinds of admittedly harmful acts should be regarded as more wrongful or harmful than others, and therefore punished more severely.

Indeed, the criminal law makes such distinctions all the time. In the context of perjury, we distinguish between misrepresentations that are literally false and those that are merely misleading, criminalizing only the former.[54] In the context of false statements, the law traditionally distinguished (though it no longer does) between lies that are exculpatory and those that are inculpatory, punishing the latter and exempting the former from liability.[55] And in the case of fraud, we sometimes distinguish between deception by act and deception by omission, regarding the former as more blameworthy, other things being equal.[56]

We make fine moral judgments in the realm of the sexual offenses as well. For example, we normally judge unwanted voyeurism as less serious than unwanted touching, unwanted touching as less serious than unwanted penetration, and unwanted penetration of an adult as less serious than unwanted penetration of a child. None of this is in any way inconsistent with a system that respects "sexual pluralism."

[54] *Bronston v. United States*, 409 U.S. 352 (1973).

[55] See *Brogan v. United States*, 522 U.S. 398 (1998) (rejecting exculpatory no doctrine).

[56] See Green, *Thirteen Ways to Steal a Bicycle* at 129–131.

C. What should count as deception about a core matter?

If the foregoing argument is correct, it suggests that there is no reason in principle why we should not base criminalization and grading decisions on judgments that some kinds of deception-induced sex are worse than others. The real problem, of course, is determining which is which.

One place to begin such an analysis is with empirical data about how people "in the street" view the wrongfulness of various kinds of deception-induced sex. As I have explained elsewhere, the point of such an approach is not that the criminal law should always follow popular opinion, or that widely held moral intuitions are necessarily correct.[57] Nor should empirical studies of public perceptions be expected to serve as a substitute for serious normative reflection about desert. Rather, I am merely suggesting that, where such data are available, they can provide a useful reference point for thinking about what kinds of conduct are more blameworthy than others, and whether they are deserving of punishment.

In the case of rape by deception, such data do in fact exist. As part of a larger work on the fundamentals of rape law, David Bryden conducted a study in which he asked respondents to consider eighteen hypothetical cases in which deception was used to obtain sex, and decide which ones should be treated as "criminal" (the study does not, however, explicitly ask respondents whether such conduct

[57] Id. at 56–57.

should be treated as "rape").[58] A majority of respondents, female and male, young and old, favored criminal penalties in only five of the eighteen cases: where the perpetrator (1) had intercourse while pretending to be conducting a gynecological examination, (2) impersonated the victim's husband, (3) lied about a venereal disease, or (4) failed to reveal a venereal disease. (The fifth case seemed to involve coercion or exploitation rather than, or in addition to, deception.) In all of the other cases, including misrepresentations about infidelity, wealth, marital status, intention to marry, intention to pay a prostitute, and even use of birth control (by a woman), a clear majority rejected criminal liability.

This study, together with the common law of rape by deception itself, provides a useful place to begin an analysis of why certain kinds of sex-by-deception cases were viewed as more blameworthy than others, what additional questions need to be asked, which kinds of cases should be treated as rape (or perhaps a lesser offense), and how such prohibitions should be formulated. (In the interest of space, and because they do not rank as criminalizable in the Bryden study, I leave to the side for now interesting cases involving misrepresentations about use of contraception and transgender status, though I intend to take these up in my book.[59])

[58] Bryden, "Redefining Rape" at 470–475, 480–487.

[59] On contraception deception, see *R. v. Hutchinson* (Canadian Supreme Court, 2014, http://scc-csc.lexum.com/scc-csc/scc-csc/en/item/13511/index.do). On transgender deception, see Aeyal Gross, "Rape by Deception and the Policing of Gender and Nationality Borders," *Law and Sexuality* 24 (2015): 1; Alex Sharpe,

D. Leading candidates for rape by deception

In this section, I consider three kinds of cases that we might want to consider treating as rape by deception. These involve sex obtained through: (1) fraudulent medical procedures, (2) spousal or other impersonation, and (3) misrepresentations regarding the offender's sexually transmitted disease.

1. Fraudulent medical procedures. There are two kinds of cases in which sex is obtained as a result of fraudulent medical procedures. Both involve a doctor or someone pretending to be a doctor. In one sort of case, the offender purports to be engaging *V* in some nonsexual act (such as a routine vaginal examination) when actually engaging *V* in intercourse. In such cases, the victim is unaware that she is having intercourse at all. As discussed above, courts almost always say that such fraud-in-the-factum cases constitute rape. In the second kind of case, the defendant tells the victim that sexual intercourse is necessary for therapeutic purposes. In such cases, the victim understands that she is having intercourse, but is deceived as to the need for such conduct. These fraud-in-the-inducement cases are rarely held to be rape.

The Bryden study considered the first sort of case, but not the second, so it is unclear how respondents would have rated the latter. I think a reasonable argument can

"Criminalising Sexual Intimacy: Transgender Defendants and the Legal Construction of Non-Consent," *Criminal Law Review* 3 (2014): 207.

be made that the first sort of case should be regarded as morally worse than the second. The first kind of deception seems closer to the core of sexual autonomy than the second. The victim in the first sort of case has not consented to the act of sexual intercourse as such, while the second has. The first victim has been denied the right to choose *whether* to have intercourse, a right which lies at the very core of our sexual autonomy. The same cannot be said of the second case. There, the victim has chosen to engage in what she knew to be intercourse, if for spurious reasons. This is not to suggest that *D*'s conduct in the phony medical necessity case is not terribly wrongful, or that it should be exempt from criminal liability (he could, for example, be prosecuted for a lesser sexual offense). It is merely to say that the crime he has committed does not seem to be rape.

There are two other factors that distinguish the phony medical procedure cases from the kind of deception-induced sex we saw in cases like *Kashur*. The first is that such acts often are committed by persons who have a special duty to the victim – such as a doctor, nurse, or other medical professional. This factor cuts in two different directions: On the one hand, it adds to the wrongfulness of the act. On the other hand, it raises the possibility that such cases could be dealt with under alternative sexual offense provisions such as those involving abuse of position of trust. The second factor is that only the most inexperienced and gullible persons are likely to be susceptible to such schemes. This factor also seems to cut in two different directions: On the one hand, it could be argued that this is exactly the kind of vulnerable victim with whom the criminal law should be most concerned. On the other hand, it might suggest that, more than in some other cases, the victim of such deception is partly to blame for her plight.

Assuming that do we want to criminalize at least some phony medical procedure cases, what should such a provision look like? The original, 1963 version of the Model Penal Code agreed with the common law position that sex obtained from a person who was "unaware that a sexual act is being committed upon" her should be a crime, though it treated it as the lesser offense of deviate sexual intercourse, rather than as rape proper.[60] The American Law Institute is currently considering a proposed revision to the sexual offense provisions. Unfortunately, the proposal expands the corresponding offense beyond what seems to me sensible. Section 213.3(2), titled "Sexual Intercourse by Exploitation," applies to cases in which the "actor represents that the act of sexual intercourse is for purposes of medical treatment or that such person is in danger of physical injury or illness which the act of sexual intercourse may serve to mitigate or

[60] Section 213.2(2). MPC § 213.3(d) also criminalizes "seduction," defined as having sex when "the other person is a female who is induced to participate by a promise of marriage which the actor does not mean to perform." The proposed revision to the MPC also creates a lesser offense of "sexual intercourse by exploitation."

prevent."[61] (I leave to the side fair labeling concerns about referring to this as "exploitation," having addressed the difference between exploitation, coercion, and deception at length elsewhere.[62])

In my view, the proposed revision paints with too broad a brush. The problem is that the phrase "for purposes of medical treatment" would seem to cover both fraudulent and arguably legitimate sex therapy. Consider, for example, the therapy depicted in the 2012 film *The Sessions*, based on a true story, in which a man suffering from polio and forced to live in an iron lung has a series of sexual encounters with a professional sex surrogate.[63] Although not without controversy, such therapy (originally described by Masters and Johnson in their 1970 textbook, *Human Sexual Inadequacy*) is viewed by many in the medical profession as effective and appropriate.[64] Under the broad language of the proposed Model Penal Cause provision, however, all such conduct would constitute Sexual Intercourse by Exploitation. (Whether it would also constitute prostitution is a separate question.) I think this is a mistake. In my view, the criminal law should not presume

[61] American Law Institute, Model Penal Code: Sexual Assault and Related Offenses, Tentative Draft No. 1 (April 30, 2014), Section 213.3(2).

[62] Stuart P. Green, *Lying, Cheating, and Stealing: A Moral Theory of White Collar Crime* (Oxford: Oxford University Press, 2006).

[63] "The Sessions" (Fox Searchlight, 2012).

[64] See T. Rosenbaum et al., "Surrogate Partner Therapy: Ethical Considerations in Sexual Medicine," *Journal of Sex Medicine* 11 (2014): 321.

to intervene in disagreements within the medical profession about the acceptability of various controversial treatments. The provision should either expressly provide that only intercourse that is *misrepresented* as therapeutic is covered, or it should create an exception to liability for bona fide treatment as recognized by the medical profession.[65]

2. Spousal Impersonation. The other major category of rape by deception at common law consists of cases in which the defendant obtains sex by impersonating the victim's spouse. Subjects in the Bryden study agreed that such cases should be treated as a crime. Some commentators have said that the reason this was treated as rape by deception is that the victim was being deceived into committing what was then a crime – namely adultery.[66] But, as stated, this is a non sequitur. Certainly, it would make sense to relieve the victim who was deceived into committing adultery of liability for that crime. But that is very different from saying that the deceiver himself should be held liable for rape.

A better explanation for why impersonation of a spouse, and not a non-spouse, was treated as rape at common law is that marital sex was the only kind of sex that was legally

[65] Thanks to Ken Simons for helping me think through these issues.

[66] See Russell Christopher and Kathryn Hope Christopher, "Adult Impersonation: Rape by Fraud as a Defense to Statutory Rape," *Northwestern University Law Review* 101 (2007): 79–80.

protected. If *V* believed she was having sex with her spouse, but was tricked into having sex with someone else, that was a matter that properly concerned the law of rape, since *V*'s legally recognized sexual autonomy was being infringed. But if *V* believed she was having sex with someone who was not her spouse, that apparently was of no concern to the common law, since *V* had no legal right to have sex with someone who was not her spouse in the first place.

In our more sexually permissive time, one would expect a broader rule. Adults are now legally entitled to have sex with almost any other adult who wishes to have sex with them (though there are a few important exceptions, as discussed below). Thus, if *V* believes that she is having (legal) sex with *A*, and is deceived into having sex with someone other than *A*, that deception would undermine a key stick in the bundle of sexual autonomy rights, regardless of whether *A* was her spouse or not. (Subjects in the Bryden study were asked only about cases of spousal impersonation, not about non-spousal impersonation. Given the way in which sexual autonomy rights have expanded since the days of the common law, it seems quite plausible that, had they been asked about such cases, they would have treated them as criminal as well.)

A recent proposed revision to the Model Penal Code seems like a step in the right direction, though it is still flawed. Unlike the provision regarding phony medical procedures (which I argued was overinclusive), this provision is underinclusive. Proposed Section 213.3(3) of the MPC defines Sexual Intercourse by Exploitation to include cases in which the "actor knowingly leads such person to believe falsely that he or she is someone *with whom such person has been sexually intimate*."[67] While sensibly broadening the offense beyond just cases in which *A* impersonates *B*'s spouse, to include impersonation of others with whom *B* might enjoy intimacy, the proposed provision is still too narrow.

Consider (a much simplified version of) the "bed trick" in Shakespeare's *Measure for Measure*: Angelo's former lover is Mariana; he called the wedding off, but she would still like to marry him. Angelo is now interested in Isabella, but the feeling is not reciprocated. Isabella and Mariana hatch a plan to deceive Angelo. Isabella sends word to Angelo that she will meet him for a sexual encounter, on the condition that their meeting occur in perfect darkness and in silence. Mariana, disguised as Isabella, goes in Isabella's place, and has sex with Angelo, who has been deceived about the identity of his sexual partner.

This case would clearly fall outside the scope of proposed Section 213.3(4), because it is not the case that the actor (Mariana) led Angelo to believe falsely that she was someone with whom Angelo had been sexually intimate.[68] Angelo had in fact previously had sexual relations with Mariana, so his belief was not false. Rather, Angelo was tricked into believing, falsely, that he would be having sex with someone with

[67] MPC Tentative Draft No. 1, Section 213.3(3) (emphasis added).
[68] Section 213.3(4).

whom he had never been intimate – namely, Isabella. Yet it is hard to see why it is any less wrongful to mislead a victim into believing (he or) she is having sex with someone with whom she has *not* previously been intimate than it is to mislead a victim into believing she is having sex with someone with whom she previously *has*.

The real wrong in these cases lies in the offender's leading the victim to believe that she is having sex with someone *other than the person with whom she believes she is having sex*, regardless of whether they have had sex in the past. For this reason, I believe that a better approach than that offered in the revised Model Penal Code provision is that contained in the English and recently revised California provisions, which define rape or sexual assault as including cases in which the defendant impersonates someone who is "known" to the victim.[69] Unlike the proposed MPC provision, the English and California provisions would apply to cases like that in *Measure for Measure*.

[69] Cal. Penal Code Section 261(5) (victim "submits under the belief that the person committing the act *is someone known to the victim other than the accused*, and this belief is induced by any artifice, pretense, or concealment practiced by the accused, with intent to induce the belief"). This formulation raises an interesting question as to whether rape by impersonation should include cases in which *D* impersonates someone who is not personally known to the victim, such a celebrity with whom she has not had contact previously. In the interest of space, I have omitted this analysis, though I intend to take it up my book. The issue is discussed in Joel Feinberg, "Victims' Excuses: The Case of Fraudulently Procured Consent," *Ethics* 96 (1986): 330, 343.

There is one further issue that needs to be considered. As noted, a rule that limited rape by deception to cases of impersonation of spouses, as opposed to non-spousal lovers, seems too narrow for a world in which non-marital sex is commonplace and legal. But what if *V* believed that she was having sex that was *illegal*? For example, suppose that *V* was in a jurisdiction that criminalized adult incest or prostitution. Or imagine that *V* was serving in the U.S. Military and thereby subject to the Uniform Code of Military Justice, which makes adultery a crime. Would it be rape by deception if *V* believed that she was having sex with her brother, a prostitute, or her adulterous lover, and was tricked into doing so with someone else?

This seems to me a close call. On the one hand, it could be argued – as it was at common law – that since *V* had no legal right to engage in such sex in the first place, such cases should fall outside the scope of rape law's protection. On the other hand, regardless of whether *V* had a legal right to engage in such sex, it might still be argued that *V* was wronged, that society still has an interest in promoting a regime that values sexual autonomy, and that the criminal justice system still has a need to prevent and punish *D*'s conduct.

The problem is analogous to one that occurs in the law of theft. Imagine that *V* has money or property stolen from him that he himself had previously stolen from a third party or earned through illegal activities such as drug dealing. Should the law regard such stealing as theft, given that

V has no “legitimate” property interest in the money or property stolen from him? I have argued elsewhere that such cases *should* be prosecuted as theft. Theft law is intended not merely, or even primarily, to protect the interests of individual property owners; that is the purpose of the private law of conversion, misappropriation, and trespass to chattel. Rather, the law of theft is intended to protect the interests that society as a whole has in preserving the system of private property. If people felt free to steal each other’s illegal drugs and stolen goods with impunity, that would undermine society’s sense of property security and potentially create a potential for violence, notwithstanding the fact that such things are illegal to own.[70]

The law of nonconsensual sexual offenses arguably follows a similar logic. Prohibitions on rape and sexual assault do more than simply protect the interests of individual victims. They are also intended to protect the interests of society as a whole in the “system” of sexual autonomy. If people who engaged in prostitution, adult incest, or adultery could be tricked into having sex with someone other than the person with whom they believed they were having sex, and if there were no consequences for such trickery, that would tend to weaken people’s sense of sexual security generally, even though the underlying conduct itself was illegal.

[70] The discussion here is borrowed from Green, *Thirteen Ways to Steal a Bicycle* at 212.

3. Lies about sexually transmitted diseases. Another significant kind of deception-induced sex that the subjects in the Bryden study said should be treated as a crime occurs in cases in which the offender misrepresents the fact that he has a sexually transmitted disease. Indeed, Bryden's subjects believed that both affirmatively lying about the fact that one has a sexually transmitted disease and failing to tell one's partner that fact should be treated as criminal.

As noted, one of the limitations of the Bryden study is that subjects were not asked to specify whether such cases should be treated as rape, or whether they should be treated as some other offense instead. In the case of misrepresentations regarding STDs, this ambiguity is quite significant. Consider the English case of *B*.[71] The defendant, who was HIV-positive, but had not disclosed this fact to his sexual partner, was charged with rape under Section 76 of the English Sexual Offences Act 2003, which provides that deception will be presumed to vitiate consent to sex only where "the defendant intentionally deceived the complainant as to the nature or purpose of the relevant act." The Court of Appeal held that rape could not lie on the facts of the case since his deceit did not go to "the nature or purpose of the relevant act." According to the court:

> Where one party to sexual activity has a sexually transmissible disease which is not disclosed to the other party any consent that may have been given to that activity by the

[71] B [2006] EWCA Crim 2945, [2007] 1 W.L.R. 1567.

> other party is not thereby vitiated. The act remains a consensual act. However, the party suffering from the sexually transmissible disease will not have any defence to any charge which may result from harm created by that sexual activity, merely by virtue of that consent, because such consent did not include consent to infection by the disease.[72]

In other words, otherwise consensual sex between *A* and *B* will not be rendered nonconsensual by *A*'s failure to disclose that he had a sexually transmissible disease, and this is so even if it could be proved that *A*'s misrepresentation regarding his STD was a but-for cause of *B*'s consenting to sex. Rather, the law should treat such nondisclosure as a nonsexual assault. For this reason, prosecutors in England are instructed to charge defendants in such cases under the nonsexual assault provisions of the Offences against the Person Act 1861, for inflicting grievous bodily harm, rather than for sexual assault or rape under the Sexual Offences Act 2003.[73]

72 Id.

73 See Sharon Cowan, "Offenses of Sex or Violence? Consent, Fraud, and HIV Transmission," *New Criminal Law Review* 17 (2014): 135 (endorsing the English approach); see also Crown Prosecution Guidelines, "Intentional or Reckless Sexual Transmission of Infection," http://www.cps.gov.uk/legal/h_to_k/intentional_or_reckless_sexual_transmission_of_infection_guidance/#Reckless1861. For a contrary view, see Atli Stannard, "When Failure to Disclose HIV-Positive Status Vitiates Consent to Sex in Canada," *Journal of Commonwealth Criminal Law* (2012): 366; Martha Shaffer, "Sex, Lies, and HIV: *Mabior* and the Concept of Sexual Fraud," *University of Toronto Law Review* 63 (2013): 467.

This seems to me basically the right approach. The real wrong in cases like *B* lies in the nonconsensual transmission, or risk of transmission, of a venereal disease, rather than in any nonconsensual sex. Imagine two cases: In one, the victim consents to sex but is deceived about the fact that her partner is HIV-positive. In the other, a victim consents to a blood transfusion but is deceived about the fact that the blood is infected with HIV. In both cases, the underlying "core" transaction is consensual; the wrong to the victim is that her health has been endangered and that she is deprived of information about such endangerment to which she is entitled. The fact that in one case the underlying transaction was a sexual encounter while in the other it was a blood transfusion is, from a moral perspective, irrelevant. The proper charge in both cases is the same: assault rather than sexual assault or rape.

This is to be contrasted to two parallel cases in which the underlying transaction is nonconsensual. In one, *V* is forced to have unwanted, unprotected sex with HIV-positive *D*. In the other, *V* is forced to undergo an unwanted transfusion of HIV-infected blood. In such cases, the victim is subjected to two distinct wrongs: unwanted sex (or an unwanted blood transfusion) *and* endangerment. Here, the offender should be prosecuted for two kinds of offense: The first, involving the unwanted underlying transaction, whether it is rape (in the case of unwanted sex) or aggravated assault (in the case of the unwanted transfusion); and the second, involving the knowing or reckless transmission of disease.

IV. Should an Adult Offender Who Is Deceived About His Juvenile Partner's Age Have a Defense to Statutory Rape?

In the previous section, we considered whether and under what circumstances we should treat as rape (or perhaps a lesser sexual, or nonsexual, offense) cases in which an offender uses deception to induce his adult victim into having sex. This section considers cases in which the offender himself is deceived into having sex with an underage victim he mistakenly believes has reached the age of consent, and as a result is prosecuted for statutory rape. Despite the different context, the methodology to be followed is similar to that used previously. We will need to ask what interests and rights are protected (or undermined) by the law of statutory rape, what wrongs and harms such conduct causes, and how those interests, rights, wrongs, and harms are affected by the so-called victim's use of deception regarding her age.

A. Statutory rape as strict liability offense

Statutory rape is normally defined as requiring proof of nothing more than that the defendant (1) had intercourse with, or penetrated (2) a juvenile below a particular age (typically, sixteen).[74] Some jurisdictions also provide that the offender must be at least some particular number of

[74] For a useful summary, see Richard A. Posner and Katharine B. Silbaugh, *A Guide to America's Sex Laws* (Chicago: University of Chicago Press, 1996), 44–64.

years of age (typically, eighteen) or at least some number of years older than the juvenile victim (typically, three). Any adult defendant who has sexual relations with a juvenile is liable for statutory rape, even if the juvenile "actually" consents (I will have more to say about what this means below). Moreover, and of particular significance here, it does not matter whether the offender actually knew that his victim was below the age of consent. Statutory rape is a strict liability offense. Under the clear majority rule, statutory rape has been committed even if the adult was unaware of – indeed, is affirmatively misled by the victim herself about – the fact that his victim is a juvenile. As we saw above, a small minority of American state jurisdictions, as well as various European jurisdictions, follow a contrary rule.

In at least some cases in which a juvenile victim lies about her age to an older sexual partner, that lie will serve as a but-for cause of the defendant's decision to have sex with the juvenile, just as the *offender*'s lie was a but-for cause of the victim's decision to have sex in the rape by deception cases discussed above. Note that, in such cases, the statutory rape defendant is being deceived not about the fact that he is having intercourse as such (as in the case of the doctor fraud cases) or about the identity of his sexual partner (as in the spousal impersonation cases). Rather, the defendant's mistake goes only to the age of his sexual partner.

One pair of commentators has suggested that, in such cases, the statutory rape offender himself has been subject to rape (by his juvenile victim).[75] But whether this is true depends on whether one believes that one who lies about one's age should be prosecuted for rape by deception. I would distinguish here between two sorts of cases: In the first, a 20-year-old obtains sex by falsely claiming to be 25. In the second, a 15-year-old obtains sex by falsely representing himself as 20. The person in the first case seems to have done nothing more morally wrong than a person who lies about the fact that he is a Navy SEAL or went to Harvard. The person in the second case, however, has done something more culpable. He has induced his partner to have sex with an underage partner and in doing so commit a crime (though it should be pointed out that under the traditional rules of accomplice liability, the juvenile victim/deceiver could not be held as complicit in his own statutory rape).[76]

Many scholars have been quite critical of the regime of statutory rape. Some are opposed to strict liability in any context.[77] Others believe that, while strict liability might be acceptable for low-stigma, low-punishment, regulatory

[75] See Christopher and Christopher, "Adult Impersonation" (arguing that, in such cases, the juvenile should be prosecuted for rape by deception).

[76] Cf. *Gebardi v. United States*, 287 U.S. 112, 119 (1932) (woman who is transported willingly across state lines for the purpose of engaging in illicit sexual intercourse is not an accomplice to the male transporter's Mann Act violation).

[77] Vera Bergelson, "A Fair Punishment for Humbert Humbert: Strict Liability and Affirmative Defenses," *New Criminal Law Review* 14 (2011): 55, 60 (expressing antipathy for regime of strict liability

offenses, it should not be used for more serious offenses like statutory rape.[78] Yet others believe that, while statutory rape laws are not necessarily unjust in principle, they are frequently enforced in an unjust manner, including, in particular, when they are used as a means to avoid bringing more serious and difficult-to-prove charges of forcible rape.[79]

Statutory rape laws have also been criticized as being paternalistic.[80] But it is important to be clear about exactly what this might mean. The most familiar kinds of paternalistic offenses are those like failing to wear a motorcycle helmet or a seatbelt: offenders, who are themselves members of the protected class, are punished for causing, or risking, harms to self. Statutory rape statutes function quite differently. Like assisted suicide statutes, they punish offenders who are not members of the protected class for causing harm

generally, but conceding that it may help prevent "certain socially undesirable conduct").

78 Catherine L. Carpenter, "On Statutory Rape, Strict Liability, and the Public Welfare Offense Model," *American University Law Review* 53 (2003): 313.

79 See, e.g., Michelle Oberman, "Turning Girls into Women: Re-Evaluating Modern Statutory Rape Law," *DePaul Journal of Health Care Law* 8 (2004): 109; Michelle Oberman, "Regulating Consensual Sex with Minors: Defining a Role for Statutory Rape," *Buffalo Law Review* 48 (2000): 703.

80 Catharine A. MacKinnon, "Reflection on Sex Equality Under Law," *Yale Law Journal* 100 (1991): 1281, 1300; Frances Olsen, "Statutory Rape: A Feminist Critique of Rights Analysis," *Texas Law Review* 63 (1984): 387, 412.

to others who are. They are paternalistic only in the sense that they apply even when members of the protected class consent to the harm. (By criminalizing potential partners, they also have the indirect effect of prohibiting sexual activity by juveniles themselves.)

I put these concerns to the side for present purposes, however, in order to focus solely on the narrower mistake-of-fact question: To wit, even assuming that strict liability is appropriately applied, in the main, to offenders who have "consensual" sex with juvenile partners, should there be an exception where the partner has affirmatively misled the offender into believing that she has reached the age of consent?[81]

B. The wrongs and harms of statutory rape

We can begin the analysis by asking both why statutory rape is a crime and why it is formulated as a strict liability offense. As before, we will want to consider the harms and wrongs the prohibited activity is said to entail.

[81] Also put to the side are interesting statutory rape cases involving defendants who are females, see Kay L. Levine, "No Penis, No Problem," *Fordham Urban Law Journal* 33 (2006): 357; defendants suffering from mental deficiencies, see Elizabeth Nevins-Saunders, "Incomprehensible Crimes: Defendants with Mental Retardation Charged with Statutory Rape," *NYU Law Review* 85 (2010): 1067; and adult defendants who are prosecuted for statutory rape when the minor with whom they have had sex has subjected them to forcible rape, see Russell L. Christopher and Kathryn H. Christopher, "The Paradox of Statutory Rape," *Indiana Law Journal* 87 (2012): 505.

Some history will be relevant here. Since at least 1576, English law has sought to criminalize sexual relations between adults and children. But the age of consent under early English common law was very low – typically, ten years of age.[82] It was not until the late nineteenth century that the law of statutory rape went through a major transformation. The "child rescue movement," established in most modern liberal democracies between approximately 1870 and 1890, was premised "upon ideas of children as innocents in need of protection from the harshness of the adult world."[83] New patterns in immigration, urbanization, and prostitution caused concerns about the welfare of young females.[84] Girls were moving into the cities, working in factories, offices, and stores, free from the supervision of family and neighbors. Social reformers believed that the potential for exploitation was great, and that legal protections needed to be enforced. Forcible rape, however, was difficult to prove. By eliminating the *mens rea* requirement, statutory rape provided an

[82] Stat. 18 Elizabeth (1576). For a useful history, see Carolyn Cocca, *Jailbait: The Politics of Statutory Rape Laws in the United States* (Albany: State University of New York, 2004).

[83] Dorothy Scott and Shirley Swain, *Confronting Cruelty: Historical Perspectives on Child Protection in Australia* (Melbourne: Melbourne University Press, 2002), 71, quoted in Belinda Carpenter, et al. "Harm, Responsibility, Age, and Consent," *New Criminal Law Review* 17 (2014): 23, 27.

[84] Estelle B. Freedman, *Redefining Rape: Sexual Violence in the Era of Suffrage and Segregation* (Cambridge, MA: Harvard University Press, 2013), at 126.

alternative route for every case in which a young female was involved.

The problem is that with the elimination of the *mens rea* requirement, questions concerning blameworthiness arise. When the defendant knows that his victim is underage, sexual relations are likely to be exploitative. But when the defendant believes that the victim has reached the age of consent, a different explanation is needed. The court in *Prince* reasoned, as we saw above, that though the defendant lacked the intent to commit statutory rape, he did have an intent to do something wrong (namely, fornication), and it was this intent to do a "lesser wrong" that was sufficient to establish the mental element necessary for statutory rape.

The extent to which the concerns of the child rescue movement are still valid today is unclear. On the one hand, society (in general) no longer views sex outside marriage as immoral in itself. And norms regarding adolescent sexuality have changed significantly: According to a recent report from the Guttmacher Institute, sixteen percent of American teenagers had sexual intercourse by the age of fifteen, one-third by the age of sixteen, and nearly half by the age of seventeen – with little difference by gender.[85] Moreover, with the elimination of the resistance requirement, forcible rape is

[85] Guttmacher Institute, "Fact Sheet: American Teens' Sexual and Reproductive Health" (May 2014), http://www.guttmacher.org/pubs/FB-ATSRH.html. These figures are slightly down from what they were a decade or so ago.

easier to prove than it was in the early part of the twentieth century – suggesting that the need for the statutory rape alternative may be less pressing (though concerns about the underenforcement of rape law persist).

On the other hand, significant concerns remain – indeed, have deepened – about the widespread sexual abuse of children, much of which goes undetected and unpunished.[86] Moreover, rates of unwanted pregnancy and STD transmission tend to be higher among adolescents than in the general population, and contraceptive use is lower.[87] And while those convicted of what we continue to call statutory *rape* are not stigmatized to the same extent as other kinds of rapists, they are hardly free of censure: among other things, they are subject to many of the same severe reporting obligations as other sexual offenders.

I do not propose to resolve these issues here. For present purposes, I shall simply assume that it is just and effective to impose criminal liability on adults who engage in sex with willing partners they know or believe to be underage, and focus on whether it is would also be proper to impose liability

[86] A. J. Sedlak et al., U.S. Department of Health and Human Services, Administration for Children and Families, "Fourth National Incidence Study of Child Abuse and Neglect" (2010), http://www.acf.hhs.gov/sites/default/files/opre/nis4_report_congress_full_pdf_jan2010.pdf; U.S. Department of Justice, Office of Justice Programs, Bureau of Justice Statistics, "National Crime Victimization Survey" (2011), http://www.bjs.gov/content/pub/pdf/cv11.pdf.

[87] Jim Leitzel, *Regulating Vice: Misguided Prohibitions and Realistic Controls* (New York: Cambridge University Press, 2008), 178–179.

on adults who are deceived by their partners into believing that such partners have reached the age of consent (also leaving to the side cases in which the offender is deceived by a third party, such as the juvenile's parent or guardian).

C. The logic of statutory rape

As noted above, the modern understanding of rape is that it involves a violation of the victim's sexual autonomy. But, in the case of children, this conception is problematic. If children do have sexual autonomy, it is autonomy of an unusually thin type. The law of statutory rape, though it does protect children from unwanted sex in at least some cases, also has the effect of *undermining* juveniles' sexual freedom by preventing them from having *wanted* sex (at least with adults).

Part of the problem here is the peculiar way in which statutory rape statutes are formulated and interpreted. Courts almost invariably say that, when juveniles have sex with adults, lack of consent should be "presumed."[88] But it is hardly clear what this means. One possible interpretation is that children, as a rule, lack the mental capacity to consent to sex. Under this view, children would be viewed as unable to consent to sex in the same way that people who are unconscious or highly intoxicated are unable to consent to sex. This understanding may well make sense in the case of small children. While such children have the capacity to consent

[88] See, e.g., *In re* M.V. 225 Cal.App.4th 1495, 1522–2 (2014); *State v. Collins*, 508 S.E.2 390, 394 (Ga. 1998).

to some acts – say, being kissed by Grandma or being shipped off to summer camp – it seems unlikely that they are capable of understanding the true nature and possible consequences of sexual intercourse. Lack of consent in this context is a result of a lack of cognitive capacity. Just as children are too immature in "mind and experience" to enter into contracts, they are too immature to have sex.[89]

But do older children of normal intelligence – above, say, the age of thirteen – also lack the mental capacity to consent to sex? It is true, as the Supreme Court has recognized in the context of the death penalty, that juvenile brains are still evolving.[90] And, certainly, many adolescents lack the emotional maturity that most adults possess. But this does not necessarily mean that juveniles should be viewed as cognitively unable to consent to sex in the same way that the unconscious, the highly intoxicated, or even small children lack the ability to consent to sex.

A more plausible understanding of the presumption that children are "incapable" of consenting to sex is that it is based on some reason independent of their cognitive capacities. The assumption seems to be that juveniles having sex with adults are so likely to be exploited that such conduct should be categorically banned. What is striking, however, is

[89] Michelle A. Sargent, Note, "Misplaced Representations: Why Misrepresentation-of-Age Statutes Must be Reinterpreted as they Apply to Children's Online Contracts," *Michigan Law Review* 112 (2013): 301.

[90] E.g., *Roper v. Simmons*, 543 U.S. 551 (2005); *Miller v. Alabama*, 132 S.Ct. 2455 (2012).

that children are deemed incapable of consenting to sex only in certain limited circumstances. Under so-called Romeo and Juliet provisions, for example, sex between teenagers has essentially been decriminalized. The implicit presumption, whether valid or not, is that exploitation is less of a danger in cases where the sexual partners are close in age.

There is also another inconsistency that needs to be noted. The law of sexual offenses makes an important distinction between cases in which a child's lack of consent is *presumed* (as in statutory rape) and cases in which it is *actually* lacking (as in forcible rape of a minor), with the latter being treated as the more serious offense. Other contexts in which lack of consent to sex is presumed reflect no such a distinction. For example, we do not distinguish between the forcible and "statutory" rape of a person who is heavily intoxicated or unconscious; we simply say that the sexual act was nonconsensual and that a rape was committed.[91] We are thus presented with something of a paradox: when a child is subject to genuinely *unwanted* sex, the presumption is that she is capable of consenting to sex; but when she is involved in *wanted* sex, the law presumes that she is *incapable* of consenting.

D. Statutory rape as regulatory offense

One way to avoid this paradox, and in the process take statutory rape law beyond its moralistic nineteenth-century

[91] Patricia J. Falk, "Rape by Drugs: A Statutory Overview and Proposals for Reform," *Arizona Law Review* 44 (2002): 131.

roots, would be to abandon the notion that the offense involves a presumption of nonconsent, and instead simply view it as analogous to other strict liability offenses that are intended to prevent harm to potentially vulnerable members of society. If this approach were followed, it might also change the way we approach cases involving deception-induced mistakes about the victim's age.

Scholars have typically divided the strict liability crimes into two basic categories: One category consists of the so-called public welfare offenses. A leading example is the adulteration or mislabeling of pharmaceuticals under the Federal Food and Drug Act.[92] Such offenses are regulatory in nature. Their penalties are typically minor, sometimes involving only a fine, and the stigma associated with them is relatively light. The other category of strict liability offenses consists of non-public-welfare crimes, leading examples of which are statutory rape and possession of child pornography.[93] These offenses carry significant stigma and relatively heavy penalties.

In thinking about the cases in which victims deceive offenders into underage sex, however, we would do better

[92] The *locus classicus* is Francis Sayre, "Public Welfare Offenses," *Columbia Law Review* 33 (1933): 55. See also Laurie L. Levenson, "Good Faith Defenses: Reshaping Strict Liability Crimes," *Cornell Law Review* 78 (1993): 401.

[93] See *United States v. Ray*, 699 F.3d 1172, 1177–78 (10th Cir. 2012) (holding that the guideline enhancement for distribution of child pornography is a strict liability provision that does not require proof of any *mens re*a to apply).

to focus not on the distinction between more or less stigmatizing, or more or less punitive, offenses, but rather on who the offense provision is primarily intended to protect. Pure regulatory provisions such as the Food and Drug Act are intended to protect the general public. Statutes that make it a crime to sell alcohol or cigarettes to juveniles seem intended to protect less the general public than individual, would-be, underage buyers of alcohol or tobacco.

The question of who a given strict liability statute is intended to protect seems relevant to the question whether mistake of fact should provide a defense. Consider first the public welfare offenses, like selling adulterated or misbranded drugs. That the defendant committed the offense by mistake does not change the fact that the public was endangered. Indeed, to allow mistake of fact as a defense in such cases would be to convert a strict liability regime into one based on negligence, even though these are the core cases to which strict liability is intended to apply. It is no surprise, then, that mistake of fact is not recognized as a defense to prosecutions brought under the Food and Drug Act.[94]

Statutes prohibiting the sale of alcohol or tobacco to juveniles present a different sort of case. Here, the risk of harm is much narrower in scope: when the seller is tricked into selling alcohol or tobacco to an underage customer, it is only (or primarily) the customer himself who is endangered, rather than the public at large. This may explain why statutes of this sort have typically been interpreted to allow a

[94] See, e.g., *United States v. Dotterweich*, 320 U.S. 277 (1943).

defense in those cases where the defendant's mistake regarding the minor's age was the result of an affirmative misrepresentation by the minor himself.[95]

Should an analogous rule apply in the case of statutory rape? I am inclined to think that it should. My argument is not based on any lack of concern about the welfare of juveniles who engage in sex. I believe that we should try to protect juveniles from themselves even when they lie about their age. The same kind of emotional immaturity that makes juveniles less than fully competent to consent to sex in the first place may also help explain a propensity to lie in such circumstances. Rather, my concern is with the unfairness and ineffectiveness of imposing statutory rape liability on the adults who are duped. A defendant who, despite his due care, is affirmatively misled into believing that his sexual partner has reached adulthood is significantly less culpable, other things being equal, than a defendant who is not so misled. In such cases, it is the adult who is being exploited by the juvenile, rather than the other way around. To prosecute the adult in such circumstances would be to compound the effects of that exploitation.

Conclusion

In this chapter, I have sought to use the law's response to deception as a means to probing the underlying logic of two

[95] See, e.g., N.J. Stat. Ann. § 33:1–77. Indeed, in some cases, the deceiving juvenile is herself liable for an offense.

key sexual offenses: rape and statutory rape. Given the theme of this volume, it seems appropriate to conclude with some thoughts about what the sexual offenses might tell us about the nature and normative force of deception itself.

First, it is not deception as such that is criminal in cases of rape, but rather sexual acts performed on the basis of deception-induced (and therefore invalid) consent. Deception in rape cases thus differs from deception in cases of perjury and false statements, where the lie itself constitutes the *actus reus* of the offense, and lack of consent is not an issue.

Second, what counts as consent-negating deception in the context of sexual offenses is not necessarily the same as what counts as consent-negating deception in other criminal contexts, such as fraud and battery. To know what impact deception has on criminal liability in each case, we need to consider the underlying rights and interests the criminal offense provision is meant to protect.

Third, despite some formal similarities, force, deception, coercion, and incapacity each negate consent to sexual conduct in different ways. We should not assume that obtaining consent to sex by means of force or coercion is necessarily equivalent, morally or legally, to obtaining consent to sex by means of deception or incapacity.

Fourth, deception in the sexual context can be used to cause harm to others and also, arguably, to self. In the case of rape, deception is used as a means to violate some aspect of another's sexual autonomy. In the case of statutory rape, the victim uses deception to facilitate what the law regards as harm to herself. Thus, judgments about the proper role that deception should play in defining liability will depend on unsettled questions concerning the harm principle and the use of criminal law for paternalistic purposes.

Finally, there are significant differences in what should count as actionable deception for purposes of rape law. Some deception probably *is* sufficient to invalidate consent for purposes of rape law: examples are misrepresentations regarding the fact of sexual penetration and the identity of one's partner. Other deception-induced sex arguably should be dealt with under more specialized, less serious offense provisions within the suite of sexual offenses: an example is misrepresentations regarding whether one is carrying a sexually transmitted disease. There are also lesser forms of misrepresentation, such as those regarding marital status, income, and professional achievement, that should arguably lie beyond the scope of the criminal law entirely.

5

Law and the Production of Deceit

William N. Eskridge Jr.*

American law famously regulates lies, deceit, misrepresentations, fraud, and so forth. On the whole, the goal of American law is to *discourage* deceit, and academic criticism tends to focus on law's failure to pursue this goal more thoroughly or more effectively. My thesis is that a more important effect and sometimes a goal of American law is to *encourage* or *produce* deceit. I shall use the term "deceit" broadly, to include not only (1) misrepresentations intended to deceive (the core definition of deceit), but also (2) material misrepresentations where intent to deceive is unclear, as well as (3) material omissions (i.e., leaving out critical information when making otherwise truthful representations).[1]

* I could not have written this chapter without the learned assistance of Erika Nyborg-Burch, Yale Law School, Class of 2016.

[1] On the many faces of deceit and the law, see, for example, Arthur A. Leff, *Swindling and Selling: The Story of Legal and Illegal Congames* (New York: Free Press, 1976).

The inspiration for my paper is America's anti-homosexual terror, a legal regime created by municipal, state, and federal authorities in the twentieth century.[2] Feeding off of and reinforcing social prejudice, American law essentially made sexually active gay men, lesbians, and bisexuals outlaws (i.e., citizens who were not only criminals but literally outside the protections of the law). From the first-hand as well as institutional accounts, we know that the law's heavy hand fueled a veritable golden age of deceit, culminating in the Supreme Court's breath-taking effort to pass off untruth as history in *Bowers v. Hardwick* and the open elevation of deceit to the level of important national policy in the "Don't Ask, Don't Tell" statute. In the latter, the nation's only President to be impeached for perjury implemented an exclusionary policy that not only *produced* a regime of deceit, but that brought lies out of the closet and elevated deceit to the status of national policy. As I shall argue, the lamentable costs of "Don't Ask, Don't Tell" are dwarfed by the costs of deceit that forms the backbone of the nation's policy toward

[2] The details of the anti-homosexual terror are laid out and conceptualized in John D'Emilio, *Sexual Politics, Sexual Communities: The Making of a Homosexual Minority in the United States 1940–1970* (Chicago: University of Chicago Press, 1983); William N. Eskridge Jr., *Gaylaw: Challenging the Apartheid of the Closet* (Cambridge, MA: Harvard, 1999); Estelle B. Freedman, " 'Uncontrolled Desires': The Response to the Sexual Psychopath, 1920–1960," *Journal of American History* 74 (1987): 83–106.

immigrants living in this country whom the government classifies as "inadmissible."[3]

The law's production of deceit comes with potentially significant costs: (1) evasion of statutory policies, (2) corruption of institutional as well as public discourse, and (3) erosion of the rule of law itself. Sometimes, those costs might well be justified, but even when justified the costs of deceit need to be considered when setting and implementing public policy. More generally, this analysis of law's production of deceit, and the costs it generates, may in turn provide strong justifications for the libertarian presumption that undergirds American public law.

How Law Produces Deceit

Consider various ways that law produces deceit, as illustrated by America's persecution of sexual minorities. For sexually active gay men and lesbians in the mid-twentieth century, the anti-homosexual legal regime produced a cornucopia of lies. Almost anything a sexually active "homosexual" did with another man or woman in the 1950s was a crime. The "suspected homosexual" usually generated a parade of lies once the authorities trained their attention

[3] Public Law 103–160, section 571(a)(1), 107 Stat. 1670 (1993), codified at 10 U.S.C. section 654 (the "Don't Ask, Don't Tell" statute); *Bowers v. Hardwick*, 478 U.S, 186 (U.S. Supreme Court, 1986) (upholding laws making consensual sodomy a felony, as applied to "homosexual sodomy" only).

on him or her. Possible criminal prosecution and a wide range of civil exclusions gave ample incentives to "homosexuals" to pass themselves off as "straight"; in this way, the law produced counterfeit identities as well as untruthful statements. Because the legal prohibitions and exclusions were both pervasive and potentially extreme, they induced deceit among the whole society of closeted "homosexuals" and their allies, even including people who did not like "homosexuals" but did not want to get involved with the state persecution either. In each of these ways, the law of the anti-homosexual terror regularly *produced* deceit – and a lot of it.

Evasive Deceit to Avoid Regulatory Requirements. The modern regulatory state cut its teeth on "homosexuals and other sex perverts" (the terminology popular in that era). Almost anything a sexually active "homosexual" did with another man or woman in the 1950s was a crime – not just consensual sodomy or oral sex, but also solicitation for sex, loitering in public restrooms or parks for "lewd" purposes, various forms of indecent exposure (including cross-dressing), publishing accounts of such activities, or even dancing or hand-holding. Although only a tiny portion of the "homosexual" activities that went on in America actually came to the attention of authorities, when they were mobilized (as they often were when people did things in public spaces) the "suspected perverts" usually lied. In 1923, for example, the New York Legislature made it a crime when any person "frequent[ed] or loiter[ed] about any public place soliciting men for the purpose of committing a crime against nature or other lewdness."[4] Thousands of men were arrested under this "degeneracy" law (as the magistrates' reports called it), and tens of thousands more men were arrested under similar laws in California, Illinois, Maryland, Massachusetts, Michigan, Missouri, Ohio, the District of Columbia, and other jurisdictions.[5] While some were probably innocent of that crime, most were in fact seeking sexual partners – but most of them lied about what they were up to. "No, I was just taking a stroll in the park." "I was drunk and did not know what I was doing." Or "I was doing nothing more than befriending a young man who seemed to be down on his luck."[6]

After World War II, the anti-homosexual terror kicked into high gear in states and municipalities all over the country.[7] The federal government followed, with the so-called "Lavender Scare," when thousands of suspected "perverts" were interrogated and purged by the local police and the FBI, federal agencies and civil service administrators,

[4] 1923 New York Laws chap. 642, codified at New York Penal Code section 722(8); see Eskridge, *Gaylaw* at 29–31.

[5] William N. Eskridge Jr., *Dishonorable Passions: Sodomy Laws in America, 1861–2003* (New York: Viking, 2008), 96–99.

[6] The befriending-young-men deceit was successful in the most (in) famous prosecution of the early twentieth century, the Newport Naval Investigations of 1991–21. Lawrence Murphy, *Perverts by Official Order: The Campaign Against Homosexuality by the U.S. Navy* (New York: Haworth Press, 1988).

[7] Eskridge, *Dishonorable Passions* at 73–108.

and military authorities.[8] What characterized this period, the high point of the terror, was the explosion of civil exclusions associated with "perverts" who were considered enemies of the state based upon their presumed violation of sodomy laws (consensual sodomy was a felony in all states outside of New York, where it was a misdemeanor). Thus, there were more questions from more state officials, with higher stakes – and, hence, many more lies from persons suspected of being "homosexual."

Because homosexuality is more acceptable and there are fewer penalties for being gay these days, the lies have abated on this front. But there remains a legacy of lies, and old enforcement patterns die hard. According to media accounts, the poster child for the continued production of lies is former Senator Larry Craig, a married conservative Mormon Republican from Idaho. Apprehended at the Minneapolis Airport for allegedly soliciting sex from a man in an adjoining bathroom stall, Senator Craig admitted to offensive behavior but transformed his apparent act of sexual solicitation into a nervous toe-tapping tic. Although the Senator was embarrassed and resigned his seat, gone are the days when he would go to jail or lose all possibility of employment for such behavior – yet media accounts suggest that he still lied.[9]

[8] David K. Johnson, *The Lavender Scare: The Cold War Persecution of Gays and Lesbians in the Federal Government* (Chicago: University of Chicago Press, 2004).

[9] Max Blumenthal, *Republic Gomorrah: Behind the Movement That Shattered the Republican Party* (New York: Nations Books, 2009),

Like gay men and lesbians seeking sexual partners on the street and in the parks in the early twentieth century, and other accused sodomites even today, the natural impulse of most people accused of a socially despised legal transgression is to lie. As illustrated by the anti-homosexual terror, the modern state has provided many more occasions for rule violators to lie, for the state has exploded with new rules, regulations, specifications for our behavior. Just like the "homosexual" in the 1940s, we encounter more rules than we are willing to obey and follow, and the state often forces us to face up to the inconsistency between those rules and our conduct – the police officer asking for an account of what you are doing in the bushes, the numerous government forms we fill out with a certification that we have told the truth on the forms, and the investigator questioning our compliance with the law. The regulatory state not only imposes truth requirements on us all, but directly puts us on the spot when we would rather say nothing. So we lie – sometimes because we do not realize there is a legal rule we are violating, more often because we do not want to suffer penalties or social stigma for violating a legal rule, and quite frequently because we do not actually believe we have done anything "wrong," rule or no rule.

The process of regulation and evasion is a dynamic process. If a regulation is easily evaded or violations are

chap. 20 (the account of Senator Craig's bathroom escapade and the press speculation).

hard to detect, then the regulation becomes either a dead letter *or* must evolve. In particular, anti-solicitation laws run the risk of desuetude, because neither party to a solicitation is likely to complain to or cooperate with the authorities unless the solicitation is unwelcome. Thus, the emerging regulatory state confronted a problem in its campaign to "purify" public spaces from sexual outlaws such as sex workers, lesbians, and gay men, all of whom developed social cues designed to avoid deeply unwelcome solicitations (e.g., the Larry Craig tap dance). By World War I, municipal, state, and federal law enforcement officials had figured out how to falsify the lies that accused sexual solicitors would concoct: the deployment of undercover police as spies and decoys, namely, eye-witnesses to solicitation – in other words, state deception to expose criminals' evasive lies. In an early deployment of this technique, the Navy in 1919 sent young seamen into the community of "fairies" surrounding the Newport Naval Station, where they were solicited for oral sex by sailors and townspeople.[10] The tactic backfired when a respected ecclesiastical defendant piously invoked the befriending-young-man defense and his counsel elicited testimony from the young men that they had participated in oral sex with the defendant. After that fiasco, police perfected the tactic of using spies and decoys, and in the process perfected the use of deceit to lure "homosexuals" out of their masquerades. Posing as interested "homosexuals" themselves, decoy or undercover

[10] Murphy, *Perverts by Official Order* at 26–29, 32–33, 77–80, 97–103.

officers would entice gay men into making an explicit offer of sex and then arrest them once the offer was made.[11]

In the armed forces, the Newport fiasco discouraged active monitoring of gay service personnel for a generation – but after World War II enforcement of more aggressively anti-homosexual policies emerged as a powerful engine for witch hunts seeking to identify and expunge sexual and gender minorities from the military.[12] The witch-hunt strategy was to pressure suspected "homosexuals" into admitting their criminal activities – and then naming other "homosexuals." As with decoy cops, deceit was central to the witch-hunting process, which depended upon the suspected "homosexual's" believing that the government had hard evidence against her or him and that the government would ruin her with public exposure. In turn, the suspect would typically lie about her comrades and herself – and sometimes would falsely confess to homosexuality.[13]

[11] Lillian Faderman and Stuart Timmons, *Gay L.A.: A History of Sexual Outlaws, Power Politics, and Lipstick Lesbians* (New York: Basic Books, 2006), 75–97; Harold Jacobs, "Note, Decoy Enforcement of Homosexual Laws," *University of Pennsylvania Law Review* 112 (1963): 259–284; Frank Wood Jr., "The Homosexual and the Police," *One*, May 1963, 21–22.

[12] Allan Bérubé, *Coming Out Under Fire: The History of Gay Men and Women in World War II* (New York: Free Press, 1990); Allan Bérubé and John D'Emilio, "The Military and Lesbians During the McCarthy Years," *Signs* 9 (1984): 759–775.

[13] For examples of the strategies followed by witch-hunting military authorities, see Michelle Benecke and Kristin Dodge, "Military Women in Nontraditional Fields: Casualties of the Armed Forces'

The central lessons of the anti-homosexual *terror* are easily generalizable: In response to any serious regulatory regime, lawbreakers will usually lie about their violations, either through concealment or (if detected) through denials of various sorts. Anticipating such deceit, regulatory authorities (if serious about enforcing that regime) will deploy a range of tactics, often involving deceit, to expose evasive concealment and lies. We see this pattern of deceit in such disparate areas of legal regulation as campaign finance, truth-in-lending, corporate regulation, and immigration.

Deceit of the Closet: Illegal Identities. There is a constant interplay between act and identity in the modern regulatory state. During Prohibition, it was illegal to manufacture or sell liquor (act), and thousands of Americans became illegal bootleggers (identity). Today, it is illegal to manufacture or a variety of illegal drugs (act), and thousands of Americans are illegal drug dealers (identity). It has long been illegal in most states to exchange the performance of sexual activities for money (act), and thousands of Americans are sex workers or "prostitutes" (identity). For all of these persons (and millions of others), legal regimes not only induce deceit about what those people are doing or planning to do, but also about their very identities. Nowhere in the law is this as clear as the regulation of "homosexuality" (a term that has connotations of both acts and identity for many Americans).

War on Homosexuals," *Harvard Women's Law Journal* 12 (1980): 215, 219–228.

Thus, the legal prohibitions of the anti-homosexual terror focused on particular activities, such as sodomy or solicitation, but the enforcement regime focused on identities, through harassment of "fairies" and "degenerates" and "inverts" (in the nineteenth century), and later "homosexuals and other sex perverts" (in the heyday of the terror). Increasingly, the letter of the law merged act and identity. Nowhere was that better illustrated than in United States military policy. Sodomy (act) has been a crime in the Uniform Code of Military Justice (UCMJ) since 1921, and enforcement of that crime has generally targeted "homosexuals" (identity). Codifying administrative practice, the Department of Defense in 1982 formalized its longstanding policy of expelling sexual minorities from the armed forces. "Homosexuality is incompatible with military service," because of such persons' "propensity to engage in homosexual conduct," which was (and remains) illegal under the UCMJ.[14] Thus, being "homosexual" is, presumptively, all that the authorities have traditionally needed to penalize a person for violating criminal sodomy laws. During the Reagan and Clinton Administrations, indeed, military officials expelled gay men and lesbians in unprecedented numbers, sometimes with no evidence of criminal activities[15] – apart from the

[14] United States Department of Defense, Directive 1332.14.1.H.1(a): Enlisted Administrative Separations (January 28, 1982).

[15] Compare the majority and dissenting opinions in *Steffan v. Perry*, 41 F.3d 677 (D.C. Cir., en banc, 1994) (the majority upholding the expulsion of an "admitted" "homosexual" and ruling that the government never has to produce evidence of any illegal act).

presumption, which by the way would also apply to heterosexuals, most of whom have engaged in UCMJ-violative oral sex.[16]

The utter conflation of act and identity for gay people was hardly limited to the armed forces. State courts stood ready to take away the biological children of parents who admitted they were lesbian, gay, or bisexual, based upon the presumption that these parents were criminal "sodomites." Public as well as private employers discharged devoted, competent employees who were exposed as "homosexuals." Admission to state bar associations and other professional groups could be denied or revoked if the authorities came face to face with an openly gay or lesbian lawyer or other professional. As the Supreme Court found in *Lawrence v. Texas* (2003), a person accused of homosexual sodomy or even just homosexuality sodomy was in the twentieth-century subject to a wide array of civil exclusions and disabilities.[17]

Accordingly, the overwhelming majority of lesbians and gay men not only lied in response to specific questions, but

16 For empirical evidence that overwhelming majorities of heterosexuals have engaged in oral sex (which the UCMJ includes as sodomy), see Edward Laumann et al., *The Social Organization of Sexuality: Sexual Practices in the United States* (Chicago: University of Chicago Press, 1994), 98–99.

17 *Lawrence v. Texas*, 539 U.S. 558, 568 (2003). For a catalogue of disabilities imposed upon gay persons at the apex of the antihomosexual terror, see Rhonda Rivera, "Our Straight-Laced Judges: The Legal Position of Homosexual Persons in the United States," *Hastings Law Journal* 50 (1999): 1015 ff. (reprinting 1979 article).

lied about their identities during the anti-homosexual terror. Consider one of thousands of examples. Born in 1933, Rose Levinson graduated from the University of Miami Law School in 1954, where she became involved with another woman. In 1951, the two women entered a "known" lesbian hangout, the Pan American, and were arrested for vagrancy. This experience, together with lurid headlines about police persecution of "homosexuals" in Miami and a second arrest for vagrancy, impelled Levinson to retreat into a strict sexual secret. When she applied to join the Florida Bar Association, the FBI interrogated her. "After they got over the initial embarrassment, they had the nerve to ask the big L question," Levinson recalled years later. "Are you a lesbian?" She expressed shock, lied through her teeth to join the bar, and lived a "discreet" life for years after that unsettling episode.[18]

This was a regime of the closet, where individuals lied not just to avoid punishment for violating a legal rule, but to avoid classification as a species of person who was, intrinsically, an outlaw or an enemy of the people. Rose Levinson and millions of other Americans in the twentieth century created lives that were saturated with deceit – negative lies denying illegal acts and a stigmatized identity, constant efforts at concealment of the soiled personhood, and lies affirming a counterfeit identity as a straight person. To

[18] James T. Sears, *Lonely Hunters: An Oral History of Lesbian and Gay Southern Life, 1948–1960* (New York: Basic Books, 1997), 24–26, 32.

this very day, most lesbians, gay men, and bisexuals in the United States are "in the closet" to family members, employers and coworkers, or neighbors – especially in states like Alabama, where continuing legal penalties interact with strong social prejudice to keep most gay people securely in the closet.

Nonetheless, after *Lawrence v. Texas,* the regime of the pervasive deceit has eased for even "discreet" gay people. Many lesbians, gay men, and bisexuals are "out of the closet," no longer lying to government officials, employers and coworkers, and family members and close friends. Those still more or less in the closet live less aggressive lives of deceit, many of them because coworkers, friends, and family members assume they are gay and they say nothing to negate (or affirm) that supposition. The easing of the regime of the closet is a consequence of the interaction between diminishing social prejudice and stereotyping and the rapid decline of state gay-discriminatory rules and practices. But just as the sexual closet has shrunk, the immigration closet has exploded in both size and intensity.

Just as "homosexuals" were, literally, outside the law for most of the twentieth century, so "illegal aliens" are, literally, outside the law today. As the government did in a bygone era for "homosexual" sodomy, so the government today seizes upon an act of nonconformity (entry into this country without following the proper procedures) and elevates it into a matter of public consequence, resulting in the criminalization of a large class of people. Immigrants who enter or remain in this country without the proper documentation are not only "outlaws," but also enemies of the republic, targeted for interrogation, possible detention, and exclusion by a dense array of complicated federal statutes.[19]

Thus, Congress has specified categories of immigrants who may not be admitted to the United States; unlawful entry and unlawful re-entry into the country are federal offenses.[20] Once here, immigrants must register with the federal government and carry proof of status on their person.[21] Federal law also authorizes states to deny

[19] *Arizona v. United States*, 132 S. Ct. 2492, 2498–2500 (2012). For laws expanding grounds of deportability and limiting the avenues of relief form deportation, see Illegal Immigration Reform and Immigrant Responsibility Act, Public Law 104–208, 110 Stat. 3009 (1996); Antiterrorism and Effective Death Penalty Act, Public Law 104–132, 110 Stat. 1214 (1996) (expanding grounds of deportability and limiting the avenues of relief from deportation); Immigration Reform and Control Act, Public Law 99–603, 100 Stat. 3359 (1986), adding, section 274a, 8 U.S.C section 1324a, to the Immigration and Nationality Act (INA), which now requires workers to furnish identify numbers and making working without documentation grounds for deportation. See also REAL ID Act, Public Law 109–13 (Div. B) sections 103, 105, 119 Stat. 231, 309–10 (2005); USA PATRIOT Act, Public Law 107–56, 115 Stat. 272 (2001).

[20] See 8 U.S.C. section 1182 (categories of immigrants excluded from entry into the United States), and sections 1325 and 1326 (making it illegal for excluded or inadmissible immigrants to enter or re-enter the United States).

[21] See id., sections 1301–1306 (registration requirements for immigrants). Failure to follow these rules is a federal misdemeanor. Id., sections 1304(e), 1306(a).

non-citizens a range of public benefits and imposes sanctions on employers who hire unauthorized workers.[22] Congress has specified which immigrants may be removed from the United States and the procedures for doing so. Persons who were inadmissible at the time of entry, have been convicted of certain crimes, or meet other criteria set by federal law are immediately removable.[23]

Under federal immigration law, a non-citizen may only be categorized as "admitted" when he or she has lawfully entered the country and an immigration officer has inspected her upon entry.[24] Thus, many immigrants are physically present in this country, but legally "inadmissible." The law recognizes the presence of these individuals only for the purpose of removing them from the country: while "inadmissible aliens" present in the United States cannot claim the rights provided to "lawfully present" individuals, the state may exercise authority over such individuals for the purposes of deporting them. There are six classes of non-citizens subject to deportation – including those who were inadmissible at the time of entry or adjustment of status, are unlawfully present, or have violated status – as well as non-citizens who have been convicted

[22] See id., sections 1622 (allowing states to deny unauthorized immigrants various public benefits), and 1324a (barring employers from employing unauthorized immigrants).

[23] See id., section 1227 (allowing removal of immigrants for a variety of reasons).

[24] See id., sections 1101(a)(13) and 1182 (a)(6)(A)(i), (a)(9)(B)(ii).

of certain criminal offenses.[25] Those who were not "admissible" when they entered the country cannot access avenues for relief from deportation,[26] and are subject instead to expedited removal proceedings.[27] While many individuals who are deported have multiple ties to the United States, and many reasons for returning, bars to re-entry for deported individuals prohibit these individuals from applying to re-enter through legal routes. As such, these bars may encourage individuals to attempt illegal entry through borders and to falsify their status once they have arrived.[28]

Because many inadmissible immigrants have come to the United States to be with their families and/or to raise their children here (often children who are themselves American citizens because they were born in the United States), they have a very powerful reason to deceive the authorities who would be inclined to detain or deport them. Like gay people during the anti-homosexual terror,

[25] See id., section 1227(a). The INA defines "conviction" for immigration purposes more broadly than in criminal cases. Ibid., sections 101(a)(48), 1101(a)(43).

[26] For example, to apply for adjustment of status, an immigrant must not have crossed the border without inspection, and must further be admissible or eligible to apply for a waiver of inadmissibility. Id., section 1255. Individuals who are aggravated felons also cannot seek voluntary departure, a procedure that allows individuals to avoid statutory prohibitions against returning after a judge issues a final order of removal. Id., section 1229(c).

[27] See id., section 1225(b)(1)(A)(I).

[28] See iid., section 1182(a)(9)(A).

inadmissible immigrants today may be loathe to tell the truth about their outlaw status; they and their families, neighbors, and employers will respond to a constant barrage of questions with lies, deceit, and misdirection. Inadmissible immigrants lie about their status and suffer lives of deceit – for the same reasons lesbian and gay people did, namely, to avoid legal punishment, possible incarceration, and social stigma. The lies, concealment, and evasion create what I should call an *immigration closet* not unlike that occupied by gay people through most of the twentieth century.[29]

Although immigration policy is largely set at the national level, state and local measures seeking to identify and punish inadmissible immigrants have created many more situations where the immigrant is subject to interrogation and, therefore, is inclined to lie in order to conceal her or his illegal status. Unlike military policy, our evolving immigration policy is one where state and local governments participate in the normative conversation, which has the effect of adding another layer of interrogation,

[29] On the ways that immigration law and enforcement create an class of fearful immigrants, whose lives are dominated by evasions, see Cecilia Menjivar and Leisy Abrego, *Legal Violence in the Lives of Immigrants: How Immigration Enforcement Affects Families, Schools, and Workplaces* (New York: Center for American Progress, December 2012); Keith Cunningham-Parmeter, "Fear of Discovery: Immigrant Workers and the Fifth Amendment," *Cornell International Law Journal* 41 (2008): 27; Antonio Vargas, "Outlaw," *New York Times*, June 26, 2011, MM22.

investigation, punishment, and exclusion that reinforces the immigration closet for many non-citizens.[30]

Federal legislation in the last twenty years has produced novel venues for deceit through new and more complicated discriminations against undocumented immigrants. Although the federal government has never recognized a right of undocumented immigrants to receive assistance of the major federal social and economic safety net programs (like food stamps), prior to 1996, agencies could provide benefits to non-citizens determined to be "permanently residing in the United States under color of the law," or PRUCOL.[31] The Personal Responsibility and Work Opportunity Reconciliation Act of 1996 (PRWORA) strongly restricted non-citizen eligibility for public benefits. The Act created a category of "not qualified" individuals, which

[30] *Arizona v. United States*, 132 S. Ct. 2492 (2012) (upholding part of the Arizona effort to add state resources to federal detection and removal of inadmissible immigrants); Douglas S. Massey, *How Arizona Became Ground Zero in the War on Immigrants*, in Carissa Byrne Hessick and Gabriel J. Chin, eds., *Strange Neighbors: The Role of the States in Immigration Enforcement and Policy* (New York: New York University Press, 2014), 40; Cristina M. Rodriguez, "Negotiating Conflict Through Federalism: Institutional and Popular Perspectives," *Yale Law Journal* 123 (2014): 2094.

[31] While never codified into law, the PRUCOL category generally applied to situations in which the Department of Homeland Security (DHS) recognized the presence of noncitizens and had made no efforts to deport these individuals. 42 U.S.C. section 1382c(a)(1)(B)(i) (2000); Social Security Administration, 20 C.F.R. sections 416.200, 416.202 (1992) (adopting the PRUCOL category for supplemental security income eligibility).

includes "lawfully present" as well as undocumented individuals, whom it prohibits from enrolling in most federal programs.[32] The law also requires state or local agencies to verify immigration and citizenship status of any applicants to these programs. In this manner, the nation's immigration laws not only exclude immigrants from protections afforded to citizens, but they also create a marginalized identity for immigrants, and impose on state and local officials obligations of interrogating this suspect group – thereby guaranteeing more occasions for undocumented immigrants to misrepresent their status.

Like the gay closet, the immigration closet is highly dynamic. Today, inadmissible immigrants are consigned to constant deceit because of their illegal identities – but the same people enter a whole new world during the nation's episodes of amnesty, when paths toward citizenship or legal residence are opened for them.[33]

[32] See Personal Responsibility and Work Opportunity Reconciliation Act of 1996, section 401, Public Law No. 104–193, 110 Stat. 2105 (1996) (codified at 8 U.S.C. section 1611).

[33] The Immigration Reform and Control Act of 1986 (IRCA) provided amnesty for undocumented immigrants who arrived before January 1, 1982 and had remained in the United States. Public Law No. 99–603, sections 201–04, 100 Stat. 3359, 3394–3411 (codified in scattered sections of 8 U.S.C.). Under IRCA, some 1.1 million people gained legal status through the Seasonal Agricultural Workers (SAWs) program, and another 1.6 million came within the more general legalization program. See Nancy Rytina, Office of Policy and Planning Statistics Division U.S. Immigration and Naturalization Service, IRCA Legalization Effects: Lawful Permanent Residence and Naturalization through

Subcultures and Social Networks of Deceit. The law produces a lot of deceitful behavior by persons seeking to evade legal requirements and, especially, persons who are outlaws (literally, outside the law). Gay people in the twentieth century and inadmissible immigrants today are examples where there were strong incentives for persons to lie about traits that the state (not to mention society) has considered critical to their identities and their outsider status in our polity. Especially where the state has created outlaw groups, the chain of lies extends further than misleading statements by members of the legally targeted group. Indeed, the web may quickly become social, as networks of deceit take shape.

The Prohibition era (1920–1933), when the manufacture, sale, and consumption of alcohol were constitutionally prohibited, was a great social experiment that sought to change the personal (drinking) habits of the American people. On the whole, the American people did not go along with this social experiment.[34] Because the demand for liquor

2001 (Washington, DC: GAO, 2002). For other examples, see Nicaraguan Adjustment and Central American Relief Act, Public Law No. 105–100, section 201–204, 111 Stat. 2160, 2193–2201 (1997) (amnesty to Nicaraguan and Cuban immigrants); Haitian Refugee Immigration Fairness Act of 1998, Public Law No. 105–277, sections 901–04, 112 Stat. 2681, 2681–538 to 2681–542 (amnesty to Haitian asylum-seekers).

[34] On Prohibition and its complicated administration, see Thomas R. Pegram, *Battling Demon Rum: The Struggles for a Dry America, 1800–1933* (New York: Ivan R. Dee, 1998); Robert Post, "Federalism, Positive Law, and the Emergence of the American

remained high and the enforcement of Prohibition was persistently low, an illegal industry flourished until the Twenty-First Amendment revoked Prohibition. To manufacture and sell a commodity that was illegal, suppliers had to lie a great deal – and complicit in their deceit was the entire supply chain, from the warehouse to the speakeasie to the customer. They were a community of deceit.[35]

Ironically, the end of Prohibition's disastrous experiment coincided with the early stages of the unfortunate regulatory experiment of the anti-homosexual terror. Lesbian and gay bars immediately became a focal point for liquor regulation that the Twenty-First Amendment reserved for state and local governments. State liquor laws generally barred licenses to establishments that were "disorderly"; bars attracting a lesbian or gay clientele were considered *per se* disorderly and were sometimes singled out by state law.[36]

State licensing rules like this one were much more vigorously enforced than Prohibition had been (ironically), and so bar owners joined with patrons to deceive the state about the nature of the clientele and the clandestine activities that went on in those establishments after hours. In the middle part of the twentieth century, bars were the center

Administrative State: Prohibition in the Taft Court Era," *William and Mary Law Review* 48 (2006): 1–55.

35 Daniel Okrent, *Last Call: The Rise and Fall of Prohibition* (New York: Scribner, 2011), 115–223; Ken Burns, A Nation of Hypocrites, Episode 3 of Prohibition (Public Broadcasting System, October 11, 2011) (documentary based upon Okrent, *Last Call*).

36 Eskridge, *Gaylaw* at 45–47, 78–80.

of the lesbian and gay subculture and were saturated with deceit. Although lesbians and gay men could let their hair down in such places, they also realized they needed to be alert to the possibility that their flirting and advances were made toward undercover cops. Fearing the loss of their licenses, the bartenders and owners made everyone alert to the possibility that state liquor agents were secretly observing their behavior. This was a triple web of deceit: in the one place where they could socialize, lesbian and gay patrons had to be careful about how much they revealed about their desires, and bar owners assisted them and sometimes required this masquerade – all because public officials (police and liquor agents) might be masquerading as gay customers. That thousands of gay and lesbian bars lost their licenses in the twentieth century is testament to the power of this network of deceit that accompanied the end of Prohibition and the emergence of visible gay subcultures.[37]

Under current law, the best example of a social network saturated with government-motivated obfuscation, misdirection, and deceit is the larger community of family, neighbors, and employers of inadmissible immigrants. The Immigration Reform and Control Act of 1986 (IRCA) makes

[37] On the monitoring of gay bars and its production of deceit by all concerned, see Nan Alamilla Boyd, *Wide Open Town: A History of Queer San Francisco to 1965* (Berkeley, CA: University of California Press, 2003), 108–147; George Chauncey, *Gay New York: Gender, Urban Culture, and the Making of the Gay Male World, 1890–1940* (New York: Basic Books, 1994).

unlawful the employment of "unauthorized aliens" and imposes upon employers requirements to document the status of persons they hire, constantly monitor their workforces, and report suspicious persons.[38]

Instead of eradicating undocumented labor, the law has led many to misrepresent their identity through falsified social security numbers, an action which can make these individuals subject to deportation as "aggravated felons," or to enter into under-the-table agreements with employers, thereby forcing undocumented individuals into a shadowy world of quasi-law or no legal protections whatsoever. In this manner, the inadmissible immigrant often becomes complicit with his or her employer in a veritable conspiracy of deceit: both want to keep the immigration authorities in the dark as to the immigrant's true status, an agenda that requires the employer and its officials to blinder themselves to the extent they can.[39]

Consider another example of the web of deceit phenomenon. Recall that PRWORA defined certain classes of immigrants, including undocumented immigrants, as *per se*

[38] Immigration Reform and Control Act, Public Law 99–603, 100 Stat. 3359 (1986), adding 8 U.S.C.A. section 1324.

[39] On webs of deceit that include employers and supervisors as well as undocumented immigrants, see Abel Valenzuela Jr. et al., "On the Corner: Day Labor in the United States" (Los Angeles: UCLA, January 2006); Steven Greenhouse, "Among Janitors, Labor Violations Go with the Job," *New York Times*, July 13, 2005; Eduardo Porter, "Here Illegally, Working Hard," *New York Times*, June 19, 2006.

unqualified to receive "federal public benefits."[40] While the PRWORA definition bars "ineligible" immigrants from accessing "retirement, welfare, health, disability, public or assisted housing, postsecondary education, food assistance, unemployment benefit, or any other similar benefit," it does not specify which federally funded initiatives are covered by the term, leaving each federal benefit-granting agency to classify its programs. In 1998, the Department of Health and Human Services (HHS) published a notice articulating thirty-one programs (including Medicaid, Medicare, and Temporary Assistance for Needy Families) the agency deemed "federal public [benefit] programs."[41] Yet other agencies have deemed certain state benefit programs that receive federal grants to provide "food assistance" to be outside of this definition. For example, the U.S. Department of Agriculture provides states with grants for Supplemental Nutrition for Women and Infant Children (WIC), without requiring states to inquire into a woman's immigration status.

The provision of WIC regardless of immigration status manifests a larger theme in government welfare policy: the law tends to make a concession to the reality of undocumented

[40] 8 U.S.C. section 1611; see id., section 1611(c)(1) (broad definition of "federal public benefit" to include federal grants and loans, licenses, and personal or family safety net benefits).

[41] Department of Health and Human Services, Personal Responsibility and Work Opportunity Reconciliation Act of 1996, Interpretation of "Federal Public Benefit," Federal Register 63 (August 4, 1998), 41658–61.

immigration when children's lives are at stake. Recognizing the right of all children to primary education, regardless of immigration status, federal law mandates provision of school breakfast and lunch to all children whose families qualify based on income alone.[42] Head Start and Early Head Start are also not considered "federal public benefits," and thus any child eligible for these programs may enroll, whether classified as qualified or not qualified.[43] Federal law also allows states to opt to provide certain other benefit programs, including emergency medical assistance and WIC, without requiring the state agencies to record immigration status.[44] All states have extended WIC to undocumented mothers, who can use the program to provide food for their children, whether citizens or immigrants. Moreover, while some agencies must report the presence of any "unlawful" immigrants when it becomes aware of their presence, the Department of Agriculture is not one of the agencies regulated under this provision of PRWORA.[45] Therefore this agency does not have

[42] 8 U.S.C. section 1615.

[43] Department of Health and Human Services, Administration on Children, Youth and Families, CCDF-ACF-PI-2008-01, http://www.acf.hhs.gov/programs/occ/resource/pi-2008-01.

[44] 8 U.S.C. section 1615.

[45] Under PRWORA section 404, the States in administering their TANF block grants, the Social Security Administration in administering SSI programs, the Department of Housing and Urban Development, and public housing agencies are supposed to report noncitizens they know to be unlawfully in the United States to the immigration authorities four times a year. Federal Register 65 (September 28, 2000), 58301–03.

to report individuals whom it suspects have violated immigration law to federal enforcement agents.

Other programs which fall under the category of "federal public benefits" are not accessible to parents who are "not qualified," but may be accessible to their children. While HHS has qualified Child Care and Development Block Grant (CCDBG) and Temporary Assistance for Needy Families (TANF) assistance as "federal public benefits," states may only consider a child's immigration status, and not the status of his or her parents, when determining whether the child is eligible for subsidies that these federal grants provide.[46] In issuing guidance on the use of Social Security Number (SSNs) of applicant parents, HHS expressed an intention to provide for all eligible children, regardless of their parents' status, and recognized that state reporting requirements could deter immigrant parents from applying. HHS explicitly specified requiring parents to furnish a SSN violated the Privacy Act, and, potentially, Title VI of the Civil Rights Act. The guidance went on to state:

> While 45 CFR 98.71(a)(13) requires States to report the Social Security Number of the family head, it is not the intention of the regulation for States to make disclosure of a Social Security Number a requirement and condition of eligibility for child care.... States must make it clear to CCDF [Child Care Development Fund] applicants that the provision of a Social Security Number is voluntary and that

[46] Department of Health and Human Services, ACYF-PI-CC-98-0.

> benefits will not be denied or withheld for the failure to furnish a Social Security Number. States also must clearly inform applicants about how the Social Security Number will be used.[47]

These provisions demonstrate the extent to which the federal government is aware of the existence of undocumented families, some of whom have children who are U.S. citizens. An undocumented parent may enroll a child without her own valid SSN, but if she attempts to access other public benefits for herself or her household, a federal agency must report her immigration violations. The law thus operates upon a fiction of providing for the well-being of citizen children while ignoring the reality of the social network in which these children live. The provision of WIC, primary education, and emergency medical services regardless of immigration status further suggests that the state cannot force all undocumented immigrants into the immigration closet without confronting the implications for human rights when it comes to the most vulnerable populations. While the law mandates that parents remain in the closet, it creates a space at the edge of the margins for their children. Yet immigrant parents and non-citizen children remain subject to deportation should a reporting agency become aware of their status, and thus even children may be pressured into the deceit of a closeted identity.

[47] Department of Health and Human Services, Administration on Children, Youth and Families, ACYF-PI-CC-00-04, http://www.acf.hhs.gov/programs/occ/resource/pi-cc-00-04.

Deceit as a Goal of Public Policy

Typically, law and its enforcement produce deceit as a consequence of the gap between what the law demands of us and how we are willing to conduct our lives; the larger the gap, the more deceit, whose production is also fueled by the confidence that deceitful evasion of the law will be successful. But sometimes deceit is the very object of law, not an impediment to its efficacy. Deceit might be a mechanism of public policy, for a number of reasons. Most obviously, deceit by law enforcement officials might be an instrument to ferret out or prove violations of law or (better yet) plans to violate the law. What I want to emphasize, however, is that deceit is also a mechanism for mediating competing values. Our nation is highly diverse, not only in terms of group identities but also in terms of values. Our diversity is not only deep and variegated, which produces group conflict and legal compromises, but is also evolving, which produces legal transitions. Lies, misrepresentations, and misdirections – three faces of deceit – can be means by which a diverse polity manages its divisions and its transitions. As before, the nation's fraught relationship with sexual minorities provides classic illustrations of this idea – and current government programs and immigration policies provide modern illustrations now that the anti-homosexual terror has ended in most jurisdictions.

Gays in the Military: "Don't Ask, Don't Tell." "Don't Ask, Don't Tell" is perhaps the most famous national policy that embraced deceit and made lying (or at the very least deliberate concealment) a public good. Based upon social antipathy to sexual variation and especially homosexuality, the traditional Department of Defense policy had been to exclude or expel "homosexuals," based upon their presumed violation of the UCMJ sodomy bar. By 1993, a lot of the social hatred had abated; and lesbian, gay, and bisexual (LGB) Americans had become a social group to be reckoned with. Indeed, LGB votes and money helped elect Governor William Clinton to be president in 1992. As payback, President Clinton in January 1993 proposed to lift the military exclusion for lesbians, gay men, and bisexuals.[48]

The president misjudged the deep hysteria that integration of gay men, in particular, into the homosocial armed forces evoked in many segments of society – not least among the young men who fantasized (in a bad way) about sharing shower facilities with gay or bisexual colleagues. Reflecting these fears, the Joint Chiefs of Staff and their allies in Congress pushed back, hard. Congressional hearings provided a forum for distinguished military commanders to reject service by openly gay or lesbian personnel. The main argument was that open homosexuality disrupted morale and unit cohesion. In a dramatic moment, Colonel Fred Peck testified that "if someone declares their homosexuality that * * * is a statement that defines a behavior." He rejected

[48] See David F. Burrelli and Jody Feder, *Homosexuals in the U.S. Military: Current Issues* (Washington, DC: Congressional Research Service, 2009).

the idea that the exclusion represented discrimination because of status, like the exclusion of African-Americans earlier in our history. Instead, he offered "another analogy," that "it would be much akin to someone in the military saying I am a racist," which would invite distrust and animosity within most units.[49] By the way, Colonel Peck was making a brilliant point about deceit as a policy goal: many soldiers are in fact racist as well as sexist, but the institutional needs of the armed forces force them to conceal their bigotry and frequently to lie about what they believe. Government programs routinely force participants into both passive and active deceit, usually with the goal of lowering the stakes of public discourse (i.e., preventing loose cannons from stirring the pot of social divisions).

The gays in the military hearings revealed a deep division within the country as well as the armed forces; LGB persons were a social group relevant to American politics, after decades of persecution, but were still not tolerated by many Americans and by most male soldiers. As a compromise, Senator Sam Nunn, Chair of the Armed Services Committee, proposed a policy of "Don't Ask, Don't Tell": consistent with the critics' claims, anti-homosexual witch hunts should stop (Don't Ask); consistent with objections raised by military officials, LGB soldiers should remain in

[49] For the testimony of Colonel Fred Peck, see Policy Concerning Homosexuality in the Armed Forces: Hearings Before the Senate Committee on the Armed Services, 103d Congress, First Session (1993), 599–602.

the closet and say nothing about their sexual orientation (Don't Tell). In July 1993, President Clinton signed onto the compromise, but with a characteristic twist. Military officials would ask *no questions* about the sexual orientation of military personnel; in turn, "homosexual" personnel should say nothing about their orientation or private activities; finally, if they *did* confess that they were "homosexuals," they would be given an opportunity to recant and rebut the presumption that they behaved like "homosexuals."[50] The statute passed by Congress in 1993 echoed the old exclusionary policy,[51] but the Defense Department immediately announced an enforcement regime along the lines laid out by the president.[52]

Although the "Don't Ask, Don't Tell" statute stopped short of openly requiring LGB military personnel to lie, the

50 See Burrelli and Feder, *Homosexuals in the U.S. Military* at 1 (quoting Senator Nunn and President Clinton, both of whom advocated "Don't Ask, Don't Tell" as a "compromise"); see also Assessment of the Plan to Life the Ban on Homosexuals in the Military: Hearings Before the Military Forces and Personnel Subcommittee of the House Committee on Armed Services, 103d Congress, First Session (July 22, 1993), 322.

51 Public Law 103–160, section 571(a)(1), 107 Stat. 1670 (1993), codified at 10 U.S.C. section 654. For an examination of the ways the 1993 "Don't Ask, Don't Tell" law was more focused on homosexual status than the previous policy was, see Janet Halley, *Don't: A Reader's Guide to the Military's Anti-Gay Policy* (Durham, NC: Duke University Press, 1999), 1–14.

52 Memorandum from Secretary Les Aspin to the Secretaries of the Military Departments et al. (December 21, 1993), implemented by amended Directives 1332.14 (separations of enlisted personnel), 1332.30 (separations of officers), and 1304.26 (enlistment).

operation of the policy made clear that deceit was its linchpin. Thus, while straight personnel could be expected to talk all they wanted about their romantic liaisons and sexual feelings, lesbian and gay personnel were required to keep the closet door tightly sealed; if the closet door cracked open in any way, they were supposed to explain it away. The day-to-day interaction among military personnel operated under a presumption of heterosexuality that required the closeted gay person not only to remain discreet about her or his own homosexuality, but also to affirmatively say or suggest their shared straightness. "Why did you not stay and watch the hot strippers last Saturday? Did you spend your weekend with another girl?" Whatever the gay soldier says in response to those quite ordinary questions will be an affirmative lie. LGB soldiers had little choice but to lie – and lie they did under the "Don't Ask, Don't Tell" regime. They lied to their colleagues, they lied to their doctors, they lied to the chaplains, they lied to their friends off base. When they didn't lie, they risked investigation or even expulsion.[53]

Supporters justified the deceit-based policy of "Don't Ask, Don't Tell" largely along cost-benefit lines. A policy seriously seeking to purge the armed forces of all LGB

[53] Tobias Barrington Wolff, "Political Representation and Accountability Under Don't Ask, Don't Tell," *Iowa Law Review* 89 (2004): 1633–1716; Tobias Barrington Wolff, "Compelled Affirmations, Free Speech, and the U.S. Military's Don't Ask, Don't Tell Policy," *Brooklyn Law Review* 63 (1997): 1141–1211, especially 1147–1166 (quoting from interviews with almost two dozen gay and lesbian veterans).

persons would have been extraordinarily expensive and disruptive; the military's mission of protecting the country and occasionally invading other countries would have been sidetracked by frequent accusations and ongoing investigations. On the other hand, a policy of open integration would have alarmed most of the young men (apparently not the young women) serving in the armed forces; always a challenge, recruitment for the all-volunteer armed forces would have been threatened by any perception that the sex-segregated armed forces were havens for "homosexuals." For a country that was still predominantly anti-gay and whose people still harbored stereotypes of gay people as predatory and selfish, the presence of openly gay men might have discredited the sex-segregated armed forces as "too gay" to be a safe place for a straight boy.

"Don't Ask, Don't Tell" was also responsive to the transitional nature of the issue. In 1963, Congress would have been shocked to learn that there were a lot of "homosexuals" in the military. In 1993, few were shocked by that, but most of the top brass remained uncomfortable if the public face of the armed forces were "too gay." The deal reached (the compromise) was that gays could serve without (much) hassle, so long as they remained discreet. This is what I have called "equality practice," whereby an excluded minority is allowed into important public institutions, but on an unequal basis.[54]

[54] William N. Eskridge Jr., *Equality Practice: Civil Unions and the Future of Gay Rights* (New York: Routledge, 2002).

As it turned out, "Don't Ask, Don't Tell" was a dynamic policy – and equality practice created conditions for taking the next step. During the Bush-Cheney Administration (2001–2009), discharges of gay and lesbian soldiers dramatically declined, as a new generation of military personnel was comfortable serving with colleagues they knew (or strongly suspected) were lesbian, gay, or bisexual. When Congress adopted a statute creating a process for repealing "Don't Ask, Don't Tell" in December 2010, it did so with bipartisan majorities and with the blessing of the policy's same-sex parents, namely, former president Clinton and former senator Nunn.[55]

Immigration: Musical Chairs with Tax Identification Numbers. There is a rough parallel to Congress's embrace of deceit in "Don't Ask, Don't Tell" in the tax regulations that developed in response to changes to the legal regime surrounding immigrant labor. IRCA mandated employers to record immigration status information for all employees on INS Form I-9s, and gave the immigration authorities power to review these documents. The Act also established civil and criminal penalties for employers who violated substantive prohibitions against hiring undocumented immigrants or who failed

[55] "Ex-Senator Reverses Opposition to Gays in the Military," *Associated Press*, December 10, 2010 (Senator Nunn's reversal on Don't Ask, Don't Tell); Meena Hartenstein, "Bill Clinton Regrets 'Don't Ask, Don't Tell' Policy, Says It Was Meant to Protect Gay Soldiers," *Daily News*, September 21, 2010 (President Clinton's reversal).

to comply with procedural recording requirements. Under the recording requirements, an employee is supposed to provide his or her SSN to establish proof of identity and eligibility to work – but of course undocumented immigrants cannot obtain a SSN.[56] In response to IRCA's identification requirements, some employers and undocumented immigrants have evaded compliance with the statute by furnishing fraudulent SSNs, while others have avoided the system completely through unreported wages.[57]

This practice reflects the evasive lies about facts and identities that pervade American law. But there is another practice that is closer to the deceit-celebrating "Don't Ask, Don't Tell" statute, through which misrepresentations and willful omissions about identity have become part of official policies. Although the Social Security Administration will not grant SSNs to undocumented immigrants living in the United States, the tax code requires that all individuals, regardless of immigration status, file income taxes.[58] The Internal Revenue Service (IRS) has created a procedural loophole, namely, the Individual Taxpayer Identifying Number (ITIN), through which to collect taxes from undocumented individuals without addressing the fact that

[56] Public Law 99–603, 100 Stat. 3359, enacting 8 U.S.C section 1324a, INA section 274A; 20 C.F.R. section 422.104(a)(2) (2005).

[57] Francine J. Lipman, "The Taxation of Undocumented Immigrants: Separate, Unequal, and Without Representation," *Harvard Latino Law Review* 9 (2006): 1–23.

[58] IRC sections 7701(a)(30), 7701(b).

these individuals use falsified SSNs to obtain work, despite formal ineligibility.[59] An ITIN does not authorize work in the United States, and cannot be used for employment tax or social security purposes.[60] Similarly, undocumented individuals cannot use the ITIN to access government benefits, nor does it provide them any formal status for immigration purposes.

The employment requirements of IRCA and the provisions of the tax code interact to create a situation in which undocumented immigrants may provide employers with legitimate ITINs for tax purposes but false SSNs for employment purposes. Section 6103 of the Internal Revenue Code prohibits the IRS from disclosing information it obtains through tax returns to other government agencies. In effect, these rules create a regulatory regime where undocumented immigrants who do not have legal work authorization are nonetheless working in this country and are paying federal income tax. Though able to comply with the tax code through the mechanisms provided in ITIN regulations, undocumented immigrants who use false or borrowed SSNs are in violation of immigration law. They remain at the mercy of ICE's decisions of when to prosecute immigration status and may not have access to remedies provided to

[59] Id., section 6109(a); 26 C.F.R section 301.6109-1(d)(3) (defining the ITIN as appropriate for use by non-citizens, and distinguishing it from a SSN); ibid., section 301.6109-1(g) (designating ITIN as distinct identification numbers for the purposes of filing with the IRS).

[60] IRS News Release IR-2003–49, 2003 I.R.B. LEXIS 141, ITIN Applicants Must Use New Form Starting April 15 (April 10, 2003).

documented workers under various federal labor statutes.[61] Moreover, without legitimate SSNs, undocumented immigrants are also barred from receiving almost all government benefits, and may not access those that are legally available for fear of deportation.

The fact that a government agency has a policy of permitting individuals to use ITINs to file taxes, while explicitly promising that it will not turn over their identities to the agency responsible for immigration enforcement, suggests both awareness of and complicity in federal policies that rely upon individuals misrepresenting themselves. Memoranda published by labor and immigration officials strengthen this impression. In November 1998, the Immigration and Naturalization Service and the Department of Labor executed a revised Memorandum of Understanding that shifted authority for policing immigration status away from the

[61] *Hoffman Plastic Compounds, Inc. v. NLRB*, 535 U.S. 137 (2002) (holding that an undocumented worker who had provided false documents to an employer and who was later fired in retaliation for union organizing, was not eligible for back pay under the National Labor Relations Act). Some employers may use *Hoffman* to argue that FLSA does not give undocumented workers a right to sue for unpaid wages for work actually performed. Other remedies that the decision may affect include FLSA remedies for anti-retaliation. However, the Department of Labor has concluded that *Hoffman Plastic* did not affect the agency's authority to enforce the statute with regards to provisions for "work actually performed." Department of Labor, Fact Sheet #48, Application of U.S. Labor Laws to Immigrant Workers: Effect of Hoffman Plastic decision on laws enforced by the Wage and Hour Division (August 19, 2002) (revised July 2008).

labor enforcement agency.[62] The Memorandum of Understanding asserted an intention on the part of both agencies to encourage enforcement of wage and hour laws without regard to immigration status. This shift further encourages misrepresentation of legal status in the workplace, while failing to address the reality that undocumented laborers remained "unlawfully" present, and in violation of IRCA, and continually subject to deportation at the discretion of the nation's immigration authorities.

Like "Don't Ask, Don't Tell," the web of deceit woven by these federal policies reflects a deep normative conflict within our polity. On the one hand, most Americans support the policy of limited immigration; many citizens harbor an intense fear that officially tolerating or (arguably) supporting undocumented immigrants will open our borders like Pandora's box. On the other hand, most Americans support a policy of compassion for people who are part of their communities, even if they did not gain admission legally and especially if they have children and extended families here. Many of *those* citizens are themselves related or feel themselves closely tied to these immigrants. Many other Americans, including businesses, profit from the presence of so many undocumented immigrants. From that social, economic, and political conflict of interests has emerged the immigration closet – a policy grounded upon deceit whose

62 See Nat'l Immigration Law Ctr., INS and Department of Labor Sign New Memorandum of Understanding on Workplace Inspections, Immigrants Rights Update, December 21, 1998, at 9.

dynamic evolution has had little connection to the rules written into the nation's immigration code.

Prison Rape. "Don't Ask, Don't Tell" and ITINs for undocumented immigrants not only tolerate deceit but raise deceit to the level of national policy. A common feature of these two regulatory schemes is that they accommodate conflicting policy commitments through a regime that explicitly tolerates and implicitly encourages deceit on the part of both institutions and individuals. A further, and particularly sad, example of this phenomenon involves an important norm and a terrible practical reality: As a nation, we strongly condemn rape and other forms of sexual assault, in prison populations as well as elsewhere – but the political community is loath to spend a lot of taxpayer money to protect prisoners against rape and other unspeakable abuses.

Illustrating this phenomenon is the Prison Rape Elimination Act of 2003 (PREA),[63] enacted without a single dissenting vote in Congress. In the statutory findings, legislators estimated that more than ten percent of the prison population is raped each year and endorsed the view that inmates need to be protected against this harm. PREA directed the Attorney General to publish rules adopting "national standards for the detection, prevention, reduction, and punishment of prison rape * * * based upon the independent judgment of the Attorney

[63] Prison Rape Elimination Act, Public Law 108–79, 117 Stat. 972 (2003), codified at 42 U.S.C. section 15601 et seq.

General, after giving due consideration to the recommended national standards provided by the Commission * * * and being informed by such data, opinions, and proposals that the Attorney General determines to be appropriate to consider."[64] Importantly, however, the standards may not "impose substantial additional costs compared to the costs presently expended by Federal, State, and local prison authorities."[65]

The face of the statute illustrates my point that government sometimes elevates deceit to the level of a public policy goal: as a practical matter, you usually cannot eliminate or even reduce the incidence of rape in prisons without investing more resources. This point is confirmed by the final PREA rule issued (after notice-and-comment rulemaking) by Attorney General Eric Holder in 2012.[66]

Consistent with the Department's implementation, PREA's statutory standards are binding on the Federal Bureau of Prisons, but are voluntary for state and local facilities. A state whose governor does not certify full compliance with the standards is subject to the loss of five percent of any DOJ grant funds that it would otherwise receive for prison purposes, unless the governor submits an assurance that such five percent will be used only to

[64] PREA section 8(a)(1)–(2), codified at 42 U.S.C. section 15607(a)(1)–(2).

[65] Ibid., section 8(a)(3), codified at 42 U.S.C. section 15607(a)(3).

[66] Department of Justice, National Standards to Prevent, Detect, and Respond to Prison Rape (May 16, 2012), codified at 28 C.F.R. Part 115.

achieve and certify full compliance with the standards in future years.[67]

As elaborated in the Department of Justice's rule, the PREA standards are process-oriented rather than result- or performance-oriented. They require facilities to (1) designate a point person responsible for coordinating protective measures, (2) develop a plan to upgrade staffing and video monitoring to prevent and detect rape, (3) create special protections for juvenile inmates, (4) ban cross-gender searches, (5) implement special training protocols for staff, (6) establish a process for coordinating the actions of first responders, medical persons, and investigators involved in any given incident of prison rape, (7) implement policies to protect against any retaliation for reporting or cooperating in the investigation of prison rapes, (8) implement no-tolerance policies for inmates who commit rape and officials who approve such behaviors, and (9) provide lesbian, gay, bisexual, transgender, and intersex inmates as well as inmates with disabilities with protections against rape and sexual abuse because of their status.

Reflecting the statute itself, the Department of Justice produced an implementation plan saturated with delusion. Notwithstanding dozens of pages of intricate cost-benefit analysis (including a labored valuation for the cost of rape

[67] PREA section 8(b), codified at 42 U.S.C. section 15607(b) (mandatory standards for federal prisons); ibid., section 8(e)(2)(A)-(B), codified at 42 U.S.C. section 15607(e)(2)(A)–(B) (voluntary standards for state prisons).

to victims) and procedural suggestions, the Department's lengthy document provides no empirical basis to believe that a single prison rape will be prevented, even if state as well as federal prisons actually adopt and enforce the guidelines. The rulemaking confirms that PREA is counterfeit policymaking, a substantially symbolic statute that pretends to tackle a serious problem. Presumably, most state as well as federal prison officials will certify that they are implementing the Department's process-based rules and that those rules are reducing prison rape – which will probably not be true (though it may be hard to falsify as well).

Like "Don't Ask, Don't Tell" and IRCA, PREA illustrates how deceit can be deployed to accommodate competing normative concerns. "Don't Ask, Don't Tell" sought to accommodate the values of equality with the military's perceived need to distance its sex-segregated units from homosexuality. IRCA sought to accommodate the value of border security with the practical needs of federal tax collectors. In the case of PREA, deceit allows public officials to reaffirm a national norm that rape is wrong, but they can reaffirm that norm without spending real money to protect a population that is politically marginal (not only disenfranchised but also, like "homosexuals" for most of the last century, scapegoated).

The Regulatory Costs of Deceit

American public policy pervasively produces deceitful behaviors, and sometimes deceit *is* the national policy.

As we have seen, deceit resulting from government policies imposes enormous costs as well as potential benefits upon the body politic. Sound public policy requires that government consider the costs of deceit and suggests that a policy's benefits be carefully evaluated in light of those costs. Indeed, a calculus of deceit yields some interesting normative hypotheses for American public law.

Evasive Deceit and the Harm Principle. Any public policy imposing duties on people and companies must consider how likely they are to deceive the government in order to evade enforcement, as well as how hard it is for the government (or private citizens) to detect and punish deceitful evasions. For an obvious example, American sodomy laws applied to private activities between consenting adults – but were almost never enforced under those circumstances, in large part because the persons involved would conceal their activities from the state and, even if detected, could often evade punishment by lying about what they were doing. In contrast, most American sodomy prosecutions were against men who allegedly forced anal sex onto nonconsenting women, men, or children or against men having sex in quasi-public places (park bushes, automobiles, bathroom stalls, porn shops) – instances where detection was more likely and where evasive deceit by the defendant was more likely to be refuted by testimony from the victim (if not consensual) or from shocked bystanders.

This simple point has vast consequences for the law. There are many human activities that disgust the body politic and that popular majorities would criminalize – but that are too expensive to enforce because of evasive deceit. This is the reason why general sodomy laws were almost never applied to private activities between consenting adults, even in the heyday of the anti-homosexual terror. Americans were certainly disgusted with "homosexual sodomy," and it did not matter where it was performed or between what parties, but law enforcement rarely prosecuted such persons. When the New York (1951) and Illinois (1961) Legislatures focused on the issue after World War II, they took consensual sodomy out of the list of criminal felonies – not because "homosexuality" was morally acceptable, but because of evasive lies by suspected "sodomites" *and* by rogue police officers. Legislatures followed this path between 1961 and 1975, when most states decriminalized consensual sodomy for this reason, usually with the support of lawyers, judges, prosecutors, and law enforcement leaders. Although it took another quarter century for the last such laws to fall, they were a casualty of evasive deceit.

The point of the sodomy reform story can be generalized. The regulatory costs of evasive deceit are an important foundation for the libertarian presumption in American public law, including constitutional law. The presumption favoring liberty says that the law ought to leave adults alone to satisfy their desires, so long as their activities do not tangibly harm other people. The stronger the human desire to do something, the more likely it is that a person will do it, notwithstanding the law, and will lie to the authorities. If no one else has been harmed, the authorities will have a much harder time detecting and proving the deceit. To take another example, once contraceptives became commercially available, the vast state and federal efforts to regulate their private use were virtually dead letters, from the very beginning.[68] This regulatory fact fueled administrative nullification, legislative repeal, and ultimately judicial invalidation of contraceptive-use laws. By the time the Supreme Court swept them all away, in its poorly reasoned decision in *Griswold v. Connecticut* (1965), they were already a dead letter.[69]

Both sodomy and contraception reveal another consequence once one considers the regulatory costs of evasive lies – the public-private distinction. American law is much better able to regulate "public" activities (where there is a third-party audience) than "private" ones (no audience or a small, intimate one). By the time the Court handed down *Griswold*, the state (Connecticut) had long ago abandoned enforcement of the anti-contraception law to "private" sexual activities within the home, but it was also the case that

[68] Andrea Tone, *Devices and Desires: A History of Contraceptives in America* (New York: Hill and Wang, 2002); Andrea Tone, "Black Market Birth Control: Contraceptive Entrepreneurship and Criminality in the Gilded Age," *Journal of American History* (2000): 435–459.

[69] *Griswold v. Connecticut*, 381 U.S. 479 (1965); see David J. Garrow, *Liberty and Sexuality: The Right to Privacy and the Making of Roe v. Wade* (New York: Macmillan, 1994), 196–269.

there was no open "public" sale of contraceptives in that state. While sodomy laws were almost never enforced against "private" intercourse within the home, they were a popular tool for harassing and arresting men soliciting sex from other men in "public" parks, restrooms, subways, and street corners.

Legislators and administrators will tend to balance the benefits of regulation against its costs, including (and often most prominently) the deceit costs. There are some public policies that yield tangible benefits – yet are not enforced and are often abandoned if the costs of deceit simply overwhelm the benefits. This is the reason many anti-gay public officials abandoned consensual sodomy laws, but this point has bite even when the benefits of regulation are commanding ones. That is, even problems that demand state regulation require a consideration of the costs of deceit – and those costs ought to influence the *kind* of regulation the state chooses to pursue.

Thus, regulation of alcohol through age-limits for supply of drinks, driving-while-under-the-influence rules, licensing of liquor-serving establishments, and the like is probably cost-justified – but broad Prohibition, namely, the criminalization of the manufacture and sale of any alcoholic beverages, is decidedly not. Both kinds of regulations are subject to evasive deceit, but the former rules enjoy more support from the adult population and are therefore more cost-effective. Indeed, almost all the historians who have studied the matter have concluded that the costs of Prohibition greatly exceeded its benefits, even if it were assumed that the ban actually reduced the consumption of alcohol.[70]

The example of alcohol has lessons for the current debate over the regulation of marijuana. The more socially acceptable and widespread marijuana use has become, the higher the deceit-based costs of enforcing criminal laws against the sale, possession, or use of that drug. Some states have legalized the drug entirely, other states and the federal government have essentially abandoned enforcement of the criminal law. An echo of the nation's regulation of homosexual intimacies as well as its regulation of alcohol consumption, the evolution of marijuana policy suggests the following dynamic for the libertarian presumption in American law: the presumption of "individual liberty" depends on how widely the "community" practices or accepts the behaviors potentially subject to the criminal sanction.

Perhaps an even broader lesson is that a proper understanding of the costs of deceit provides a foundation for economics- and incentive-based solutions to many problems, instead of command-and-control rules. The penalty for entering the United States without proper documentation is, potentially, very high – detention (often in jails housing criminal inmates) and then deportation. Has this penalty structure produced a lot of benefits, at acceptable costs? The evidence is overwhelmingly negative: this

[70] For example, see Karen Blumenthal, *Bootleg: Murder, Moonshine, and the Lawless Years of Prohibition* (New York: Macmillan, 2011).

penalty structure has not prevented millions of immigrants from entering the country without proper admission, and it has imposed terrible human costs, including staggering costs of deceit.[71]

This kind of cost-benefit calculus inspired the proponents of the DREAM Act and of President Obama's executive order providing a path to citizenship for many undocumented immigrants and their families. Go one step further: Why not a regime that emphasizes monetary incentives for immigrants to enter the country legally and for many inadmissible immigrants to "earn" their citizenship through avenues of public service and other contributions?

Deceitful Identities: Pluralism and the Closet. There is a bigger way to think about the costs of deceit. The most dramatic effect of the anti-homosexual terror was that people not only had to lie about themselves, but also were motivated by legal and social pressure to create phony identities. Millions of Americans in the twentieth century lied about their sexual orientation to themselves as well as their families, neighbors, and employers. Millions of others understood their sexual orientation to

[71] Daniel Kanstroom, *Aftermath: Deportation Law and the New American Diaspora* (New York: Oxford University Press, 2012); M. Kathleen Dingeman-Cerda and Susan Bibler Coutin, "The Ruptures of Return: Deportation's Confounding Effects," in Charis E. Kurbin et al., eds., *Punishing Immigrants: Policy, Politics, and Injustice* (New York: New York University Press, 2012), 113, 120, 132; Massey, *How Arizona Became Ground Zero*.

be not straight but lied to straight society, while entering the underground life of variation. These "costs of the closet" were not just the product of a parade of individual lies, but were the consequence of identity presentation that was fundamentally deceitful.

The costs of the closet were staggering. For starters, living a life grounded upon lies about one's romantic preferences imposed huge psychic costs on sexual minorities – and usually upon their loved ones as well. Thus, millions of these closeted lesbian or gay people married someone of the "opposite" sex, most of whom were probably straight. Not only were these marriages founded upon deep lies, but the lies often produced terribly unhappy marriages, to the eternal bewilderment of the spouses who were not privy to the secret identities.

The costs of the closet also included enormous social welfare costs. To take one dramatic example, the closeted lives of most of the early victims of AIDS facilitated the spread of the HIV virus and retarded public health efforts to trace the advance of the disease and isolate it. Another example is the epidemic of child molestation by closeted Roman Catholic priests in the post-World War II era, when the priesthood was an attractive calling for men who were attracted to minors but deeply closeted about those forbidden desires. When closeted pedophile priests found they could not control their sexual impulses, they lied about their crimes and found cover from their frightened victims, from ecclesiastical officials who covered up their crimes and provided them with fresh venues for predation, and even from parents and parishioners who could not imagine that respected priests could do such things.[72]

The example of child-abusing adults in positions of authority (from priests to coaches to family members) suggests that some identities ought to be stigmatized and the acts constituting those identities considered reprehensible. But our point is that the state needs to be *very careful* about what kind of persons the state decides to create as a class of *outlaws*. In the 1950s, not only did the anti-homosexual government regulatory apparatus not distinguish between the lesbian or gay man seeking consensual adult relationships from the predatory child molester, but the state deliberately threw those very different kinds of people into the same category. Demonizing a minority without good reason is not only unjust treatment of the minority, but insanity for the larger community, for such policies create turmoil, resentment, and scapegoating. Illustrating the last point, the state's focus on adult homosexual relations between 1945 and 1969 diverted private as well as public regulatory attention away from pedophile priests, coaches, and family members who were molesting girls and boys.[73]

[72] Jason Berry, *Lead Us Not into Temptation; Catholic Priests and the Sexual Abuse of Children* (Urbana: University of Illinois Press, 2000); David France, *Our Fathers: The Secret Life of the Roman Catholic Church in an Age of Scandal* (New York: Broadway Books, 2004).

[73] Eskridge, *Dishonorable Passions* at 88–108, 374–375.

Similar risks are associated with our current immigration policy, which creates an "immigration closet" populated by hundreds of thousands, if not millions, of people. Like gay people in the prior century, inadmissible immigrants and their families today must hide an important feature of their identities because they are not in compliance with legal rules and because the penalties for violation are high. Indeed, the immigration closet strikes me as more suffocating than the gay closet had been. In practice, the penalties are more severe today for inadmissible immigrants than they were for most sexually active gay or lesbian persons in the previous era. Sexual and gender minorities suffered from police harassment and sometimes lost their jobs; inadmissible immigrants not only suffer these harms, but if apprehended may be incarcerated and often will be deported. Because so many inadmissible immigrants have children (who are a primary reason to enter this country), the state's response disrupts the lives of those children as well as the adults involved with the deported immigrant.[74]

The costs of the closet are borne by the polity as well as the persons within the polity. In our country, most of the

[74] For a detailed and hard-hitting analysis of the devastating effects of the immigration closet on the health and lives of tens of thousands of children, see Sara Satinsky et al., *Family Unity, Family Health: How Family-Focused Immigration Reform Will Mean Better Health for Children and Families* (Washington, DC: Human Impact Partners, June 2013). See also Ajay Chaudry et al., *Facing Our Future: Children in the Aftermath of Immigration Enforcement* (Washington, DC: Urban Institute, February 2010).

inadmissible immigrants are ethnically Latino. A portion of the Latino community within the United States consists of inadmissible immigrants, their families, and their larger social and even employment networks – all of which engage in a vigorous effort to deceive the government and much of the community. It is estimated that between 11 and 12 million persons in this country are undocumented immigrants, the large majority of whom are Spanish-speaking.[75]

Thus, state-produced deception may operate at the group level, not just the individual level. By creating an enormous subclass of denizens who are demonized and persecuted, the federal and state governments are risking the productive pluralism that has been the backbone of American greatness – namely, constant influx of new groups, eager to make it in this country and putting pressure on established groups to keep up.[76]

[75] Office of Immigration Statistics, Policy Directorate, U.S. Department of Homeland Security, Michael Hoefer et al., *Estimates of the Unauthorized Immigrant Population Residing in the United States: January 2011* (Washington, DC: GAO, March 2012).

[76] In his opinion for the Court in *United States v. Arizona*, 132 U.S. 2492 (2012), Justice Kennedy recognized that the "history of the United States is in part made of the stories, talents, and lasting contributions of those who crossed oceans and deserts to come here." Id. at 2510. Recent scholarship has focused upon the contributions that immigrants make to the growth and development of the nation's economy. See Jason Furman and Danielle Gray, "Ten Ways Immigrants Help Build and Strengthen Our Economy," The White House Blog (July 12, 2012) http://www.whitehouse.gov/blog/2012/07/12/ten-ways-immigrants-help-build-and-strengthen-our-economy (identifying ten contributions immigrants make to the overall economic well-being of the

The foregoing analysis does not necessarily insist that the United States throw over its immigration laws and admit all comers (though that is a possible policy). Instead, the analysis suggests that the punitive approaches entrenched in existing law create closets for many persons and for important subgroups in the community. The waves of deceit entailed in those closets represent a significant social and political as well as personal cost of those policies and need to be considered as the country moves forward.

Webs of Deceit Undermine the Rule of Law. Another way of thinking about law's production of deceit is to consider the effects that it has on the rule of law. The rule of law is not self-sustaining; it requires nurturing and attention.

country, including creating businesses that supply jobs, adding innovation to the market, raising overall market wages and increasing GDP); Patrick Oakford, *Top 5 Reasons Why Immigration Reform Means More Tax Revenues* (Washington, DC: Center for American Progress, April 15, 2014) (documenting that unauthorized migrants pay more than $13 billion in payroll taxes each year); see also Bruce P. Corrie, "A New Paradigm for Immigrant Policy: Immigrant Capital A Case Study of People of Mexican Origin in Minnesota," *William Mitchell Law Review* 35 (2008): 283 (categorizing immigrant capital into consumer capital, productive capital, entrepreneurial capital, fiscal capital, global capital, cultural capital, and civic capital, and applying this framework to quantify contributions Mexican immigrants have made in the state of Minnesota). For a study providing evidence that immigrants and their children will be crucial contributors to the workforce in the future, in part because this demographic will meet the changing demands of the labor market, see Dowell Myers et al., *The Contributions of Immigrants and Their Children to the American Workforce and Jobs of the Future* (Washington, DC: Center for American Progress, June 19, 2013).

For bootleggers and drinkers during Prohibition, for sexual minorities during the terror, and for undocumented immigrants today, the law's draconian measures not only turned and continue to turn socially productive people into outlaws, but also have tended to create an outlaw culture that may swallow up the rule of law. Consider several dimensions of this phenomenon.

Start with Sissela Bok's principle of veracity, namely, that individuals and institutions ought to strongly presume against lying. Thus, it was ethically wrong for President Clinton and Congress, when they enacted the "Don't Ask, Don't Tell" statute, to announce (on the face of the statute) that the "presence in the armed forces of persons who demonstrate a propensity or intent to engage in homosexual acts would create an unacceptable risk to the high standards of morale, good order and discipline, and unit cohesion that are the essence of military capability." Bok would criticize this statement as one that the president and Senator Nunn knew to be false, as they both supported the idea of "Don't Ask, Don't Tell" – which entailed leaving in the military almost all the "persons who demonstrate a propensity or intent to engage in homosexual acts." The reasons that Bok gives for criticizing such a statement are ones that have particular relevance for the rule of law.[77]

[77] Sissela Bok, *Lying: Moral Choice in Public and Private Life* (New York: Pantheon Books, 1978); Sissela Bok, *Secrets: On the Ethics of Concealment and Revelation* (New York: Pantheon Books, 1983). See 10 U.S.C. section 654(a)(15) (finding of fact in the "Don't Ask, Don't Tell" statute, quoted in text).

Central to her case for the veracity principle, Bok asks us to appreciate the social value of truth-telling. We tend to trust the veracity of what we hear. When someone lies to us, not only have we been harmed by taking actions that we should not have taken, but we become less prone to trust future representations. Note the parallel between the rule of law and Bok's case for the veracity principle. Both rely on predictability and trust. When the law itself embraces deceit, as the "Don't Ask, Don't Tell" Act did on several levels, the law undermines the conditions for its own flourishing. The bipartisan repeal of that law in 2010–2011 was not only justified by considerations of justice (for sexual minorities) and efficiency (avoiding turmoil in the armed forces), but also by the rule of law itself.[78]

The current stalemate on immigration policy reflects this Bokian concern on an ever larger level, because it implicates the *democratic rule of law*. Existing statutory rules produce webs of deceit that extend well beyond immigrant communities, to include employers and large companies, state and local officials, and federal executive department officials. In my view, immigration reforms, of the kind pressed by Presidents Bush and Obama, would address these concerns – but those reforms have been rejected in

[78] On the critical importance of trust to the rule of law, see especially Tom R. Tyler, *Why People Obey the Law?* 2nd ed. (Princeton, NJ: Princeton University Press, 2006).

Congress, and without sufficient justification. Responding to Congress's inaction, the Obama Administration in 2012 adopted the Deferred Action for Childhood Arrivals (DACA) program, which "defers" deportation of inadmissible immigrants who arrived in this country as children (during a specified time period) and allows them to secure work permits.[79]

The DACA program, and any expansion of it, illustrate the important role that deceit plays in the fate of a democratic rule of law. To begin with, this program not only seeks to protect children from the humiliations, risks, and degradation of their illegal status, but also seeks to protect the nation's democratic pluralism. Without the DACA program, the odds are that these millions of children will remain in this country, but living in the immigration closet that will prevent their personal flourishing. The DACA program potentially reduces the personal deceit-based costs for these persons – and in the process aspires to free a sizable chunk of the body politic from the political and social alienation that the immigration closet foments. To the extent that the DACA

[79] Janet Napolitano, Secretary of Homeland Security, Memorandum: Exercising Prosecutorial Discretion with Respect to Individuals Who Came to the United States as Children (June 15, 2012); Department of Homeland Security, U.S. Citizenship and Immigration Services, Consideration of Deferred Action for Childhood Arrivals (DACA), http://www.uscis.gov/humanitarian/consideration-deferred-action-childhood-arrivals-daca#filingprocess (viewed August 1, 2014).

program also ratifies the patterns of (non)enforcement that authorities have already been following, it also has the Bokian virtue of bringing official policy in line with actual policy.

Conversely, the DACA program might be a milder example of deceit as a matter of official government policy. The point, and apparently the intended purpose, of DACA is not "deferral" of deportation, but rather amnesty from deportation. Like "Don't Ask, Don't Tell," DACA is equality practice, providing space for more humane treatment of vulnerable human beings but without assuring them complete equality, yet. As with "Don't Ask, Don't Tell," DACA is a transitional program whose fate depends on how well it works and how Americans respond to the policy. Indeed, the President in November 2014 extended the DACA program to include adult immigrants who are inadmissible but who are raising children who are citizens.

It is notable that President Obama did not create DACA through an executive order or through a White House memorandum to the Secretary of Homeland Security. Instead, the secretary simply announced the program, apparently after coordination and discussions with the White House. Especially in light of the president's expansion of DACA to include millions of inadmissible adult immigrants, this amnesty under the guise of deferral poses a larger challenge to the "democratic" features of the rule of law, especially the constitutional principle that the broadly accountable

Congress must sign on to any major change in American legal rules. Even those sympathetic to the president's policy need to recognize the legitimacy costs and risks that major unilateral executive action will polarize the politics of immigration reform even further than before.[80]

[80] For an examples of such a critique, see Robert J. Delahunty and John C. Yoo, "Dream On: The Obama Administration's Nonenforcement of Immigration Laws, the DREAM Act, and the Take Care Clause," *Texas Law Review* 91 (2013): 781; but see Shoba Sivaprasad Wadhia, "In Defense of DACA, Deferred Action, and the Dream Act," *Texas Law Review* 91 (2013) (responding to Delahunty and Yoo). ICE officers and agents also challenged the policy as in violation of immigration law. The plaintiffs claimed that DACA violates their obligation to initiate the removal process against those not lawfully present, and argues that the law only grants executive discretion once the once these proceedings have begun. See, e.g., *Crane v. Napolitano*, 920 F.Supp.2d 724 (N.D. Tex. 2013) (motion to dismiss granted in part).

Afterword

Law, Lies, and Law Schools

Montré D. Carodine

I am most grateful to our colleague, Professor Austin Sarat, for putting together yet another dynamic conference. This was probably one of my favorite in this exciting and important series that Professor Sarat has brought to our law school because it strikes at the very heart of what the law is in reality versus what it purports to be. The chapters in this book and the conference discussions based on those chapters were wonderfully varied and diverse: through these robust exchanges, we have explored deceptions that our country's Founding Fathers did or did not engage in when laying the legal foundation for this country's very existence, deception in our courtrooms by witnesses, lies by and to the government, lies that the government produces or draws out of people, the role of deception in relation to rape and statutory rape law, and how the law deals with all of those complex issues.

I am drawn particularly to the theme of discussion that has focused on the impact of the law's lies on the victims of those lies. The victimization that law's lies perpetuate has been a recurrent theme in this book, as it was in the conference on which this book is based. For example, Professor Mary Anne Franks began her paper by stating quite simply that America is built on a lie, essentially that our foundational legal principles in this country are rooted in lies. While I won't completely rehash the wonderful debate that followed her presentation, I will say that the deceptions of our country's very founding do indeed continue to haunt us today. So, in many ways, we are not only beneficiaries of the brilliance of our Founding Fathers, but we are victims of their deceptions. That's the impact of harmful lies and deception when not rectified – they continue to flourish, even generations removed from the original lies.

What I do want to focus on is how law schools and legal educators can begin "at home," if you will, in dealing with the ways that we ourselves, law schools that is, deceive the public and the harm that we ourselves do as law schools. We are, after all, a foundational institution, so what we do at law schools matter. Future leaders in the law – legislators, judges, lawyers, law professors – get their start in developing their legal thinking and philosophies in law school.

Of late, law schools ourselves have been called to task for deceptive practices ranging from outright lying in the reporting of employment numbers[1] to deceiving students into believing that traditional legal education actually prepares them for the practice of law.[2] One recent graduate sharply put it this way to a national publication: Law schools will lie to you. Do not believe a word that comes from law schools, law deans, or law professors.[3] The

[1] Ben Trachtenberg, "Law School Marketing and Legal Ethics," *Nebraska Law Review* 91 (2013): 866, 872 (noting that misleading statistics have pervaded the business-as-usual reporting by law schools of their graduates' employment outcomes and salaries, which is among the most important information for prospective applicants deciding whether and where to attend law school"); Christopher Polchin, "Comment, Raising the 'Bar' on Law School Data Reporting: Solutions to the Transparency Problem," *Penn State Law Review* 117 (2012): 201, 202, 207–210 (discussing the attention that has been placed on deceptive job reporting practices by law schools because of the difficult legal job market); Maura Dolan, "Law School Graduates Aren't Finding Much on the Employment Docket" *Los Angeles Times*, April 1, 2013, http://articles.latimes.com/2013/apr/01/local/la-me-law-grads-20130402; Juggalo Law, "Law Schools Lie ... Or a Rug. A Dog on a Rug," April 26, 2011, http://abovethelaw.com/2011/04/law-schools-lie-like-a-dog-or-a-rug-a-dog-on-a-rug/ (then recent law graduate arguing that "[l]aw schools have been lying through their teeth about employment statistics for years now").

[2] David Segal, "What They Don't Teach Law Students: Lawyering," *New York Times*, November 19, 2011, http://www.nytimes.com/2011/11/20/business/after-law-school-associates-learn-to-be-lawyers.html?pagewanted=all&_r=0.

[3] Erin Fuchs, "I Consider Law School a Waste of My Life and an Extraordinary Waste of Money," Business Insider, December 14, 2013, http://www.businessinsider.com/is-law-school-worth-the-money-2013-12?IR=T.

criticism hurled at the legal academy, much of it deserved, has sparked an entire movement – a national discussion on the future of legal education. The bringing to light of our own deception in the legal academy has led to a steep decline in enrollment and applications to law school.[4] The crisis in legal education has caused law schools to become more introspective and to examine ourselves.[5] There are other areas in which we need to do that – to self-reflect on ways in which we are not living up to our purported ideals. Our students learn from our examples – and again, they are the ones who will develop the laws and legal institutions of tomorrow – their reliance on deceit and deceptive practices or their efforts to avoid this path could very well depend on the nature of the very institutions that train them in the law.

Aside from deceiving our students, law schools often deceive and victimize ourselves while also deceiving our external constituencies. The treatment of minority and women professors is ripe territory for discussing law

[4] Martha Neil, "Law School Applications Down 37 Percent since 2010; First-Year Class Could Be Smallest in 40 Years," *ABA Journal*, July 22, 2014, http://www.abajournal.com/news/article/law_school_appli cations_down_8_percent_new_lsac_survey_shows_theyve_dropped.

[5] Owen Praskievicz and Christina Thomas, "20 Most Innovative Law Schools," *The National Jurist*, September 2012, http://www .nxtbook.com/nxtbooks/cypress/nationaljurist0912/index.php#/28 ("Driven by sharp criticism, a challenging job market, and a significant drop in applications during the last two years, law schools are moving forward with innovative ideas that were quashed only a few years ago").

schools' internal/external deceptions. Last year, a book entitled *Presumed Incompetent: The Intersection of Race and Class for Women in the Academy*, burst onto the national scene and sparked lively discussions across the country.[6] The book contains a number of chapters written by women professors, many of color, and some of whom are law professors. Others are professors in various other disciplines at universities nationwide. What connected all of these women were the striking similarities of their experiences of oppression and harassment at their respective institutions. Moreover, their stories struck a chord throughout the nation because they were also strikingly similar to the experiences of many women professors of color across the country who may have never met the authors. The authors of the various chapters in the book told stories of harsh treatment by colleagues and some students, who (as the title of the book expresses) presumed their incompetence despite their qualifications and their actual competence. There were also stories about the racialized and gendered hierarchy at law schools across the country – ways in which women and minorities are often called upon to do a disproportionate share of service on committees and elsewhere. In line with the *Presumed Incompetent* movement, just this

[6] *Presumed Incompetent: The Intersections of Race and Class for Women in Academia* (Gabriella Gutiérrez y Muhs, Yolanda Flores Niemann, Carmen G. González and Angela P. Harris eds., 2012).

summer, the listserv for the Association of American Law Schools (AALS) women's section exploded with e-mails from women (including minority women) across the country discussing their experiences of oppression on law school faculties.

One story that was not in the groundbreaking book discussed above or told on the listserv exchange, but that would have fit right in with both, is the story of a woman of color who was asked by the dean of her law school to serve on a hiring committee. She had been asked to serve on hiring committees a number of times – as is typical for people of color, who are often pressured to serve on these committees for "diversity purposes." She agreed and went to what she thought was the first meeting only to find out that the committee had already been meeting for a month and reviewing candidates, she was told by her colleagues that indeed she was asked to be on the committee only when the human resources department for the university rejected the formally constituted committee because it did not include an African-American person.

The dean admitted this to be the reason for asking her to be on the committee. The professor felt embarrassed and humiliated to have been the object of such blatant tokenism. What value could she add the committee, which had already reviewed and deliberated on several candidates? Moreover, in the future, was she – only one of a very small percentage of African-Americans on the faculty – always expected to be on this committee, which any faculty member knows is probably the most work intensive faculty committee. When was she supposed to do research and write, if this was the case? After all, the presumption of being a scholarly lightweight is often a problem that plagues women of color, as the book *Presumed Incompetent* makes clear.

More fundamentally, would she be perpetuating a lie for the law school and the university which, like most institutions of higher learning across the country, touts itself as an institution that embrace and value diversity? And what does it mean to embrace and value diversity – to overwork and objectify the few racial minorities at an institution to promote an image of being an inclusive institution?

My point with this story, the stories that came to light in *Presumed Incompetent* and this summer on the listserv for the AALS women's listserv, as well as the reform that has been sparked because of the "law school as a scam" movement, is that the law will continue to lie, deceive, and victimize, as long as law schools continue to be deceptive institutions. As was repeatedly noted during our conference discussions, lying is deeply embedded in our profession. Indeed, it is the negative quality that we're most known for – hence all of the lawyer jokes, which should make us very uncomfortable.

I am reminded of that public service commercial about teenage drug abuse where the teenager who is abusing drugs (or maybe alcohol), poignantly tells his father that he learned this behavior from watching his father. Our students are watching – it was fitting that we have this discussion about law and lies at a law school. My hope is that law schools will become more vigilant in self-policing and addressing our own deceptions – deceptions that are causing real harm to real people and the profession. Our society will be all the better for our efforts.

Index

Index